LEARNING FROM THE WORLD'S BEST CENTRAL BANKERS

CENTRAL BANKERS

PRINCIPLES AND POLICIES
FOR SUBDUING INFLATION

LEARNING
FROM THE
WORLD'S BEST
CENTRAL BANKERS

PRINCIPLES AND POLICIES
FOR SUBDUING INFLATION

GEORGE M. VON FURSTENBERG
Rudy Professor of Economics
Indiana University
Bloomington, Indiana 47405, USA

AND

MICHAEL K. ULAN
U.S. Department of State
Washington, D.C. 20520, USA

Kluwer Academic Publishers
Boston/Dordrecht/London

332.112
V94 L

Distributors for North, Central and South America:
Kluwer Academic Publishers
101 Philip Drive
Assinippi Park
Norwell, Massachusetts 02061 USA
Telephone (781) 871-6600
Fax (781) 871-6528
E-Mail <kluwer@wkap.com>

Distributors for all other countries:
Kluwer Academic Publishers Group
Distribution Centre
Post Office Box 322
3300 AH Dordrecht, THE NETHERLANDS
Telephone 31 78 6392 392
Fax 31 78 6546 474
E-Mail <orderdept@wkap.nl>

 Electronic Services <http://www.wkap.nl>

Library of Congress Cataloging-in-Publication Data

A C.I.P. Catalogue record for this book is available
from the Library of Congress.

Printed on acid-free paper.

Printed in the United States of America.

*The views expressed are those of the authors and not those of the Department
of State or the U.S. Government. At Indiana University, Stephanie G'Schwind
was the style editor, Mary Blizzard the designer, and Eve Hermann the compositor.*

To my parents, Kaspar and Elisabeth,
Freiherr and Freifrau von Fürstenberg, in memoriam,
and to two of my professors at Princeton University,
Edward J. Kane and Burton G. Malkiel,
who taught me to appreciate great personalities,
and to my wife, Gabrielle, and son, Philip, who know
that saying nice things is a joy, even in writing.

George M. von Furstenberg

To my mother, Dorothy Ulan,
and in memory of my father, Martin Ulan,
who supported and encouraged me
in everything I have sought to do.

Michael K. Ulan

CONTENTS

FOREWORD

BURTON G. MALKIEL
Chemical Bank Chairman's Professor of Economics
Princeton University

Central bankers have often believed that they are the Rodney Dangerfields of public officials—they seldom receive respect from the public or from elected officials. Particularly in the days of high inflation and substantial unemployment, they were held responsible for everything that ailed the world's economies. And monetarists often suggested that nations would be far better off if central bankers were replaced by robots who would do nothing more than ensure that the money supply was increased at a fixed percent each year.

Our views have changed considerably over the past two decades. The main reason is that, thanks in substantial part to the efforts of central bankers, inflation has generally been contained. With the reduction in inflation and the recent relative stability of price levels in most developed nations, risk premiums have tended to decline sharply. Moreover, unemployment rates, at least in the Western Hemisphere, have decreased substantially. Finally, even many economists who consider themselves monetarists now tend to be less certain of the stability of the link between the money supply and economic activity. Thus, there is greater appreciation of the critical role of judgment in the conduct of monetary policy and a general belief that the judgments central bankers have made have generally been sound. Indeed, the Chairman of the Federal Reserve finds his picture on the cover of a variety of news and financial magazines and is praised as an admiral who has successfully kept the economy on an even keel. And throughout the world, central bankers have probably never been more trusted than they are today.

The growing reputation of central bankers has led von Furstenberg and Ulan to believe that there is much to be learned from examining the ways in which central bankers practice their profession. So they proceeded to ask what are arguably the world's seven best central bankers from various countries throughout the world what they considered to be their finest achievements and how they went about gaining support for policies designed to maintain price stability. They obtained excellent cooperation from John Crow of Canada, Roberto Zahler of Chile, Alan Greenspan of the United States, Helmut Schlesinger of Germany, Markus Lusser of Switzerland, Donald Brash of New Zealand, and Yasushi Mieno of Japan. They offer here a series of essays in which they present what central bankers have to say for themselves and the lessons they believe they can teach about monetary policy—not what economists, politicians, or journalists like to say about them.

Learning from gifted practitioners is common in many fields where personal skills and the quality of judgment and execution matter so critically. It is particularly important in fields such as central banking, where gaining political support, maintaining independence, and establishing credibility often make the difference between success and failure. Indeed, we see that while analyses and modeling may help, these leaders rely mainly on qualities of human judgment, schooled instinct, developed taste, and probity of character to deal with the conduct of monetary policy in our complex, interdependent world.

In this volume, we find a fascinating treatment of how the governors have tackled the hardest dilemmas of policy-making in their own specific political settings. We learn how the bankers themselves believe they have earned and preserved credibility and how they have maintained and expanded their base of popular support. We read in their own words how they have attempted to inspire trust and how they have secured and defended the independence of their institutions. We read how they have tried to mitigate exogenous supply shocks and cope with regulatory failures, unstable surges of capital flows, extremes in asset valuations, and financial crises. Perhaps one of the most interesting lessons we learn is that central bankers must refuse to accept credit for fortuitous successes lest they will be blamed and lose credibility when things beyond their control go wrong.

The study of great individuals and the lessons that can be learned from their leadership is not always considered fashionable. I believe, however, that the essays in this volume can be of enormous value to academic economists, students, and especially future leaders in banking, finance, and government service. No student of monetary theory and policy will want to miss this fascinating work in which the world's most gifted central bankers speak so eloquently about their trade.

INTRODUCTION TO THE WORLD'S BEST CENTRAL BANKERS

Central bankers play a prominent role in many societies; a few of them even become oracles or celebrities. Yet they are commonly accorded little respect as educators and role models. This volume hopes to change that. For the world's best central bankers, portrayed here, teach and lead impressively, doing so with insight, courage, quality, and conviction. They are commendable role models for those with high aspirations. There is much to learn from them about securing credibility in business, banking, and finance all over the world, as well as for training to fight two- and three-front public-relations campaigns on one's home turf with principles intact.

A CENTRAL BANKER'S WORST FRIENDS

Central banks may be independent from direct interference by other parts of their government, but that does not keep their top figures from being lionized, instrumentalized, and patronized by reporters, politicians, and economists.

For example, financial correspondents in many countries assiduously comb through central bank statements for clues about the future course of monetary policy and interest rates. What a central banker has to say about the outlook for the economy or deeper issues matters to them only insofar as it helps forecast what policy the central bank might try to implement next. The main reason correspondents pay attention to the very latest releases is that they are hoping to find some clue as to the direction of interest rates.

Elected politicians do another kind of job on central bankers. They either treat their central banker as a convenient scapegoat or try to coopt the rhetoric of rectitude, depending on the curtain call and fund raiser. They rarely look for either information or education but cherish the opportunity alternately to berate and to befriend an official whose prominence and reputation may well exceed their own. Populist snarling at high or rising interest rates is politically much more attractive across the political spectrum than lauding the central bank's vigilance and preemptive strikes against inflation. Politicians, like Shakespeare's king, like inflation dead but hate those who kill it if there is any economic bloodletting at all.

Economists, present company of course excepted, tend to be equally bad friends. Most central bank professionals are trained as economists and four out of the seven best central bankers chosen for this volume have a doctorate in the subject. Yet academic treatments of the leadership role and responsibilities of central bankers have tended to be condescending. Some on the diehard fringe still call for gold and commodity index standards to knock central bankers out of discretionary action. They see central bankers as termites irresistibly driven to hollowing out sound money, feasting in a consumptive progress until its pillars come down. The favorite caricature conjured up in article after article—even in the internationally dominant U.S. economic mainstream—is a little less extreme but not much more respectful: It casts central bankers as lying in wait to spring positive inflation surprises on an intentionally confused public to give the economy some froth with extra injections of money. Central bankers certainly must have understood at some level that such a fix may stimulate economic activity for a time, but ultimately will result in greater inflation. But left to their own time-inconsistent incentives, they just could not stay with low inflation anyway, charged mainstream economists, because the good of breaking out on the upside came before the bad of coming down again. The bad, however, was deeply discounted by these fly-by-night operators of central banks who had political agendas pinned on them by economists. Assuming there is this endemic inflation bias, central bankers need either a constitutional straightjacket or iron charter to restrain them, or economists to shame them.

The following quote (from Marvin Goodfriend and Robert G. King, *NBER Macroeconomics Annual 1997,* Cambridge, Mass: MIT Press, 1997, pp. 274-75) gives a sense of the type of aspersions cast by many economists in the past and why they are now getting less and less believable to the profession:

> Inflation scares are easy to understand from the perspective of
> the new synthesis. A central bank has an incentive to cheat on its
> commitment to price stability in the NNS [no nonsense?] model

because a monetary policy action can reduce the markup distortion and increase employment. [A number of economists] might argue that a central bank without a precommitment technology could not sustain a low-inflation equilibrium at all. At a minimum, their argument suggests that the incentive to cheat makes price setters hypersensitive to policy mistakes in a way that makes a low-inflation equilibrium extremely fragile.

It seems to us that NNS reasoning coupled with recent monetary policy developments weakens considerably the force of such a point. We think that central banks such as the Federal Reserve today largely internalize the long-run costs of cheating. As a result of the Volcker Fed's taking responsibility for inflation in the late 1970s and successfully bringing it down, the [central bank] is now widely held to be responsible for inflation. Moreover, the low-inflation experience since then has demonstrated clearly the long-run benefits of price stability. Hence, we believe that the temptation for the [central bank] to cheat on its low-inflation commitment is much weaker than in the past.

If two distinguished academic economists, both of whom list a Federal Reserve Bank as among their current affiliations, can grant no more than the partial absolution that the best central banks "today largely internalize the long-run costs of cheating," one can readily envision the suspicions still harbored in much of the rest of the profession. Alan Blinder, with his recent book *Central Banking in Theory and Practice* (Cambridge, Mass: MIT Press, 1998), is among the most splendid and knowledgeable exceptions.

While economists working at research universities in the United States tend to be set against inflation and politically conservative, economists working elsewhere may reflect and pitch other viewpoints, depending on their employer. Caught in a multi-front war, central bankers therefore easily find themselves attacked from several sides: too tough or not tough enough on inflation, too weak and slow or too strong and fast in reacting to signs of trouble, taking too few or too many risks with price stability, or favoring this or that group and interest or ideology too much—and the laboring class least of all.

HOW WE CAME TO BE APPRECIATIVE

Canadians tended to get at Governor John W. Crow, mainly pummeling him for recession and higher unemployment, when he headed the Bank of Canada from 1987 to 1994. Some of the critics would not stop flailing at him for years afterward. The first of the two authors happened to work at the University of Toronto from 1994 to 1995, where he witnessed the sickening spectacle of the governor's being vilified in the press and even by a part of the economics profession. In truth Governor Crow had saved Canada years of further grief and showed that if monetary policy can reform, fiscal policy must not be far behind. In fact, it appeared obvious that the lessons he taught would stick and could be ignored only at Canada's peril by his successor. So we sought to make his acquaintance and asked him to identify his most profound and principled writings in order to work on an essay not of haughty criticism but of discerning appreciation. We also asked him to identify works that were most authentically his own rather than approximations of his views crafted by staff.

The governor, though certainly not looking for a public defender or paying this matter much mind, agreed to point out a few of his key addresses and eventually to comment on what we had drafted, but doing so only very sparingly. As the project began to intrigue the first author further and after the second author, from the U.S. Department of State, had agreed to join up, we asked Governor Crow to identify other governors around the world whom he considered as sharing the depth of his commitment to sound money. Like Governor Crow, these governors were to champion the cause of self-disciplined government that takes its educational role seriously and seeks to convince, rather than blind side, the public. The other governors—a term we reserve for heads of central banks—represented in this volume are those he named. He might have named more from past or present if we had not asked him to stop when there was a total of seven.

We proceeded with all the other governors as we had with Governor Crow, down to asking for their portrait photo and a short personal biography that was more than the usual dry list of career stops. Gratefully, we received the cooperation of all of them, communicating either directly or through their present (Chairman Alan Greenspan) or former (Governor Yasushi Mieno of Japan) staff. There were detailed rounds of comments from Dr. Helmut Schlesinger, former president of the German Bundesbank, and from Dr. Donald T. Brash, the current governor of the Reserve Bank of New Zealand. Dr. Roberto Zahler, former governor of the Central Bank of Chile, reacted more tersely, somewhat in the manner of Governor Crow. One former governor (Dr. Markus Lusser of Switzerland) unexpectedly passed away in April 1998, five days after sending us a total of ten single-spaced pages of comments on an earlier draft. Unlike all the other governors, he would not be able to review, and eventually (at least tacitly) to approve of, how we had integrated his comments as we revised the relevant chapter. So we have inserted excerpts from his elaborations, clearly marked as his own, as a sign of respect.

REVERSE LEARNING

Once upon a time it was not unusual for advanced training in the military to include studying strategy and tactics employed in the battles of Napoleon, though not in the way students of voice might learn from the delivery of Enrico Caruso, or clergy might be fortified by studying the lives of the saints. While it is not easy to explain this to Napoleon, "great men" are now definitely "out," not just banished. Instead, institutions and financial incentives are to serve as a near-perfect substitute for character and integrity. New Zealanders have toyed with a scheme, rather more pathetic than humiliating, of paying the governor on performance, as though the only way to make sure he would do the right thing was to have that thing line his pockets. A vice president of a regional Federal Reserve Bank in the United States dismissed our project by advising us to focus instead on studying the design of "monetary institutions that will protect us from those central bankers who are not so great." He had a point, of course, but investing in devices protecting from rogues and mediocrities is not the same as providing a vision of greatness.

While we are not necessarily opposed to attempts at automating virtue and forcibly restraining those who might do something, we doubt that tight shackles and deep depressants can keep top decision makers morally or functionally fit. If the leadership of any institution rigidly sticks with the institution's rules of motion once it has been recognized that things have taken a wrong turn, both that leadership and the institution quickly lose legitimacy. If the central bank must pursue an activist policy to target inflation as commonly maintained (e.g., Goodfriend and King, p. 277), its leadership has to make many difficult judgment calls that defy automation. Such judgment needs to be appreciated and trained. For this reason we do not apologize for seeing training benefits in the respectful study of successful elites. These elites are employed in something more important than minding the mechanics or following formal rules and orders. By accepting the ultimate challenge of being responsible for an important social outcome, they have denied themselves such subterfuge.

Academics live by the standard of arguability, meaning that internal logical consistency is required but any good sense of relevance for applications or a trained sense of responsibility in policy advice are extra. Central bankers do not have the luxury of choosing to be irrelevant or irresponsible with no harm done. So perhaps the most thoughtful and successful among them have something to teach the teachers, and reverse learning is an appropriate response. If academics should occasionally deign to learn from gifted practitioners, then students could learn from both of them all the more.

What, then, are the lessons? This book is about letting the world's best central bankers speak first because they do so eloquently and with much needed shading and elaboration. But we owe at least a good try in this introduction at compressing their wisdom to a set of simple guides or points of orientation. These are rough and ready guidelines of the kind Napoleon might have given to the entire cavalry, if not to every foot soldier. Chapters 1 through 7 contain them, and much more, in the authentic and polished form given to them largely by the governors themselves.

THE OVERRIDING PRINCIPLE AND PURPOSE

(1) The central bank's purpose is to provide for stable money in a sound financial system. Governors from Lusser of Switzerland to Zahler of Chile have used almost those exact words.

(2) While unexpected outbreaks of inflation may give the economy a lift if they are due to unanticipated boosts to demand rather than adverse shocks to supply, the cumulative costs of containing such outbreaks far exceed their short-lived benefits. Governors Crow of Canada, Schlesinger of Germany (long before he became governor), and Brash of New Zealand were equally emphatic on this. The other governors perhaps no longer needed to be quite so emphatic since the point had already largely been taken by their public.

(3) Continuing inflation imposes a loss of efficiency and precision on economic arrangements and raises investment risk. While systematically higher inflation may not lead to a permanent reduc-

tion in the annual rates of economic growth, it will reduce such rates long enough to leave the level of output and income appreciably below where it would have been if noninflationary conditions had been maintained. Learning to live with inflation is a study in endless masochism.

(4) Tolerating continuing high rates of inflation is a sure sign of bad government and instability, tantamount to a breach of the social peace and public trust.

(5) Surges in foreign capital flows, exchange-rate distortions, and asset-price inflation pose exceptionally difficult problems of strategic and regulatory management, including staying on a steady course of avoiding inflation in the prices of goods and services. Governors Zahler of Chile and Lusser of Switzerland had to contend with such problems, while Governor Mieno of Japan confronted them head on. Chairman Greenspan may have to cope with them a second time before his third full term expires in the year 2000. The need to cope with adverse low-probability events that may disrupt the intermediation process and then cause cumulative damage to complex interdependent economic and financial systems means that prudent discretion and trust in the helm of the central bank are indispensable to maintain and restore confidence in a crisis. Automatic pilots are not reassuring and do not work very well when caught flying low over a previously dormant but now suddenly erupting volcano.

(6) Major bank failures, government bail-outs of the financial system, and overworked lender-of-last-resort functions pose a clear and present danger to the central bank's reputation for competence and technical fitness, which is another aspect of credibility. They also pose a threat to the steady pursuit of approximate stability of the general price level. Precisely because of the central bank's vital interest in a well-provisioned and supervised banking and financial system with the correct regulatory rewards and punishments, it should avoid role conflicts by not being the principal regulator itself. Both the German and the Swiss governors represented in this volume welcomed the fact that their respective central banks were unencumbered with any direct responsibility for the supervision of banks.

(7) The line of what represents approximate price level stability has now been drawn at no more than 2 percent per annum on average over a period of three to five years. Governor Crow of Canada pioneered this unequivocal and numerically precise multi-year inflation targeting. Of the seven countries represented in this book, only Chile

still operates with higher, but declining, target levels of inflation. Most governors believe that measured inflation overstates true inflation that would need to be compensated to preserve constancy of living standards by about one percentage point per annum.

GUIDELINES FROM CENTRAL BANKERS' OWN PRACTICE FOR EARNING AND PRESERVING CREDIBILITY

(1) Clearly state and justify both your tactical and strategic objectives, but do not delay action or be seen to hesitate until your justifications are accepted.

(2) Explain the degree of control and risk you see in reaching these objectives and with what precision and provisos you expect to be able to meet them within the stated time frame.

(3) Let yourself be called to account by stipulating in advance what degree of responsibility you accept for reaching the announced short- and medium-run objectives. Repeat precisely for what you propose to be responsible and what the central bank cannot possibly guarantee, overcome, or achieve on its own. Governor Crow of Canada was a master at explaining to the Canadian public that a record of approximate price stability is all they can demand from their central bank: while that may be the best possible framework for achieving other good things, the central bank cannot produce those. Whenever successful governors begin to acquire the aura of omnipotence, they should worry and protest loudly. For if they accept credit for all good things in economics and financial markets, they will also be blamed for all bad things outside their purview.

(4) If factors outside your control, such as adverse supply shocks, impinge on your reaching your short-term objectives, explain how, and how fast, you expect to be able to get back on track in those dimensions for which you have accepted responsibility.

(5) If you fail to reach your objective and there is no valid and convincing excuse, do not try to construct one. Instead, own up publicly, but not overly apologetically, to any errors and state how you propose to guard against them in the future. Governors Brash of New Zealand and Lusser of Switzerland are prime examples of such leveling with the public, which elevates the public discourse and raises the level of participation.

(6) To make something lasting out of central-bank independence and to discourage your successor from ever wasting the reputation

capital so far accumulated, you have to help make inflation thoroughly and irreversibly unpopular. You keep working on this by explaining over and over that inflation is bound to be harmful on balance until this truth is widely shared and firmly anchored in public consciousness and institutions.

(7) Remain dignified and seemingly above the fray even when dealing with any unprincipled or grandstanding elements of your central bank council, contending with backbiting from the Finance Ministry, or when facing vitriol from critics with parliamentary immunity or a media license. Patiently repeat the principles and convictions essential for the conduct of monetary policy and the nation's welfare, and uphold your convictions in word and deed, being prepared to offer your resignation to publicly protest any violation of basic principle as a last resort.

ON MONETARISM

(1) Some central bankers have found it useful to demonstrate accountability and strategic resolve by announcing money-supply targets.

(2) The narrower the concept of money and the closer it is to comprising just the chief liabilities of the central bank, the more controllable the concept but also the further it is away from the objectives anyone ultimately cares about.

(3) No central bank has ever maintained a record of faithfully meeting either its narrow-money or its broad-money targets for very long. Even the German Bundesbank, which has stuck with preannounced annual money-supply growth-targets from the mid-1970s until the beginning of 1999, when the DM was suffused into the Euro, has missed—presumably chosen to miss—its annual money-supply growth-target ranges about half the time according to its own rating for 1975 to 1996.

(4) Meeting money-supply targets while missing a more substantive objective, such as gaining or maintaining approximate stability of the price level, is no excuse: it provides little political cover. Violating such intermediate targets when ultimate objectives are achieved is immediately excused. The governor of the Swiss National Bank used violations of money-supply targets as a convenient prompt to provide an update on the stance of monetary policy to the public.

(5) Central banks that have a reputation for competence and

integrity cannot gain additional credibility by announcing the recipe that they plan to follow to achieve price stability, particularly if the recipe keeps having to be adjusted to current developments as they taste their cooking.

(6) Nevertheless, central banks do well to stress that, by managing their balance sheet, they are quite able to move the economy to the nominal outcomes they desire over a period of two to three years and that they have to operate in a forward-looking manner given the lags with which their actions take full effect.

(7) The central bank should strive to make expectations of price-level stability the rock on which nominal wage-contracts and sticky-price contracts are founded. One of the benefits is that indexation can be avoided in the private sector when the central bank safeguards price-level stability in all but exceptional circumstances that call for temporary deviations from inflation rates near zero.

ON SECURING CENTRAL BANK INDEPENDENCE

(1) Independence cannot be bestowed by constitutions or central bank charters alone but must be earned by demonstrating superior performance and incorruptibility.

(2) An independent weakling as head of a central bank is a contradiction in attributes.

(3) Even nominally independent boards and councils of central banks are designed to limit the independence of their heads and to allow political influence to enter. Governor Zahler of Chile chose to resign to protest the actions of his central bank council.

(4) Central bankers owe their freedom of action to the people's trust in their superior management abilities and in the honesty of their intentions. They must continually try to explain and press their cause, and to court public opinion, to assure that they will not be pushed aside. A silent plebiscite is being held on central bankers all the time, and independence does not mean that central bankers can ignore the implicit vote count. Governor Lusser even looked forward to an explicit popular referendum on central bank independence in Switzerland. A central bank, like the European Central Bank, which presides over a monetary area comprising a number of countries, needs to develop broad-based popular support for price stability to safeguard its independence; it must not regard national governments as reliable and sufficient backing.

INTRODUCTION

XXI

(5) Central bankers wishing to be reappointed must be popular with financial pundits and with the media that are often taken to represent "the people." They should keep some distance from the latest elected government even if that government has strong support. Governor Crow of Canada failed to be reappointed by a new government that came in strong and thought him unpopular. Failing to be reappointed is a political price well worth paying for leaving a lasting legacy of the right principles and practices to an entire nation.

(6) Independent central banks flourish in democracies where they are supported by the consent, indeed appreciation, of "the people," who bestow immediate legitimacy. A record of accomplishment will give central banks an independent political power-base. Maintaining independence means continuous investments in preserving that base. All of the central bankers featured in this volume function in vibrant democracies.

(7) International fora and bureaucracies of international financial institutions that attempt to organize international monetary coordination detract from the quality and immediacy of the confidential and trusting working relationships that already exist between the world's best central bankers. Here, too, a central bank's independence is entirely compatible with national and international connectedness and cooperation, provided it is not forced on any of the participating central banks against their better judgment from outside.

ORGANIZATION OF BOOK

The following essays, organized by time and region, honor the work and ideas of the seven best current or recent central bank governors in the world. Starting with the Western Hemisphere, part I proceeds from Canada's Governor Crow (1987 to 1994) to Chile's Governor Zahler (1991 to 1996) and on to the United States' Chairman Greenspan (1987 to present). Part II, Europe, covers Presidents Schlesinger (1991 to 1993) of the German Bundesbank in chapter 4 and Lusser (1988 to 1996) of Switzerland in chapter 5. Finally, part III deals with outstanding governors in the "Far East:" Governor Mieno (1989 to 1994) of Japan in chapter 6, and in chapter 7, Governor Brash (1988 to present) of New Zealand.

The chronological and partly overlapping order within each of the three parts provides a sense of the evolution of official thinking about principles and practices of monetary management in the region. The geographical grouping, particularly of Canada with the United States, and Switzerland with Germany, shows the close links between neighboring countries of greatly different size that sometimes complicate, but always affect, the making of monetary policy. Chile is the only developing country whose governor is represented here, and Chile is by far the fastest growing of the seven countries. But with its former governor trained at the University of Chicago and a good friend of Governor Crow, the networking is close, as it has tended to be between all the world's best central bankers.

Just as Governor Zahler fits easily with North America, and Chile with the North American Free Trade Agreement, Governor Brash of New Zealand fits well with both Europe and America, and not with its conceptual antipodes. Having spent some part of his professional life in New York, Governor Mieno is no stranger to the rest of them either, and Schlesinger, like the others, has made many professional trips and speeches in the United States and Switzerland. Because of his many years of service, prominence, and humanity, Chairman Greenspan has been at the center of this network for twelve years already.

ABOUT THE AUTHORS

George M. von Furstenberg was born in the western part of Germany during World War II. In 1961 he arrived as a nineteen-year-old immigrant, alone in New York to make it the hard way—study, work, and no play—first at Columbia University's School of General Studies and then at Princeton University, from which he received a Ph.D. in economics in 1967, one year after becoming a U.S. citizen. Since then, several years of work at the International Monetary Fund (Division Chief, 1978 to 1983) and at various U.S. government agencies, including the U.S. President's Council of Economic Advisers (Senior Staff Economist, 1978 to 1983) and the Department of State (1989 to 1990), have alternated with his academic pursuits. He has had Fulbright research and teaching fellowships to both Poland and Canada and has been featured in successive editions of *Who's Who in America* and in the forthcoming, better late than never, edition of *Who's Who in Economics*.

A prolific writer and frequent editor, his interests are consequently policy-oriented, broad, and international. He is, however, passionate about sharing in the teaching and examination of his core subjects of macroeconomic theory and international finance at Indiana University in Bloomington. There he has been a full professor since 1973 and a titled professor since 1983. He is deeply involved with his doctoral students and their professional success, currently working with them on NAFTA expansion, monetary union, and financial integration topics.

Michael K. Ulan was born in Chester, Pennsylvania, in 1946 and grew up in the Philadelphia area. Arriving on the campus of Lafayette College in Easton, Pennsylvania, in September 1963, he thought that economics was an abstract, philosophical subject. Despite misgivings, he took the economics principles course at the suggestion of a cousin and found that the discipline was anything but irrelevant to the real world, though it often tries to be. A few years later (including one spent at the London School of Economics), he left Lafayette with a B.A. in economics, magna cum laude. Along the way he was elected to Phi Beta Kappa. After graduation, he headed down the Delaware River to Philadelphia and graduate studies at the University of Pennsylvania, where he earned a Ph.D. in economics, intending to become a college professor.

Since academic jobs were scarce when he completed his dissertation, he chose a civil service career. He worked at the Departments of Labor and Commerce before joining the State Department's policy-analysis staff in 1981. Policy analysis challenged him to produce clear, cogent memoranda on a wide range of topics—quickly. At State, however, he also found a place where he could do some longer-term research. As International Economist, he has written and co-authored articles in the area of international trade and finance, on international investment, and on the proper measurement of economic variables. His work at the State Department with William G. Dewald, who later became Director of Research of the Federal Reserve Bank of St. Louis, helped persuade the Department of Commerce to change the way it measures the nation's international investment position. No wonder then that he moved to State's investment office when the policy-analysis group of which he was a member was disbanded. Nonetheless, as this volume indicates, the range of his professional interests remains broad. Of course none of the views expressed in this volume—to the extent we have added any to those of the governors represented here—is to be attributed to the U.S. Department of State or to the U.S. Government.

PART I
WESTERN HEMISPHERE

LEADING CANADA TO PRICE STABILITY: GOVERNOR CROW'S CRUSADE

GEORGE M. VON FURSTENBERG AND MICHAEL K. ULAN

CONTENTS

John W. Crow
Governor, Bank of Canada, 1987–1994

John W. Crow was born in London, England, in 1937. After primary and grammar school studies there, he completed two years (1956 to 1958) of national service in the Royal Air Force, receiving a commission as Pilot Officer, which did not, he hastens to add, qualify him to fly a plane. Rather, most of his service was spent attending the Joint Services School of Languages, where he qualified as a military and civil-service interpreter in Russian. Oxford University was next, where he graduated in Philosophy, Politics, and Economics (PPE) in 1961, besides captaining the college soccer team.

He went from Oxford to the International Monetary Fund in Washington, D.C., where he first worked mainly with Latin American countries, increasing his fluency in Spanish. On his (forced) retirement from active soccer, he took up cricket, playing for the Washington Cricket Club and also becoming its Treasurer. In 1969 he transferred to the North American Division of the Fund, covering Canada, the United States, and Mexico, and in 1970 he became Division Chief. In this position, he followed Canadian economic policy closely and made frequent visits to Ottawa to discuss exchange-rate matters. At this time, Canada went onto a flexible exchange rate, whereas the Bretton Woods pegged-rate regime was still the rule in most of the world.

These visits led to an offer to join the Bank of Canada staff, as deputy chief of the Research Department. Mr. Crow accepted this offer and moved to Ottawa in 1973, becoming Chief of the department soon after. He continued to advance rapidly, being appointed Adviser to the Governor in 1979, Deputy Governor in 1981, and Senior Deputy Governor in 1984 before becoming the Governor of the Bank of Canada for a seven-year term ending January 31, 1994. In 1993 he was elected Chair of the central bank Governors of the Group of Ten (G-10) countries, a position he relinquished when his term as governor ended.

After more than thirty years in public service, Mr. Crow now is busy with a wide range of activities in the private sector. He and his wife, Ruth Crow (née Kent), enjoy life in Toronto, where they find time for theater, opera, and gardening. They have two children.

LEADING CANADA TO PRICE STABILITY: GOVERNOR CROW'S CRUSADE

PREFACE

This study set the pattern for the studies presented here that celebrate the exemplary achievements of certain heads of central banking organizations. To be included in this project, the central bank presidents, chairs, or governors must have made important recent contributions to the theory, credible achievement, and defense of approximate price-level stability as the overriding macroeconomic goal of monetary policy.

John W. Crow, Governor of the Bank of Canada for a single seven-year term starting in 1987 and ending on January 31, 1994, distinguished himself in that select group. He agreed to identify the most pivotal and comprehensive addresses or statements delivered during his tenure, which, while taken through many drafts with his staff, remained his own in both substance and writing. In a letter dated November 18, 1994, we asked the governor to identify specifically those contributions that

> explained how he conceptualized, motivated, planned, publicly justified and executed the steadfast pursuit of the goal of getting down to approximate price-level stability when confronted with various economic challenges, including unexpected disturbances, or short- and medium-term costs associated with making the transition to lower inflation credible and durable.

The four contributions selected by the governor are identified in the references section at the end of this chapter; they are referred to by number throughout. All but one of these addresses were first delivered outside Canada, and all draw universal lessons from the Canadian experience.

Our interest in the governor's writings stems from the belief that economic science and society can gain by close and respectful study of the actions of those distinguished individuals—gifted practitioners—who have succeeded brilliantly in articulating and conducting macroeconomic policy; academics sometimes call this "reverse learning." For this reason, the point of this essay is to let the governor be heard and his good counsel be acknowledged. We relate, however, some of the evaluations of the governor's work in Canada, both appreciative and critical, less to provide mechanical balance than to show that a "prophet," or politician who did good by the long term, is rarely given credit in his own country or time. However, principled policies of price level stability that endeavor to raise future macroeconomic efficiency and predictability are slowly being recognized as an invaluable legacy, first in other countries and then in his own.

INTRODUCTION

How Macroeconomics Evolved up to Governor
Crow's Appointment

In the decade of macroeconomic hubris, from approximately 1956 to 1966, control appeared to be not only possible to economists but increasingly perfectible through their research. While problems arising from uncertainty in the private sector and from the vagaries of consumer and business confidence were not denied, they were viewed as challenges to stability that could eventually be met. Only popular superstitions blocking timely applications of the requisite monetary and fiscal policies might still have to be overcome. Then the profession could triumph and achieve goals of stability by means of government servants suitably instructed.

For a time economists demanded, and received, much respect.

Ten years later, the sense of being in close control had crumbled, but the obstinacy of the people and their representatives was not to blame. Instead, the tuning fork of policy activism, consisting of a stable Phillips Curve and reliable policy multipliers, had proved dissonant with experience. This famous curve, which refers to a downward-sloping relationship between the unemployment rate and the rate of change in money wage rates, discovered by Phillips (1958) of the London School of Economics in British data, often had been misunderstood to imply that faster wage and price inflation helped reduce unemployment so that "loosening up" on both monetary and fiscal fronts would combat cyclical unemployment. By 1976 (when Lucas wrote his famous "Critique"), it had become clear to all but a few that, as a profession giving policy advice, economists were in way over their heads.

First, doubts were raised about the ability of economists to inform policy makers about the likely consequences of their actions, by means of prior evaluations with econometric models. Then an attack, under the guise of classical economics, succeeded in reducing discretionary attempts at demand management to something worse than futility: The new orthodoxy held that exercising discretion could only disturb. Policy makers were told to stick by simple and transparent rules and not to listen to any economist who dared recommend otherwise. All economists could do was to help tie policy makers to such rules so as not to leave them exposed to the temptation of "time inconsistency"—a euphemism for when politicians cheat by letting instant voter gratification subvert their original, socially optimal, plans. Having come to believe that credibility is determined by the strength of the ties that bind sinful actors to virtue, economists were quick to offer an assortment of constitutional shackles or changes in Central Bank Acts.

Economists, who had once ventured to save the economy from its own instability, now made a pitch to save it from policy activism and activist politicians. Part of their audience was not amused and concluded that the time had come to save both the world and politicians from economists. Macroeconomists, who had once been riding high, being "in" way over their heads, now were down and definitely "out." Many forsook dealing with concrete macroeconomic policy issues entirely in favor of counterfactual environments of their own making in which they could experiment out of sight.

When one influential macroeconometrician (Sims, 1986) charged that economists tend to put forward policy conclusions and forecasts as if they were surer of them than they ought to be, based on any objective evidence, he was already firing over trenches from which no self-respecting academic economist dared look up anymore. So when

John Crow was appointed Governor of the Bank of Canada on February 1, 1987, there was little the economics profession had with which to invest him. A research economist himself, he would have to find his own way as policy maker.

THE CENTRAL BANKER'S IMPLICIT
CONTRACT WITH THE PUBLIC

From Bad Instrument Landings to Commitment
to a Single Objective

Thrown into a murky campaign—Canada's price level had slightly more than doubled by any measure from 1976 to 1986—with weapons and firepower whose reliability and strength were being made increasingly uncertain by financial innovation, the governor had a difficult start. The record of inflation, given in Table 1, showed Canada in the 1970s and 1980s to be no better than the average for industrial countries, and being down at the level of some international average has never been good enough for Canada or for John Crow personally. He briefly surveyed (1, pp. 3–4) the earlier type of policy activism that had lingered in the seventies with ever-declining self-assurance. The success of that type of activism had been predicated on the unspoken assumption that the public knew only one game, blind man's buff. Without themselves being recognized or getting caught, policy makers could then nudge the public into whatever they decided to be the right stance. As even the seemingly best of the combinations of economic variables that could be reached in this way became ever more disagreeable, the blindfolds came off and the game was up: People started to see inflation coming when stimulus to real activity was intended (1, p. 4). In a number of countries they began to adopt a sullen, "show me" attitude toward political promises of good behavior. For policy makers, on the other hand, "there was genuine uncertainty as to exactly what role Canadian monetary policy should play" (3, p.13), particularly after the Canadian dollar was allowed to float, starting in 1970.

With the old *modus operandi* discredited, no new game plan was immediately at hand. From 1975 to 1982 the makers of monetary policy first tried to pretend that they would cease playing. They would just preprogram the path of what was at first believed to be a closely controllable intermediate target, M1, which is an aggregate

Table 1

Canadian and Industrial-Country-Average Inflation Rates, 1971–1997
(from preceding year in percent)

Date	Canada	Industrial Countries
1971	3.1	5.3
1972	4.9	4.8
1973	7.5	7.9
1974	11.0	13.4
1975	10.8	11.4
1976	7.3	8.6
1977	8.1	8.8
1978	8.9	7.5
1979	9.2	9.7
1980	10.2	12.4
1981	12.5	10.4
1982	10.8	7.7
1983	5.9	5.2
1984	4.3	5.0
1985	4.0	4.4
1986	4.1	2.6
1987	4.4	3.2
1988	4.0	3.5
1989	9.5	4.6
1990	0.5	5.2
1991	5.6	4.4
1992	1.5	3.2
1993	1.9	2.8
1994	0.2	2.3
1995	2.2	2.5
1996	1.5	2.3
1997	1.8	1.7

Source: International Monetary Fund, *International Financial Statistics Database*, March 25, 1998.

of currency and checkable deposits often referred to as "narrow money." But presetting an intermediate target close to the levers of control turned out to be out of touch with the final target the public cared about: M1 targeting failed to deliver any semblance of price stability and was ultimately dropped. Years later a solution was still wanting. As Governor Crow noted (1, p. 7) dryly in his 1988 Hanson lecture at the University of Alberta:

[W]e have yet to find an aggregate that could take over the role, previously assigned to M1, of being a formal intermediate target for policy, that is, with preannounced target bands stretching out from a specific base period.

If there were to be an intermediate target or, rather, set of targets to which to direct the money supply, at least some of them would have to be much closer to the final target than to direct policy instruments to assure success. As the governor put it toward the end of his tenure, "Monetary policy is the most market-oriented, and therefore most indirect perhaps, of all public economic policies" (4, p. 58). Indeed, the search for a mechanism that could be relied upon to convert preannounced instrument use into preconceived ends appeared increasingly hopeless, perhaps even misguided from the start. Monetary policy makers, it appeared, could not be told to drive with locked steering wheel and fixed cruise control if they were also to be held responsible for getting safely to an agreed destination (2, p. 8).

In actuality, when the governor took over, it was far from clear that there was an agreed-upon destination. If anchors had been cast before, they had frequently failed to grip bottom or been lost at sea. Reading between the lines (1, p. 7), in the day-to-day implementation of monetary policy, the longer-term objectives of monetary policy tended to be lost from view. In addition, past guidance systems were becoming unreliable and obsolete. Faced with this predicament, Governor Crow did what a good general would do in a comparable situation. He clearly defined the strategic objective, reviewed what he had to work with, and then designed a battle plan. That plan, while flexible as to means, was unyielding in the pursuit of price stability as the chosen end:

> Monetary policy should be conducted so as to achieve a pace of monetary expansion that promotes stability in the value of money. This means pursuing a policy aimed at achieving and maintaining stable prices (1, p. 3).

The governor thus immediately articulated "a clear and consistent framework for monetary policy, into which the particular central bank actions are shown to fit and are seen to fit" (4, p. 61).

It is commonly observed that, in recent years, a number of advanced industrial countries have steered toward the goal of price stability. But price stability was not entrenched as the overriding goal of monetary policy in Canada when Governor Crow assumed office. His predecessor had left neither ringing speeches nor a credible record to that effect while Governor Crow left both. The preamble to the Bank of Canada Act suggests a number of goals (2, p. 6). Price stability was not yet seen

GEORGE M. VON FURSTENBERG & MICHAEL K. ULAN

as a kind of structural contribution to an effective market economy
. . . [or] as an investment that would, so far as the institution of
money and monetary exchange could, promote a range of objectives, such as high employment and rising living standards, that
go under the head of economic progress (2, p. 5).

It took Governor Crow (2, p. 6) to start the long process of
persuading the body politic that

price stability [is] the means by which those goals can best be
achieved through what we have got to work with—namely, our
central bank balance sheet, nothing less and nothing more.

He thereby reduced a multitude of goals, from the viewpoint of accepting operational control, to just one. Surely the central bank would
be held accountable by people acting through markets, but he was at
least going to define the criterion by which it should be judged.

What were the hoped-for benefits of achieving a close approximation to price stability, defined in 1991 as inflation heading to
"clearly below 2 percent" for practical purposes?

[B]ecause inflation creates distortions [in relative prices], output
will be higher over time in conditions of price stability than in
those of inflation (1, p. 3). The fundamental case for pursuing
price stability thus rests on the benefits of a trustworthy monetary standard in an economy based on money (1, p. 3). [Such a
policy] also provides a necessary anchor for market expectations
(4, p. 61). [S]tability in the value of money, and sustained
confidence in its future value, will make domestic financial systems, and the international links among such systems, generally
work better as well. This itself contributes to better economic
performance and also facilitates the prudential tasks we undertake (4, p. 69). [T]he advantages in absorbing shocks that a flexible
exchange rate can provide are likely to be realized only if that
exchange rate is anchored by a monetary policy directed at domestic price stability (3, p. 14). I doubt whether one can do better than having each country consistently pursue policies oriented
toward domestic price stability (4, p. 65). Such an international
framework provides a solid monetary basis for relatively stable
exchange rates (4, pp. 65–66). For once, it puts the economic
policy horse before the exchange rate cart (3, p. 19).

The higher the rate of inflation, the governor warned, the less predictable its behavior. Confidence in the predictability of the future value of money is undermined by inflation and cannot be restored without eliminating inflation because "a commitment to a steady inflation rate [appreciably above zero] is ultimately not credible" (1, p. 4).

In his justly famous Hanson Memorial lecture (1, p. 4), the governor elaborated on why aiming to stabilize inflation at any appreciable rate is a political-economy disaster and a delusion:

> [I]f the authorities were unwilling to act to get the rate of inflation down from, for example, 4 percent, why should anyone believe they would be any more willing to get it back to 4 percent if for one reason or another upward pressures on prices led the inflation rate to rise to 5 percent? And so on.

By his exacting standard, Governor Crow's target of heading toward an inflation rate "clearly below 2 percent" after 1995 was to become credible already well before that year. Canada's consumer price inflation averaged 1.5 percent per annum already from the middle of 1991 to the first quarter of 1994. When the new, sensible-liberal government of Prime Minister Chrétien appointed Gordon Thiessen to succeed Crow at the end of January 1994, they appointed someone who could afford to speak more softly since all the heavy lifting had already been done. But Thiessen held the same big stick over any resurgence of inflation that Governor Crow had used to beat it down. When Governor Crow's seven-year term ended, the core inflation rate (adjusted for cuts in tobacco tax rates) was down to 1.5 percent while the measured inflation rate actually fell to zero on a twelve-month basis in early 1994. The governor would prefer us to focus on year-over-year or even longer average rates of change (2, p. 5). Even so, all the specific targets for the reduction of inflation jointly announced by the central bank and the government in early 1991 (2, p. 6) had been more than met.

"It Pays to Advertise" (2, p. 6) and *The Consent of the Governed*

The governor had defined a singular objective, with the crucial instrument—managing the balance sheet of the central bank and thereby the terms on which the central bank supplies liquidity to the market—unambiguously dedicated to one target. Indeed, "[s]ince monetary policy involves the use of a single tool, providing liquidity to the financial system, one might well ask how monetary policy could be expected to achieve more than one economic objective" (2, p. 4). Yet, politically, the central bank is never fortified against conflicting demands by force of logic alone. Rather, the governor had to fight to make an exclusive coupling to price stability acceptable within the government.

In a representative democracy this is done not primarily by doing battle with ministries or by lobbying influential politicians from within. Rather, the key to self-protection is to convince important constituencies outside government that the central bank is acting in their own, well-understood long-term interest, and in that of the country. These core constituencies, which include many silent and unorganized people—not usually trade unions, nor even business, builders, or bankers associations—are difficult to mobilize. Yet they provide an indispensable back-up for defending the central bank against unprincipled impositions from other units of government.

How does a central bank win a following that could provide firm cover? Financial columnists or economic commentators in the media frequently are important catalysts of public opinion. Some of them are able to draw the lessons of experience ahead of the general public. With luck, popular insistence on price stability may become firm, and institutions that reliably produce stable prices may be valued. A central bank needs to be seen as true to its word and as a symbol of self-restrained and competent government that other units of government, particularly those concerned with taxing and spending, would do well to emulate. It is protected against attacks from within as long as this reputation holds up. To earn and preserve its *de facto* independence, it must prove itself morally and technically fit to act, and to achieve as promised, both now and in the future, barring all but the most extraordinary upheavals.

The Minister of Finance has an explicit directive power through which it can override the Bank of Canada's monetary policy decisions, thereby precipitating the resignation of its governor (2, pp. 8–9). Yet it would never conceive of openly laying a hand on a central bank, whose prestige and competence, in its area of responsibility, far exceeds that of any other unit of government. Any egregious attempt to step on the prerogatives of the central bank or to use new appointments for transparently partisan ends and short-term advantage would be instantly punished by financial markets. If the central bank is valued highly enough, retribution at the ballot box might follow in due course.

Formally independent or not, the central bank is thus always on probation with the public. It needs to be concerned with all aspects of credibility, both in terms of avoiding time inconsistency, further discussed below, and by demonstrating technical and moral competence and public leadership—crucial to its ability and willingness to deliver on its stated commitments with a steady hand. To protect its credibility, a central bank should not overstate what it can be expected to do or how precisely it can deliver, while giving its best effort, in an uncertain environment. Governor Crow publicly dismissed the notion that "monetary policy exerts its influence in any precise or mechanistic way" (1, p. 5). Instead, he compared the conduct of monetary policy to "driving in a rainstorm with defective windshield wipers. It can be done, but only very carefully" (1, p. 6).

The central bank, with best effort and intelligence, may also not be able to anticipate and neutralize all possible sources of systemic risk, foreign and domestic. Nevertheless, it must be seen as highly vigilant, doing everything in its power to forestall payments-and-settlements crises of the financial system that could undermine its reputation for competence and control. "The less real lending of last resort we do . . . the better" (4, p. 58).

Each one of Governor Crow's four addresses considered here has much to say on the need to establish and maintain credibility. Almost his entire 1993 lecture at the University of Pretoria is a treatise on political economy and on the art of public persuasion, too little practiced:

> Without a clear legislative objective, the central bank obviously must go to great pains to set out as clearly as it possibly can the basis on which policy *is* being made. Only by doing this can it provide the public and government with the wherewithal for properly assessing its performance (2, p. 9). Such . . . means of public communication (including, I might add, lectures) give the central bank the opportunity to explain how its actions are contributing to the objective that has been established for monetary policy (2, p. 10).

There is a corollary to this: A voting public that has not been made to understand and care about the objective of price stability will not long enjoy the services of a central banker who provides it. There are many examples of central bankers who, with a wink and a nod, have made inflation with their independence. Governor Crow did not become one of them.

THE ECONOMIC SYSTEM AND WHAT TO DO ABOUT DISTURBANCES

Overview

Central bankers are not nearly as tempted toward time inconsistency as economists like to warn. This sin is committed if originally right-thinking central bankers who know that inflation could only be harmful and costly to reverse in the long run nonetheless later agree to risk their reputation for the sake of short-term stimulation. Most central bankers would regard it as absurd to be cast as lying in wait with inflation surprises to spring on a duped, hamstrung, or intentionally confounded public. Yet inflation has been far from negligible in most countries, including Canada, until quite recently. Without continued determined and competent action, it always comes back in countries in which political survival, as decided by voters, is not yet firmly predicated on its avoidance. For this reason, the credibility of central bankers cannot depend solely on the degree of independence provided in their charter or on the sincerity of their good intentions. Rather, the quality of their understanding of the economic system and the tools they have to work with largely determine their success.

Governor Crow has gone to considerable length to provide glimpses of the model that informs him. This model, he explained (1, p. 6), is not an abstract of the Quarterly Projection Model, or of any other macroeconometric model, devised and maintained by his staff. Rather, it is an outline of the links between key variables and how these variables can be tethered reliably to a nominal anchor in view of specific disturbances that may affect them. Furthermore, different parts of the constellation become visible at different times, and structures may shift, calling for changes in the calibration of policy responses. The public then needs to be assured that steadfastness in pursuit of the goal of price stability is strengthened, not weakened, by allowing flexibility in the choice of appropriate means and dosage.

Governor Crow provided this element of accountability and assurance by sharing his reflections on past episodes and what they taught him (1, pp. 7–11; 3, pp. 14–18). These event studies sought to identify the factors involved in any change and to explain how particular challenges to stability were answered by monetary policy. At the same time, there is a strong sense of continuity, reinforced by careful reassertion of the goal, its rationale, and of the basic capability to achieve it. Such frequent reaffirmation precludes cover-up and opportunistically shifting ground to disclaim responsibility.

The governor's clarity in communicating the basis for his actions has encouraged us to write down the basic model that might be apt to characterize his thinking in a general way. We will attempt to outline his views on (1) exchange-rate determination; (2) determinants of the money-supply process; (3) factors determining the inflation rate whose level constitutes the policy target; and (4) the system constraints, which are aggregate demand and supply relations specified in real rather than nominal terms.

Assuming the resulting model can be closed or made amenable to simulations with actual data, an economist would be tempted to evaluate first the quality of the specification of the model and then the benefits of following the policy embedded in it. For instance, the damage done to price stability by different types of exogenous shocks under the existing modified-feedback rule might be compared to what it would be under an automatic rule, such as fixed or preannounced rates of growth of the money supply. Alternatively, various modifications of the feedback rule could be suggested to achieve a closer approximation to the optimum configuration in view of the expected variance-covariance pattern of disturbances. Once the intended rate of growth of the money supply had been identified, there would be the implementation problem of achieving it through the banking system with the least amount of signal confusion and control error.

Instead of engaging in a broad-ranging evaluation of alternatives for monetary policy, we will here be content with just extracting a model from the governor's speeches to gauge its economic character, parentage, and coherence. Academic respectability, while not a central banker's most pressing concern, could still be an element in support of credibility. Economists are probably not alone in wanting to be sure that a governor, who did well, made his or her— or rather, the nation's—own good fortune, and did not just happen to catch a favorable wind.

While the technical presentation of the model is left to another publication (von Furstenberg, 1998), a detailed outline of its main features, organized by subject, will reveal how it derives from the governor's thinking. Readers who are impatient with detailed discussions of economic specifications and more interested in issues of political economy should proceed directly to the next main section.

Exchange-Rate Determination

Of all bilateral exchange rates, the exchange value of the Canadian for the U.S. dollar is the main subject of government policy concerns. The Canadian-dollar index against the G-10 currencies is published by the Bank of Canada on the basis 1981=100, a level briefly surpassed in 1991. Its year-end 1997 level of 79 indicates substantial exchange rate depreciation of the Canadian dollar relative to the currencies of the other nine countries since 1991. While the index is "nominal," i.e., not adjusted for differences in inflation rates of the countries contributing to the index with Canada, its "real" counterpart would give a similar reading because differences in inflation rates, particularly with the United States, have been small. The Group of Ten industrial countries consists of the better-known G-7 (Canada, the United States, the United Kingdom, Germany, France, Italy, and Japan; since Russia was first included at the 1997 Denver Summit, this group is now also known as G-8) plus Belgium, the Netherlands, and Sweden, and, since 1984, Switzerland, with yet more countries scheduled to be added. Represented by finance ministers and central bank governors, these G-10 countries are regarded as most active in international finance and in the design of international monetary and banking systems and standards. Organizational and manpower support for much of the work of this group is provided by the Bank for International Settlements (BIS) in Basle, Switzerland. While the "effective" exchange rate index with the G-10 countries is referred to officially, that index moves closely with the U.S. dollar value of the Canadian dollar, given that the weight of the U.S. dollar in the effective exchange rate index is about 80 percent.

Cross-border market and financial integration between Canada and the United States is so close that Governor Crow tends to refer to Canada's exchange rates in the singular and not as a multilateral composite. He has identified three types of factors that may buffet this rate:

> First, there may be *fundamental developments*, including adverse developments, that call for downward adjustments in the real

exchange rate "through which the loss of real income was generalized throughout the Canadian economy" (1, p. 8). For example, after 1990, "with softness in commodity prices, our terms of trade were down from their earlier highs" (3, p. 17). Earlier there had been "positive market assessments of the Canadian dollar in the light of the boom in a whole range of the industrial materials that Canada exports" (3, p. 17).

Shocks such as the U.S. fiscal profligacy shock of the mid-1980s or the German fiscal profligacy shock since unification of the country in 1990, by fundamentally altering capital import requirements, also affect exchange rate fundamentals (4, pp. 64–65). He thus tended to believe that, more often than not, exchange rates, and financial markets, are right in line with fundamentals, often carrying messages to which policy makers need to listen with care. A view of fundamentals that is restricted to "purchasing power parity or a movement in the current account, may not be giving the right answer" (4, p. 64).

However, unlike a change in "real" fundamentals that alters the long-run equilibrium exchange rate, a change in the capital imports a country might "need" to reconcile smoothly with its government's policy may not be what financial markets allow it to get. These markets will not offer acceptable terms if the country is seen to cling to a course that is ultimately unsustainable. For this reason, "policy" effects on the exchange rate are frequently distinguished from "fundamental" effects, if not without strain.

Second, *monetary policy and demand shocks* may arise at home or spill in from elsewhere, particularly from the United States. These may affect interest rates and exchange rates interactively. Indeed, "exchange markets, and money markets also, can move around significantly in response to shifts in perceptions and/or anticipations about monetary policy as well as in response to the actions themselves" (3, p. 16). "[T]he degree of exchange rate response will also depend on how long the [new] policy stance is expected to last and on how firmly views are held about the future course of the Canadian dollar" (1, p. 5). Though *non*monetary and *non*policy factors may, of course, have consequences for interest and hence exchange rates also (3, p.17), the influence of monetary policy shocks, including foreign shocks, is conveyed through changes in the U.S.–Canadian short-term interest differential. Changes in the expected *persistence* of a policy or demand change are captured by changes in the coefficient on that interest differential.

Third, a variety of additional factors that defy easy labeling may affect exchange rates. For instance, large fiscal and current-account imbalances may add to uncertainties in financial markets and keep the state of inflationary expectations fragile (1, pp. 8–9). However, it is not easy to define how changes in such factors, expected or unexpected, affect exchange rate changes, though they may be linked systematically to the volatility of such changes. Seemingly spontaneous capital flows may occur, and "herd instinct" (4, p. 64) may amplify the disturbance. Bubble paths and "extrapolative expectations" (1, p. 8; 3, p.18) may give real exchange rates the appearance of a random walk for a time, delaying the return to fundamentals. Hence there is an *error component* in changes in the exchange rate that represents a catch-all for processes that are difficult to explain or pin down. If there is a fundamental equilibrium to the level of the real exchange rate, any such error must reverse itself eventually.

Having completed the inventory of factors mentioned prominently by the governor as bearing on exchange rate movements, the question arises whether this rendition is fully compatible with the theory of efficient asset markets. This theory states that any excess over the riskless rate of return prevailing on liquid investments in financial markets must be attributed to nondiversifiable risks, so that, if risks can be fully hedged, there should be no predictable advantage in shifting investments from one currency into another. Governor Crow clearly pointed to the key element of that theory when he noted (1, p. 8) that, other things given,

> any change in Canadian short-term interest rates relative to those in the United States will be possible only to the extent that there is an offsetting movement between the current exchange rate and that expected to prevail at the relevant maturity date for the investment.

Detailed technical examination (in von Furstenberg, 1998) has shown that in a matter going from the broad sweep of rhetoric down to detail, the governor's reasoning passes the test of academic respectability with flying colors. Because what follows relates to either his area of immediate responsibility, the money supply process, or relations whose economic underpinnings are rather more easily recognized [as "distinctly mainline, market-oriented" (1, p. 5)], no further "audits" of this kind appear necessary. Rather, the focus in what follows will be on how the governor fits the money-supply process into a coherent view of the economy and on what the implied model says about coping with disturbances.

The Money Supply Process

In determining the stance of monetary policy, Governor Crow clearly distinguishes between *tactical* and *strategic* decision elements (3, p. 18). Tactical decisions have to do with providing some offsets to short-term disturbances that could otherwise throw the economy off its intended path toward target. They lead to a reaction function telling how to ride waves in a storm. Strategic decisions focus on ultimately achieving the target. They make sure that the anchor holds and stays in place even if the anchor cable is long and the ship is never still. Because monetary policy effects on prices are subject to "long and variable lags" (2, p. 4) that may be distributed "over more than two years" (2, p. 7), the main focus must be on the intermediate term. Nevertheless, both the tactical and the strategic elements combine to determine the setting of monetary policy:

> In gauging the impact of its monetary policy actions on demand and inflation, the central bank must . . . keep an eye on both interest rates and the exchange rate. [W]hen, for example, monetary conditions need to be tightened, . . . to the extent that [an appreciation of] the exchange rate takes part of the load, less needs to be done through interest rates. We use the term "monetary conditions" to characterize the transmission of that joint interest rate and exchange rate effect (3, p. 16). [T]he term . . . does not for us *define* in any lasting sense monetary policy and its purposes any more than do interest rates by themselves or does the exchange rate by itself. . . . Our fundamental interest is in seeing to it that our monetary policy actions, working as they do through money markets and other financial markets, contribute to sustained good economic performance in Canada by helping to maintain confidence in the future value of our money (3, p. 17). In these circumstances it is more essential than ever to provide policy with a framework that is directed as clearly as possible at ensuring moderate expansion in dollar spending in the Canadian economy (1, p. 10).

There are indications here that, as a first approximation to estimating growth in the demand for real money balances—money balances adjusted for inflation—under noninflationary conditions, the long-run real income elasticity of demand for real balances (the percentage change in the demand for real balances caused by a 1 percent change in real income), frequently estimated to be close to one, is applied to the target rate of growth of real output. This yields the rate of growth of the money supply that accords with the underlying cycle-average ("potential") growth rate of the economy if the long-term target for the inflation rate is zero. As already indicated, Governor Crow does not view the normal or potential rate of growth of output as immutable. He even expects that a reliably noninflationary monetary policy could make a small but positive contribution in this regard. There may also be permanent shifts in the time path of the income-velocity of money (the ratio of Gross Domestic Product to the money supply) from time to time. In addition, there is a strong "error-learning" or correction component in policy formation. If that component is more reactive than forward-looking, it would imply, for instance, that money-supply growth is cut in response to having experienced excessive inflation, or real-output growth above potential, in the recent past. Strict accountability for the outcome, approximate price stability, thus implies that the governor must have the flexibility to secure it.

Linking money-supply growth with trend rates of real economic growth and having it react to undesired changes, particularly in the price level, does not reveal what exactly the monetary authorities must do to their liabilities (CB money) to achieve a close coupling. There are some random elements in the transmission of Bank of Canada instrument settings to financial markets that can be interpreted as unintended disturbances to the money supply. Here money is defined in the normal way as an aggregate much broader than central-bank money. Hence an error term in money supply, and correction of last period's intermediate control error that has now become apparent, must be included. In this way the looseness of a central bank's operational control over broad-based money growth is taken into account.

Strong faith in the predictability of that aggregate's income velocity would give "[m]onetary aggregates . . . a significant role to play in this strategy" (1, p.10) of ending inflation. Indeed, emphasizing long-term strategic elements would be compatible with rates of growth of the money supply, which are announced for one period ahead within a range whose width might be two times the standard deviation of the money-supply control error.

Turning to the tactical components, what then should monetary policy do if, say, there is a real depreciation of the Canadian dollar? (A real depreciation of the Canadian dollar occurs when the number of units of foreign goods and services that can be purchased for one unit of Canadian goods and services falls.) Governor Crow has emphasized that the real consumption wage must fall, or be held back, if such a real depreciation is to materialize from nominal exchange-rate depreciation (3, p. 16). Indeed, nominal and real exchange rates must move hand in hand if the domestic inflation targets are not to be disturbed. Real depreciation means that the real earnings of workers—in terms of their buying power over the tradable goods they produce and consume, and hence costs to their employers—must fall if resources are to be transferred to the production of traded goods such as exportables and import substitutes. But if depreciation raises the price of traded goods, including imports, relative to nontraded goods, and the price of the latter is sticky downwards, real depreciation also presents a direct threat to price stability (1, pp. 9–10).

Unless counteracted, this threat is compounded by the ultimately stimulative effects of real depreciation on aggregate demand. Real personal-consumption expenditures would initially fall on account of the income effects of the adverse change in the terms of trade, with imports bearing the brunt of the reduction. Nevertheless, the increase in international competitiveness would soon raise employment and income if there were sufficient slack in the economy. The reason is that net exports would tend to rise even though foreign direct investment in the Canadian economy could increase as well. Any reduction in the cost of Canadian assets to foreigners relative to their prospective earnings stream in international markets could make expanding in Canada more attractive. But since financial investors wanting to reduce the growth in their Canadian exposure presumably were behind the initial real depreciation of the Canadian dollar to start with, crosscurrents in the international capital accounts would still lead to a reduction in net capital imports and in the deficit on current account.

Given prior balance, aggregate demand thus would increase above the desired level in Governor Crow's analysis. A rise in the (annualized) real interest rate, such as in the three-month commercial paper rate net of the inflation rate expected for the three months ahead, by one percentage point for every 3-percent depreciation in the real exchange rate index, could then be designed to offset this disturbance. Such a combination of developments would leave Canada's monetary conditions index (see Freedman, 1994) unchanged. Given a sudden depreciation of the real exchange rate, the reduction in money-supply growth helps raise the real interest rate in the short run to buffer aggregate demand against the exchange-rate disturbance.

Nominal interest rates and exchange rates, which are the normal rates, unadjusted for inflation, that are quoted in financial markets, are highly volatile in the short run compared with the inertial momentum characterizing prices of goods and services, particularly prices of finished goods, over short periods immediately ahead. For this reason, movements in real and in nominal interest and exchange rates need not be distinguished as a practical matter at high frequencies of observation. The expected inflation rate can change potentially in an instant, merely as a result of a major, usually political, shock or announcement, but the broad-based inflation rate affected lies farther out and is not the one immediately ahead or next to be reported. Hence Governor Crow does not make the distinction between real and nominal rates in this context, though changes in real rates are clearly intended.

If it were perceived that increases in interest rates and exchange depreciation could both be purely nominal, the combination of these two changes would signal a rise in expected inflation. "[W]hen strong expectations of high inflation develop, interest rates that otherwise look high are not really so in regard to economic behaviour" (1, p. 6). Such a rise in expected inflation would have to be counteracted by a contractive monetary policy's temporarily raising nominal interest rates even further. But success in wringing expectations of increased inflation out of the system would eventually produce a large fall in nominal interest rates. "[O]ne of the eventual results . . . [of such a policy] is in fact, so far as monetary policy can deliver them, low interest rates, not high ones" (4, p. 62). Once investors have confidence in what the central bank is doing to protect the price level, "it may be plausible to argue that the additional liquidity greases the wheels of the financial market, acting to encourage a decline in interest rates across the maturity spectrum" (4, p. 61). At the same time it would allow *real* interest rates to fall to levels that are necessarily determined by nonmonetary factors in the long run.

The Determinants of Inflation and Aggregate Supply

Because expectations drive financial markets in ways that are difficult to guide or predict closely, the Bank of Canada can never be sure how any of its actions that add to or subtract from liquidity will be interpreted and processed by the market. "In particular, because interest rates are inherently forward looking, it depends on what happens to the views of investors and savers in the process" (4, p. 60). "[M]arkets provide a valid independent view, even a 'quote,' on the economic and financial situation" (4, p. 64).

Inflation is also often determined as a part of a forward-looking process, with expected inflation inversely related to the demand for real money balances because it is more expensive to store purchasing power in the form of money balances when they are expected to lose buying power more rapidly. As a result, any change in the rate of inflation expected for the future affects the level of prices set right now, as well as the pay raises negotiated for the contract period ahead. Nevertheless central bankers wisely decline to presume that their credibility is so firm that they can factor obliging expectations into the success of their programs as soon as they are appointed. In theory, a public that is confident that any outbreak of inflation will soon be squelched by the monetary authorities reacts with less inflation to any given cause. Yet one reason that Governor Crow was wary of underplaying inflation risks and staking changes in the rate of inflation on changes in forward-looking expectations may be the desire to avoid "wishful thinking" (4, p. 64):

> [G]iven history, . . . [skeptical] views on the chances that a better inflation performance can be sustained are likely to be particularly slow to change. This means that the Bank of Canada has to move carefully and purposefully if it is to encourage a sustained improvement in those expectations. . . . [B]uilding trust in money takes time (4, p. 62).

Economists who lament policy makers' tendency to ignore the effects of changes in expected inflation when inflation is on the way up, may recognize it as prudent when inflation is on the way down. Still, the governor overfulfilled his interim goals, on the way to reducing inflation toward the vanishing point, because in determining the degree of effort to be made he opted not to factor in adjustments in expectations. The extra effect he got from this effort may indicate that he

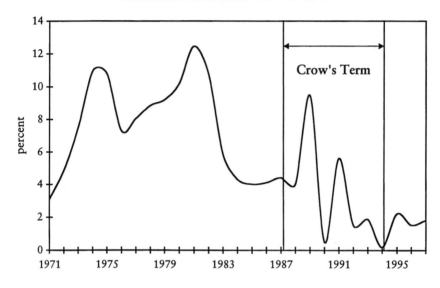

Canadian Inflation 1971–1997

Figure 1
Source: International Monetary Fund,
International Financial Statistics Database, March 25, 1998.

impressed private-sector expectations with his policy. The accomplishments during his term in subduing inflation are evident from Figure 1.

There are also technical reasons why Governor Crow and his successor may have gained more support for avoiding inflation. In an increasingly cashless society with deregulated financial markets and floating interest rates, nominal own rates of return on money move ever more closely with the T-bill and related rates, and hence with the expected rate of inflation embodied in them. With reserve requirements on bank deposits removed and the Bank Rate floating (4, p. 59), rates paid on bank liabilities float as well. Inflation and money issue thus no longer are able to yield much seignorage to the government. Rather, inflation, by driving up the government's nominal interest costs, only adds to the government deficit, and to its political discomfort, under conventional accounting that does not adjust for changes in the real value of government debt. Hence the inclination may grow for units of government other than the central bank to support a policy of strict avoidance of inflation.

What contemporaneous and past factors then contribute to

measured rates of inflation? In an open economy, a simultaneous change in nominal and real exchange rates generally affects inflation in such a way as to reverse part of the initial real change over time. Past levels of output and employment in relation to sustainable noninflationary levels and the current momentum of the real economy also may cause the overall rate of inflation to change. This view emerges from the governor's reference to slack (1, p. 9) as well as to unsustainable rates of expansion (1, pp. 10–11) as conditioning inflation dynamics. He sees long and variable lags in the transmission, to inflation, of changes in the supply of settlement balances to financial institutions. Such actions "directly influence the very shortest-term interest rates in the Canadian money market" [then] the whole spectrum of "rates of return on a wide variety of assets and liabilities and, through them, the exchange value of the Canadian dollar" (1, p. 5). "[The effects] spread to aggregate demand in the economy and finally to inflation" (2, p. 7), so that "monetary actions do take time to exert their effects on spending" (1, p. 6). Spending that grows faster than potential output and carries output past its long-term sustainable ("potential") level adds to inflation.

Factors Contributing to Changes in Aggregate Demand

A positive link between output growth and changes in inflation can be viewed as an aggregate supply relation, for instance, when labor contracts are such that surprise inflation for a time lowers real wages and thereby raises employment and output. A negative link could be established through the reduction in real balances (money balances divided by the price index) and through the rise in real interest rates and the real exchange appreciation that the policy reflex of monetary tightening in response to unexpected inflation could induce. Changes in interest and exchange rates, beyond those needed to correct inflationary biases that may have become apparent, in turn, influence the money supply process through the "tactical" terms, creating an interdependent system.

Starting with the demand for real balances, Governor Crow notes that aggregates at least as broad as M2 (essentially the sum of currency in circulation, checking and checkable deposits, and savings deposits) have "[s]ince the end of 1984 . . . returned to a path much more in line with the growth of nominal spending" (1, p. 10). M1 (essentially M2 minus savings deposits) growth, by contrast, can be greatly affected, but in a manner that is difficult to predict, by substitution between those adjustable-interest-bearing components contained only in M2, and the low- or no-interest-bearing components of money comprising much of M1 (1, p. 7).

The systematic long-term elements of the money supply equation must mirror those of the corresponding money demand equation at zero inflation. Since Governor Crow explicitly dismisses the possibility of disequilibrium between the supply and demand for money (1, p. 5), rates of change in demand and supply of nominal balances are always equal, given the free movement of interest and exchange rates. However, unlike in elementary textbook models, the growth in nominal money supply is endogenous, meaning dependent on the internal working of the economy and the (interest, inflation, and exchange) rate outcomes is yields.

The governor has explored these workings by considering the determinants of the main components of aggregate demand. The presumption of strong negative effects of real interest rates, primarily on business investment, and weaker, but on balance positive, effects of real depreciation on net exports and other components of aggregate demand appeared already in the specification of the money-supply process. The *tactical* part of that process was to maintain aggregate-demand balance. In addition, there may be changes in "autonomous" elements, such as fiscal and other components of aggregate demand, that were not technically within the governor's purview. Wealth and real-balance effects, though barely hinted at, could be included in this catch-all term as well. Its movements could then indicate added, or reduced, stimulus to aggregate demand from a variety of sources, including external shocks to aggregate demand.

THE QUALITY OF POLICY

Having extracted a small conceptual model from the governor's addresses, the final questions are where and how it might have been helpful. Few central bankers organize their thinking and decision processes in a manner analogous to solving a fully specified model. Even fewer, with any experience, would ever commit publicly to any such formal model and the constraints and limitations it would impose. Nevertheless, the previous sections have shown that outstanding governors do not seek to avoid public scrutiny. Rather, they choose to give many indications of their general lines of thought, whether or not such candor is convenient for others:

> As regards accountability through communication, I doubt if anyone would disagree that a body with public policy responsibilities should be as clear as possible regarding the basis for its actions (2, p. 9).

On account of this candor, there is a good chance that the model abstracted from Governor Crow's four speeches does, in fact, succeed in providing a faithful characterization of his approach.

It may then be interesting to focus on policy and to ask how the model is equipped to react to specific disturbances, say, in monetary relations and government spending. The objective is not to give an *ex post* conditional forecast of what the governor might have done if he had acted on the prompting of the model attributed to him. Rather the purpose is to distinguish areas where the model might give strong guidance from those in which its guidance is less cogent.

Countering Disturbances Arising in the Monetary Sector

The governor has emphasized the looseness of the relation between what the central bank does and what happens to interest rates (4, p. 60). Hence the relation between these actions and their effect on the quantity of broad-based money (including many types of deposit and certificate-of-deposit claims on banks and related financial institutions and not just checkable deposits issued by banks) may be judged equally loose. For this reason, the first relevant policy experiment involves analyzing the consequences of an unintended, and initially unobserved, money supply shock arising in the transmission from open-market operations (the central bank's purchase or sale of government securities) to broad money.

The model implies that, with a positive shock of this kind, the rate of inflation increases to the extent real output grows faster in the short run. When there is an unintended increase in the nominal money supply, inflation and the growth rate of output would both be nudged up, but real money balances demanded and supplied would at first still show an increase. However, all of that increase would quickly be reduced because both the money-supply-induced decline in the real interest rate and depreciation of the exchange rate would induce (contractive) monetary countermeasures. High-frequency signals about changes in the rates prevailing in the market would immediately induce some correction of the positive money-supply error and all its consequences. Full correction would come one period later as last period's unintended change in the money supply is undone to put the money supply back on the track originally intended. Thus both the goals of short-term stabilization and long-term fidelity to price stability would be well served.

Fiscal Mismanagement: What Can a Governor Do?

The last experiment designed to show how the system would respond involves a fiscal shock that expands aggregate demand. It is no longer clear to most macroeconomists how such a shock would be administered since any permanent increase in government spending would imply a matching permanent increase in taxes on a present-value basis. It would create growing uncertainty about the future distribution of tax burdens and may reduce a country's advantage as a work, business, production, incorporation, and residence location. Still, most economists believe that any increase in government spending on goods and services that is believed to be temporary would expand current aggregate demand on balance, though possibly by a fraction, rather than a multiple of itself.

Good as it is in relation to monetary management, the previous model was clearly not developed for fiscal-policy planning, nor is it capable of yielding a reliable assessment except under special conditions. These are circumstances where, as in the United States in the mid-1980s and as in Germany in the early 1990s, a policy of fiscal expansion led to higher real interest rates and a sharp real appreciation of the exchange rate while capital imports surged and the money supply showed little growth. Governor Crow discussed such foreign circumstances in his 1993 address at the Reserve Bank of India (4, pp. 64–65). If the previous model remained applicable, in Canada such a fiscal policy would have induced some short-term tactical accommodation on account of the joint rise in real interest rates and the exchange rate.

Yet such accommodation is not what an inappropriately unbalanced fiscal policy may deserve, nor is a real appreciation of the currency bound to follow a fiscal expansion. Even the model most commonly used for analyzing the international effects of a country's macroeconomic policies (known as Mundell-Fleming; the governor, however, prefers the opposite, chronologically correct, ordering of names) need not suggest such an outcome (see von Furstenberg, 1998). Should international investors, Canadian and others, greet fiscal expansion by marking down the Canadian dollar, the money supply function would call, correctly, for a contraction of the money supply.

Conversely, Canada's much needed turn to fiscal conservatism, 1995 to 1996, was greeted by some appreciation of its dollar and brought a measure of interest-rate relief. Subsequently, however, as interest rates in Canada continued to decline to low levels not seen since 1971 to 1972, Canada's effective exchange rate index fell sharply, signifying steep depreciation, even though the news on fiscal deficit control remained highly favorable.

In principle, the central bank can do little directly to contain unsustainable fiscal deficits or to improve relevant political incentives. There are limits to the degree to which a central bank that prides itself in command independence from other units of government can issue them report cards that amount to censure. Its public complaints about the government's fiscal policy tend to be veiled and guarded unless the government intends to use central bank criticism for its own plans. Yet governors cannot avoid fiscal issues entirely. There is no one among them who has embraced the ("Ricardian") belief that fiscal balance, or the choice of tax versus debt financing, should not be a macroeconomic concern. Instead, they know that fiscal mismanagement represents a clear and present danger not only to their provisional independence, but also to the effectiveness and calculability of what they do. For instance, rising interest rates on short-term government debt may create positive income effects for net financial investors that weaken the negative interest-rate effect of monetary policy on aggregate demand. A large public debt may keep financial markets on tenterhooks.

Fiscal and monetary issues thus remain entangled even now that attempts to exploit monetary-fiscal policy trade-offs, at unchanged expectations of inflation, have long been recognized as unrealistic (1, p. 4). Indeed, fiscal discipline helps preserve monetary discipline, and there is a need for mutual reinforcement, not trade-offs, between them. Governor Crow observed already in 1988 that the economy was becoming "more acutely sensitive to the disagreeable arithmetic thrown up by cumulating deficits and the resulting rise in debt and debt service burdens" (1, p. 4). He hinted that large fiscal and current account imbalances gnaw at the credibility of government in a way that also threatens to erode the expectational support needed for effective monetary actions (1, p. 8).

From his lecture pulpit, Governor Crow did what he could to

issue even stronger warnings before fiscal problems would get out of hand:

> As regards fiscal policy, the imperative is to steer wide of the risks of cumulative pressures on debt and deficits. In Canada, continuing the budgetary effort directed at reducing such pressures is important. It is important not just for stability in financial markets and, it might be argued, for reinforcing confidence in monetary policy. It is important also for ensuring that government does not absorb an excessive proportion of private savings, forcing an unduly large share of Canada's investment needs to be financed abroad (1, p. 4).

This forthright warning was not heeded by the Mulroney government, which had become too weak to be conservative or otherwise of use. In 1993, the last full year of Governor Crow's tenure, Canada's current account deficit was equal to between 70 and 80 percent of its total net investment in fixed capital and inventories, depending on how a statistical discrepancy is allocated. The government deficit, on the national income accounts basis, "absorbed" 86 percent of total net private saving. If there was to be any regret for the governor, it was that, unlike in his area of responsibility, the fiscal side did not reform as promised. Ironically it was left to the new government of Prime Minister Chrétien, which chose not to reappoint Governor Crow, to turn Canada decisively away from a headlong course into crises provoked by unsustainably high levels of internal and external debt. In this process of renewal and reform, the new ideas provided by some of Canada's western provinces and competition within the federal system also played a salutary part.

CANADIAN APPRAISALS

Shortly after Governor Crow's term ended, Canada's leading national daily, *The Globe and Mail*, asked its expert panel of bank-watchers to appraise Governor Crow's tenure and to advise his successor, Gordon Thiessen. The comments of three academic economists and of three others prominently involved in economic and social affairs and studies were then reported in an article by Kidd (1994, pp. 38–40). Freeman (1995), a reporter in the parliamentary bureau of *The Globe and Mail,* unfavorably contrasted Governor Crow's *public style* with that of his successor, while noting similarities in their policies and objectives. More substantive evaluations of Canada's transition to noninflationary growth are provided by Laidler and Robson (1993; 1994). The Bank of Canada does not play a direct role in the supervision or restructuring of Canada's increasingly centralized, but dynamic, financial services industry; we refer to Chant (1997) and Neufeld and Hassanwalia (1997) for comprehensive treatments of this important subject.

One additional characterization of Governor Crow's tenure was delivered on April 3, 1995, by a prominent economist formerly with Nomura Canada (Leo de Bever) and is repeated here with his permission. A similar, but more prosaic, assessment appeared earlier in an editorial by Peter Cook (*The Globe and Mail*, January 9, 1995, p. B2). Excerpts from each comment follow in order, without repeating points already made earlier.

1. [S]ociety has many more goals than just price stability. . . . [P]olicy makers must devise policies so as to minimize adjustment costs. On this basis, Bank of Canada policy has not been a great success. Canada's manufacturing sector was devastated [by the combination of high interest rates and appreciation of the exchange rate]. If Thiessen proves no more cooperative than Crow was, then he, too, should step aside.

2. [T]he accumulation of inflation-fighting credibility has been costly in terms of other economic and social goals. But this credibility is now an asset, lending the bank short-term maneuverability to ensure that broader priorities are not left behind in the pursuit of zero inflation.

3. The task for the next seven years is to consolidate past achievements, and that will not be easy. Canada had a highly credible central banker in the person of John Crow. What it needs is a more credible central bank and currency. Canada has neither of these yet. Anyone who doubts this should look at the extremely high interest rates on long-term Canadian bonds. . . . First, we must depersonalize monetary policy. Price stability needs to be seen as the goal of an institution—the Bank of Canada—and not merely of its current governor. . . . The second, more important prerequisite for establishing the credibility of the Canadian currency is political support for the Bank. Without [a cred-

ible plan to deal with our public sector's dangerous levels of debt and deficit] government borrowing will, in due course, overwhelm monetary restraint, and the hard-won gains of the past seven years will be wasted.

4. Internationally, Crow was a big crowd-pleaser. Luckily for Ottawa, that fan loyalty has shifted quickly to Thiessen, the man seen mostly as Crow by another name.

5. [J]ust like other small trading countries such as Austria and the Netherlands, Canada should fix the value of its currency at a realistic level—say 70 cents (U.S.)—relative to its major trading partner. This would allow our interest rates to decrease toward U.S. levels.

6. As governor, I would have accepted a higher but stable inflation rate, which would have lowered both unemployment and public debt. John Crow's preoccupation with zero inflation has cost this country enormously. For Thiessen and the government to continue that preoccupation would be absolutely disastrous.

7. Foreign investors viewed Governor Crow like Atlas: He would hold the country up high, eliminate inflation, and make the exchange rate levitate.

If the quotes are indicative of the division of informed opinion and opinion leaders in Canada, the continued pursuit of price-level stability is still far from secure, with only a minority favoring disciplined adherence to that goal. Economists of station (e.g., Fortin, 1996) have been particularly hard to convince or to reconcile. For the most part, therefore, the governor led Canada toward price stability kicking and screaming, years before his precious destination came to be appreciated in all major industrial countries and quite a few developing countries besides.

THE LEGACY

The evaluation of Governor Crow's record in his own country has continued to be mixed, even hostile. But his achievements on the price front have received history's high compliment of having become a permanent feature of the political landscape and of national pride and aspirations that no amount of polemics can effectively question or remove. Indeed, as the data of Table 1 showed, Governor Crow's bequest of a credible low-inflation regime to his fellow Canadians has not been squandered by his successor, Governor Thiessen. Instead, Governor Crow helped jolt Canada into a high-energy period of disciplined government reform and retrenchment that has yielded much gain after, admittedly, a protracted period of pain.

It has become hard to imagine that future Canadian governments or central bankers would dare return the country to double-digit inflation, or even something lower such as the treacherous 4 percent inflation, "and so on," Crow had warned about in his famous Hanson lecture, cited earlier. Rather, protestations to the contrary notwithstanding, the country as a whole has embraced the principled pursuit of price stability.

Instead of U.S. inflation rates defining the lowest rates that could possibly be hoped for in North America, Canada is in the process of developing an independent reputation for hard money. That reputation is beginning to be as enviable vis-à-vis the United States as Switzerland's is with regard to Germany. Canada's average annual inflation rate over the ten-year period of 1987 to 1997 was 2.8 percent, while the U.S. rate was 3.5 percent. For the second half of this period the difference was even greater: 1.0 percent consumer price inflation annually in Canada compared with 2.8 percent in the United States on average for 1992 to 1997. While the market for over twenty-five years had required higher nominal interest rates on otherwise comparable Canadian-dollar versus U.S.-dollar denominated paper, particularly at the long end, this is no longer true in 1997 to 1998. It has taken a long while from the time Governor Crow helped lay the foundations, but Canada is now getting credit where credit is due.

REFERENCES

Chant, John F. 1997. "Canada's Economy and Financial System: Recent and Prospective Developments and the Policy Issues They Pose." Pp. 2–43 in George M. von Furstenberg, ed., *The banking and financial structure in the NAFTA countries and Chile.* Boston: Kluwer Academic Publishers.

Crow, John W.

(1) *The Work of Canadian Monetary Policy. La Politique Monétaire à L'Oeuvre au Canada.* "Eric J. Hanson Memorial Lecture," delivered [at

the University of Alberta, Edmonton, Alberta] by John W. Crow, Governor of the Bank of Canada, January 18, 1988. Pamphlet distributed by the Bank of Canada, pp. 3–11. Also published in *Bank of Canada Review*, February 1988, pp. 3–17.

(2) *Monetary Policy, and the Responsibilities and Accountability of Central Banks. La Politique Monétaire, le Mandat des Banques Centrales et l'Obligation qu'elles ont de Rendre Compte.* "The Gerhard de Kock Memorial Lecture by John W. Crow, Governor of the Bank of Canada, University of Pretoria, Pretoria, South Africa, 10 February 1993." Pp. 3–10 (F:3–12) in *Institutional Arrangements and Policy Objectives of Central Banks: A Canadian Perspective. Le Cadre Institutionnel et les Objectifs Stratégiques des Banques Centrales: Une Perspective Canadienne.* Pamphlet distributed by the Bank of Canada. Also published in *Bank of Canada Review*, Spring 1993, pp. 21–30.

(3) *Monetary Policy Under a Floating Exchange Rate Regime: The Canadian Experience. La Politique Monétaire dans un Régime de Taux de Change Flottants: L'Expérience Canadienne.* "Lecture by John W. Crow, Governor of the Bank of Canada, at the Stockholm School of Economics, Stockholm, Sweden, 22 April 1993." Pp. 11–19 (F:13–22) in *Institutional Arrangements and Policy Objectives of Central Banks: A Canadian Perspective. Le Cadre Institutionnel et les Objectifs Stratégiques des Banques Centrales: Une Perspective Canadienne.* Pamphlet distributed by the Bank of Canada. Also published in *Bank of Canada Review*, Summer 1993, pp. 37–47.

(4) *Central Banks, Monetary Policy, and the Financial System. Les Banques Centrales, la Politique Monétaire et le Système Financier.* "C. D. Deshmukh Memorial Lecture by John W. Crow, Governor of the Bank of Canada, Reserve Bank of India, Bombay, India, 22 November 1993." *Bank of Canada Review*, Winter 1993–1994, pp. 57–69.

Fortin, Pierre. 1996. "The Great Canadian Slump." Presidential Address to the Annual Meeting of the Canadian Economics Association (June). Published in *Canadian Journal of Economics* 29 (November).

Freedman, Charles. 1994. "The Use of Indicators and of the Monetary Conditions Index in Canada." Pp. 458–76 in Tomás J. T. Baliňo and Carlo Cottarelli, eds., *Frameworks for monetary stability*. Washington, D.C.: International Monetary Fund.

Freeman, Alan. 1995. "The Buck Starts Here," *Canadian Banker* 102 (January/February):16–21.

Kidd, Kenneth. 1994. "No More Mr. Ice Guy." *The Globe and Mail Report on Business Magazine*. Toronto: Globe and Mail (February):33–40.

Laidler, David E. W., and Robson, William B. P. 1993. "Re-entry in Progress: Canada's Transition to Noninflationary Growth." C. D. Howe Institute *Commentary*, No. 51 (August). Toronto: C. D. Howe Institute.

_____, and _____. 1994. "The One to Three Percent Solution: Canadian Monetary Policy under the New Regime." C. D. Howe Institute *Commentary* No. 59 (March). Toronto: C. D. Howe Institute.

Lucas, Robert E., Jr. 1976. "Econometric Policy Evaluation: A Critique."

Pp. 19–46 in Karl Brunner and Allan H. Meltzer, eds., *The Phillips curve and labor markets.* Carnegie- Rochester Conference on Public Policy Vol. 1. Amsterdam: North-Holland.

Neufeld, Edward P., and Hassanwalia, Harry. 1997. "Challenges for the Further Restructuring of the Financial Services Industry in Canada." Pp. 44–106 in George M. von Furstenberg, ed., *The banking and financial structure in the NAFTA countries and Chile.* Boston: Kluwer Academic Publishers.

Phillips, A. W. 1958. "The Relationship between Unemployment and the Rate of Change in Money Wages in the United Kingdom 1861–1957," *Economica* 25 (November): 283–99.

Sims, Christopher A. 1986. "Are Forecasting Models Usable for Policy Analysis?" *Federal Reserve Bank of Minneapolis Quarterly Review* 10 (Winter): 2–16.

von Furstenberg, George M. 1998. "Price Stability: How Canada's Governor Crow Approached It," *Journal of Policy Modeling* 20 (June): 335–360.

COURAGE AND CONVICTION: CHILE'S GOVERNOR ZAHLER

GEORGE M. VON FURSTENBERG AND MICHAEL K. ULAN

CONTENTS

Dr. Roberto Zahler
Governor, Central Bank of Chile, 1991–1996

Roberto Zahler was born in 1948 in Santiago, Chile, the son of immigrants. His father was born in what is today Slovakia, and his mother in Ukraine. He received his primary and secondary education in a British school in Santiago and began college as an engineering student, switching to economics when he realized he possessed "almost nil spatial imagination." He received his undergraduate degree from the University of Chile and his M.A. and Ph.D. degrees from the University of Chicago.

Dr. Zahler began his professional career with a short stint at the Central Bank between 1969 and 1972, while he was still an undergraduate student. After finishing graduate school in 1974, he joined the faculty of the University of Chile, where he taught macroeconomics and monetary policy. Four years later, he joined the staff of the United Nations Economic Commission for Latin America and the Caribbean (ECLAC), where he rose to the post of Chief Regional Adviser in Monetary and Financial Policy. While at ECLAC, he served also as a consultant to the World Bank, Interamerican Development Bank, International Labor Organization, and the Ford Foundation.

Roberto Zahler was appointed to the Board of Governors of the Central Bank of Chile in December 1989. He became Vice Chairman of the Central Bank in March 1990 and began a five-year term as Governor of the Central Bank of Chile in December 1991. He participated actively in meetings of the Latin American Central Bank Governors and the activities of the Bank for International Settlements, the central banks' central bank, in Basle, Switzerland. Under his stewardship, the Central Bank of Chile reduced inflation by half, and the country succeeded in its goal of keeping the current-account deficit below 4 percent of Gross Domestic Product, on the average, during his term in office. He resigned as governor six months prior to the end of his term, citing situations that made it impossible for him "to continue leading the central bank according to what I think are basic principles."

After leaving the Central Bank, Dr. Zahler turned to the private sector, where he was appointed Chairman of the Board of Directors of Siemens-Chile in March 1997. He started his own consulting firm, Zahler & Co., in May of that year.

An opponent of the military regime that ruled Chile between 1973 and 1989, he also served as vice president of the Chilean Institute of Humanistic Studies from 1980 to 1993.

COURAGE AND CONVICTION: CHILE'S GOVERNOR ZAHLER

PREFACE

As President of the Board of Councillors of the Central Bank of Chile, Roberto Zahler had two explicit statutory objectives: price stability and the normal functioning of internal and external payments. He saw price stability not as an end in itself but as a *sine qua non* for achieving other economic goals, such as stable, sustainable economic growth. Implicitly, he also sought to give substance to the independence of the Central Bank, which had been established *de jure* or *pro forma*, but not necessarily *de facto*, only two years before he became the head of the Bank. While this may appear a tall order, particularly in a developing economy, Dr. Zahler succeeded admirably: he halved the inflation rate and presided over an opening of Chile's foreign-investment regime. His resignation on principle, when he saw the independence and integrity of the Board of Councillors threatened, left the government of Chile to find a replacement who could maintain the prestige and reputation for independence and integrity that the Bank had attained under his leadership. By sacrificing his person, Zahler saved the program.

INTRODUCTION

Roberto Zahler is another of the central bank heads identified in this study "who showed a disciplined, reflected commitment to the goal of effectively and predictably stable prices." As we did with the other central bank heads, we asked him to identify those of his statements that he regarded as adding up to a comprehensive exposition of his approach to monetary policy. In his response, dated July 25, 1995, he stated:

> I am proud that you have appreciated our disciplined and reflected commitment to the goal of effectively and predictably stable prices, and I hope very much that our efforts in subduing inflation will be valuable for other practitioners of economics and central banking.

Roberto Zahler became a member of the governing board of the Central Bank of Chile in December 1989 and headed the board between December 1991 and his resignation on June 28, 1996, six months prior to the end of his term. Starting after the coup d'état of 1973, and continuing during the workout from the severe banking and economic crisis of the early 1980s, the Chilean economy underwent market-oriented structural reform and modernization in many sectors, first under authoritarian and then under democratic rule. These reforms bore great fruit. Real GDP doubled from 1983 to 1994 and continued to grow at a highly satisfactory rate thereafter. Encouraged by this success, which made it a leader and role model for the Americas, the government relaxed or eliminated many of the remaining controls in the financial sector during Zahler's tenure at the Central Bank. As a result, the depth, organization, and sophistication of financial intermediation have improved rapidly. Chile is thus becoming an exporter of models of financial and savings organization and of financial services in the region. It has also become a beacon of price stability, although in memory of former, uncertain and inflationary, times, a variety of indexed units of account, in particular the UF, are still used in a variety of contracts.

Dr. Zahler sent us both published articles and some of his speeches dealing with his philosophy of central banking and the situation of the Chilean economy. This chapter first reviews the macroeconomic situation in Chile, then discusses the extent to which the Central Bank of Chile is independent of the government. Next, we present Roberto Zahler's views on monetary policy and its objectives and discuss Zahler's conduct of monetary policy. Finally, we assess his record as head of the Central Bank of Chile and discuss his legacy.

THE ECONOMIC BACKGROUND

For the time being Chile is still a developing country—not yet an industrialized nation. The state of its small, open economy depends to a great extent on events outside its borders. During the past quarter-century, its economy has seen boom and bust, nationalization and free-market reform, rampant inflation, and movements toward price stability. Between 1971 and 1996, the compound annual

Table 1

Chilean, Industrial-Country, and Developing Western Hemisphere Average
Inflation Rates, 1971–1997
(from preceding year in percent)

Date	Chile	Industrial Countries	Developing Western Hemisphere
1971	20.0	5.3	13.7
1972	74.8	4.8	17.5
1973	361.5	7.9	25.5
1974	504.7	13.4	29.9
1975	374.7	11.4	37.2
1976	211.8	8.6	52.0
1977	91.9	8.8	44.4
1978	40.1	7.5	37.5
1979	33.4	9.7	41.7
1980	35.1	12.4	51.5
1981	19.7	10.4	57.4
1982	9.9	7.7	66.3
1983	27.3	5.2	99.0
1984	19.9	5.0	111.8
1985	30.7	4.4	130.2
1986	19.5	2.6	88.7
1987	19.9	3.2	123.0
1988	14.7	3.5	114.6
1989	17.0	4.6	79.8
1990	26.0	5.2	504.7
1991	21.8	4.4	148.1
1992	15.4	3.2	170.8
1993	12.7	2.8	239.2
1994	11.4	2.3	299.5
1995	8.2	2.5	51.2
1996	7.4	2.3	23.8
1997	6.3	1.7	N.A.

N.A.: Not Available
Source: International Monetary Fund, 1998b.

Chilean Inflation 1971–1997

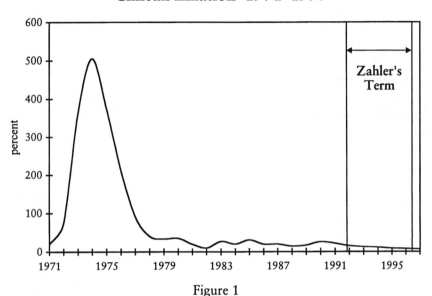

Figure 1
Source: International Monetary Fund,
International Financial Statistics Database, March 25, 1998.

rate of growth in Chile's Gross Domestic Product (GDP), 3.5 percent, was greater than that of the International Monetary Fund's Industrial-Country aggregate, 2.7 percent (International Monetary Fund,
1998b). Notwithstanding several declines in real GDP that were far
more severe than those of other developing economies in the Western
Hemisphere, the rate of growth of Chile's GDP is nearly equal to the
growth rate for developing economies in the Western Hemisphere
taken as a group (3.6 percent). The declines in Chile's GDP during
1972 and 1973 were related to problems associated with President
Salvadore Allende's statist economic policies. The contractions in
Chile's output during 1975 and 1982 (the latter of which continued
into the following year) were associated with recessions in the nation's
industrial trading partners, and, in the second instance, the Latin
American "debt crisis," which caused the flow of foreign investment
to the nation to evaporate. Since 1983, however, with a 5.8-percent
compound annual rate of growth, the rise in Chile's real GDP has
been more than twice as fast as those of the industrial countries or
developing areas of the Western Hemisphere.

As shown in Table 1, inflation in Chile has been far higher than in the industrial countries. Between the late 1970s and the granting of a new charter to the Central Bank of Chile in 1989, it remained higher than that in industrial nations but not out of line with the rates of inflation in many other developing nations. Inflation in the Fund's Developing-Western-Hemisphere aggregate since the mid-1980s has been skewed by extremely rapid price increases—several thousand percent per year—in a few countries, e.g., Bolivia in 1984 and 1985, Nicaragua from 1988 to 1991, Peru in 1989 and 1990, and Brazil from 1989 to 1990 and 1992 to 1994 (International Monetary Fund, 1997, pp. 114–15). Since the turn of the decade, however, Chile's inflation rate has consistently trended downward, by 1995 reaching a level nearly 70 percent lower than it was in 1990, thanks to a consistent anti-inflation policy undertaken by the Central Bank. Figure 1 contrasts the recent record of low inflation with the high inflation of earlier years.

HOW INDEPENDENT IS THE CENTRAL BANK OF CHILE?

The Central Bank of Chile was created by Decree Law Number 486 August 21, 1925, as "part of a general reform to the finance and banking system," which included Chile's return to the gold standard. Through the end of 1931, the Bank's primary job was to maintain the convertibility of the peso into gold (6, pp. 1–2). At the end of 1931, however, steep declines in the nation's exports and the inflow of foreign investment led to the suspension of convertibility. Beginning at that time, monetary policy was used more actively to promote fuller employment of resources and financing of the fiscal deficit through both direct and indirect credits to the government. At the same time, inflation tended to accelerate, "thereby initiating a period of chronic inflation which has continued almost uninterruptedly throughout the past six decades" (6, p. 2).

In 1953, the Bank was rechartered. Under the terms of its new charter, the Bank was given a more active role in the development of the Chilean economy; it was explicitly authorized (within limits) to extend credit to the Treasury and state entities. Dr. Zahler notes, "Perhaps it is not a coincidence that the beginning [of] this new institutional phase was accompanied by a significant acceleration in the rate of inflation" (6, p. 2). In December 1989, the Central Bank of Chile received its third charter; this document made the institution independent of the government and specified that the Bank should ensure the stability of the currency and the normal functioning of the domestic and international payments system (6, p. 2). The Central Bank of Chile became not only the first independent central bank in Latin America but also the first in the entire developing world (*New York Times*, December 11, 1989, p. D3; *Financial Times*, November 28, 1990). This independence was a "parting gift" of General Pinochet's regime, designed to place the Bank beyond the control of politicians and ensure the continuation of a free-market economy in Chile (*Financial Times*, November 28, 1990).

The Bank's former director of research, Juan Andreas Fontaine, asserts, however, that the Bank's independence is more tenuous than that of either the U.S. Federal Reserve System or the German Bundesbank because its financial position is not solid. In Fontaine's view, another banking crisis like that of 1982—as a result of which the then-military government pumped $8 billion into the banks to help the financial institutions remain solvent and liquid—could cause serious losses to the Central Bank *(Financial Times*, November 28, 1990; *Christian Science Monitor*, March 17, 1995). In 1982, $8 billion was just under one third of Chile's GDP. In addition to the reason cited by Fontaine, the Central Bank of Chile's independence is more tenuous than that of the U.S. or German institutions because Chile lacks the tradition of an independent monetary authority.

In June 1996, six months prior to the end of his term, Roberto Zahler resigned as the President of the Central Bank of Chile, referring in his resignation statement to "situations in recent months which have made it impossible for me to continue leading the central bank according to what I think are basic principles necessary for the exercise of the presidency of this institution of issue" (tr. from *Diario la Epoca,* June 29, 1996. p. A1 cont.). Although President Zahler did not give specific reasons for his early departure from office, reportedly his resignation was precipitated by the negotiations to settle a dispute pertaining to the repayment of some of the funds lent by the Central Bank of Chile to commercial banks during the bank bailout of 1982 to 1983, a dispute that included the allegation that some members of the Central Bank's Governing Council had conflicts of interest in the matter (*Financial Times*, July 3, 1996, p. 6; U.S. Department of State, 1996, p. 1).

A 1989 law set the annual repayment of the subordinated debt of the commercial banks to the Central Bank arising from the bailout at a fixed percentage of each bank's profits with no deadline for full repayment (*Christian Science Monitor*, March 17, 1995). Of the thirteen banks that owed bailout funds to the Central Bank, six had taken advantage of "generous conditions" and the booming economy to repay their debt; two of the remaining seven, the Banco de Chile—the country's largest—and the Banco de Santiago, owed 70 percent of the $4.5 billion in bailout debt still outstanding. The 1989 statute also allowed the banks to convert some of their profits into new shares at book (rather than market) value. In recent years, the Banco de Chile and the Banco de Santiago took advantage of the option to issue new shares, thereby reducing their designated profits—and their required payments to the Central Bank of Chile; President Zahler estimated that this conversion of bank profits had cost the Central Bank $100 million in 1994 and would cost the Bank $200 million in 1995. In March 1995, the government said it would freeze "much-needed" legislation to modernize the banking system until the debt dispute was settled, and Dr. Zahler said that the Central Bank would sue banks issuing new shares to reduce their required payments to the Central Bank if the repayment issues were not resolved. In January 1995, the Chilean government passed a law requiring the full repayment of the loans to the Central Bank within forty years; the following month, after an appeal by thirty-one opposition members of Congress, the statute was declared an unconstitutional violation of private-property rights by the Constitutional Tribunal.

In the wake of the Tribunal's decision, the Central Bank was negotiating loan repayments with the commercial banks. Reports in the Chilean press indicate that four of the five members of the governing council of the Central Bank were willing to give the private banks generous repayment terms, but President Zahler was holding out to make the banks repay an amount closer to the face value of their debt (U.S. Department of State, 1996, p. 1). Some of the press reports suggest conflicts of interest on the part of some of the four councillors; one was said to own stock in one of the private banks involved in the dispute. Others hint that policy differences with the Ministry of Finance may also have played a role behind the scenes, either setting the stage for Zahler's resignation or contributing to its ready acceptance. Certainly the Minister of Finance's (Hacienda) dismissive public-service announcement, *"las personas pasan, las instituciones quedan* [people go, institutions stay]," immediately afterward was not entirely reassuring in this regard. While the press reports do not prove that the Central Bank of Chile lacks independence from the remainder of the government, to the extent that they are accurate, they do indicate a lack of integrity on the part of members of the Bank's governing body. Such a situation can be as costly to the Bank's integrity in the pursuit of monetary-policy goals—and to private economic agents' perceptions of central-bank integrity—as subservience to the wishes of the government of the day. For when there is less than complete confidence in a central bank's high standards and incorruptibility, it will not have the broad-based support on which its independence ultimately rests.

President Zahler's resignation statement refers to several unidentified "situations" that prompted him to leave office. Another incident that may have contributed to his decision was an April 1996 vote of the directors of the Central Bank on raising interest rates in Chile. The *Financial Times* reports that the two directors it describes as "closest to the government" were "believed to have voted against Mr. Zahler on a new round of interest rate rises" (*Financial Times*, July 3, 1996, p. 6). In this instance, some observers might infer that the directors cited in the newspaper article were acting on behalf of the government rather than voting for the monetary policy they believed was in the best interest of Chile. If these two directors are widely perceived as "close to the government" and they did behave as indicated in the *Financial Times* article, the integrity and independence of the central bank could well be questioned. Should private economic agents conclude that members of the governing board of the Central Bank of Chile lack either integrity or independence of the government, there could be adverse consequences for the Chilean economy: inflation expectations could increase, and foreign investors might decide that Chile is a less-than-desirable place in which to place their funds. Either outcome would likely reduce future growth in the country's GDP.

To summarize, the answer to the question posed at the beginning of this section, "How independent is the Central Bank of Chile?" is not entirely clear. *De jure*, it is independent of the government; *de facto*, the reported behavior of some members of its governing body leaves some room for doubt. We have dwelled on this matter because questions of the institutional design supporting the independence of the central bank are very important all over the world. At the present time, they are being actively debated in Europe, where the "independent" head of the European Central Bank, with a mandate to pursue stability of the price level, faces a central bank council where eleven out of seventeen members represent each of the eleven member countries. In addition, a separate advisory group is attached alongside this structure to press national policy priorities and otherwise to interfere in the decision process with agendas of its own.

PRINCIPLES OF MONETARY POLICY

President Zahler notes that its Constitutional Charter assigns the Central Bank of Chile two objectives: price stability and the normal functioning of internal and external payments (3, p. 5). In this context,

> Normality in the functioning of external payments means we must avoid a deterioration in the balance of payments which might endanger the normal development both of our overseas trade and of our financial commitments with the rest of the world.

Zahler states that the Central Bank's objectives are oriented toward "guaranteeing public confidence in the payment system" (6, p. 3). In his view, such confidence is a prerequisite for the efficient working of the economy and economic development of the nation, and the control of inflation is a "fundamental element of this public confidence." In a letter to one of the authors, the President of the Central Bank of Chile defines his inflation objective as attaining "an inflation rate in a gradual fashion, similar to that of the industrialized countries, i.e., on the order of 2 percent to 3 percent per year" (7, p. 1).

The instrument specified in Chilean law for maintaining normality in the functioning of the payments system is the exchange rate of the peso (3, p. 5). With respect to the Bank's use of the exchange rate, President Zahler (3, p. 6) states:

> Our interventions in the currency market—so called *dirty floating*—have not and will not be intended to break trends, but rather to smooth out excessive exchange rate volatility caused by specific events or over-reactions of the market. Proof of this is the marginal nature of such interventions.

Dr. Zahler's immediate exchange-rate objective is to hold the effective exchange rate—a trade-weighted index of the foreign-exchange value of the peso against the currencies of its major trading partners—within a 10-percent band on either side of a central level (4,

p. 79). The exchange rate target was designed "to achieve a 'moderate' and sustainable current account of the balance of payments deficit," and the exchange-rate target was not part of the anti-inflation program of Chile's central bank (7, p. 1). The currencies included in the index that the Central Bank follows are the U.S. dollar, the mark, and the yen. The weights of the currencies in the index were changed—on November 30, 1994—to dollar, 45 percent; mark, 30 percent; and yen, 25 percent (Banco Central de Chile, 1994, p. 5), with the German mark soon to be replaced by the Euro with the same weight.

Any change in the real exchange rate will affect the domestic price level (i.e., add to or subtract from inflation) directly through its effects on prices in the traded-goods sector and indirectly through its effects on output in both the traded and nontraded-goods sectors of the economy. A rise in the real exchange rate of the peso makes Chile's imports cheaper and puts downward pressure on domestic prices; a fall in the peso's exchange rate does the opposite. Considering productivity growth and the sustainability of the current-account deficit, government authorities recently decided to build into the rule that determines the central value of the target band an annual real appreciation of 2 percent, which is considered the productivity-growth differential between Chile and the rest of the world (Budnevich Le-Fort and Landerretche Moreno, 1997, pp. 120–21). Hence, the authorities expect that the secular movement of the real exchange rate of the peso will help reduce inflation. Unlike the nominal exchange rate, which expresses the number of units of one currency that are needed to purchase a unit of another currency (or basket of currencies), the real exchange rate of a currency takes into account relative inflation rates in the respective economies and measures the number of units of domestic goods and services that must be produced to purchase a unit of foreign goods and services.

Why Is Price Stability Important?

President Zahler (3, p. 2) states that price stability is not an end in itself:

> The principal objective of the economic authorities as a whole is to achieve greater development in the country and to improve the conditions and quality of life of all the population, and these goals are mainly achieved through higher economic growth.

Some critics of price stability as an objective of monetary policy maintain that focusing on price stability retards economic growth, but Zahler responds that, while inflationary monetary policy can stimulate growth in the short run, it harms growth prospects in the long run; moreover, economic theory and empirical studies have demonstrated that price stability has a positive effect on economic growth in the medium and long terms (3, pp. 2–3). President Zahler points out that an independent central bank can focus its policy on the long term. In addition to its deleterious effects on growth beyond the short run, inflation functions as a regressive tax, with its greatest adverse effect on the poorest members of society; hence, price stability has a "positive effect" on income distribution and, therefore, "helps to build a society with greater opportunities for everyone." Thus, "an institution like the Central Bank, working toward the achievement of the anti-inflation goal, is without doubt contributing to the country's medium- and long-term economic development."

According to the Chilean central banker, even though monetary policy "may keep a stable course," inflation tends to fluctuate and impose both microeconomic and macroeconomic costs, interfering with the efficient working of markets and affecting the exchange rate, interest rates, and wages. Since all prices do not rise at the same rate, relative prices of goods and services will change as the aggregate price level rises, and such inflation-induced volatility of relative prices "harms the efficiency of resource allocation, introduces friction into credit and labour markets, engenders uncertainty which delays and reduces investment and shortens contracts, and shortens the effective business planning horizon" (6, p. 3). In addition to imposing economic costs, inflation causes social strains in a nation since the poor tend to be hurt more by inflation than others in society.

Zahler makes two further points about the Bank's anti-inflation policy: it is the medium- and long-term trend of inflation—and not month-to-month wiggles in the Consumer Price Index (CPI)—on which the Bank focused during his presidency; and it was the policy of the Central Bank of Chile to reduce inflation gradually (3, pp. 3–4). On the latter point, he asserts (3, p. 4) that prudence and gradualism are fundamental to the Bank's efforts:

> It is not in our interest to show spectacular results which may be reversed at the first sign of trouble. We have preferred gradual progress, but on a solid and stable base, where what is achieved is consolidated.

In this connection, he notes that, by mid-1996, the Central Bank had "consolidated inflation at a rate not seen in Chile in decades" and that the last two times the inflation rate had been reduced to a figure near the then-current level of around 12 percent, "the accumulated imbalances were such that in a few months everything that had been gained was dramatically lost" (3, p. 4). Elaborating on his concern that anti-inflationary monetary policy not produce or aggravate imbalances in the Chilean economy, President Zahler (6, pp. 4–5) states:

> A fundamental criterion of the Central Bank's anti-inflationary policy is that it should not be a source of significant imbalance in other areas of [the] economy. Achievements on inflation cannot be at the expense of generating a substantial increase in levels of unemployment and idle capacity, maladjustment in financial markets or an unsustainable deterioration in external accounts. Such internal or external imbalances would imply not only high costs in themselves, but would also erode the credibility of the stabilization effort, raising doubts about its sustainability and delaying its effects, and in the end it would turn out to be counterproductive if stabilization had to be abandoned in mid-course.

A gradual and sustained policy to reduce the rate at which prices are rising allows contracts to incorporate declining Central Bank inflation targets, minimizes risks of generating imbalances in other markets, and ensures the permanence of progress already made toward price stability (6, p. 5). Since 1990, the first full year that the Bank operated under its new charter, each September, the Central Bank of Chile has announced its inflation goal for the following year—in terms of the December-to-December change in the nation's CPI (Budnevich Le-Fort and Landerretche Moreno, 1997, p. 117). These targets, together with the actual December-to-December changes in the Index are presented in Table 2 below.

Indexing and the Quest for Price Stability

Indexing an economy (i.e., linking nominal wages, savings-account balances, etc., to a price index like the CPI) can help protect people against inflationary surprises and reduce the redistributive effects of inflation. It is not uncommon for governments or monetary authorities in developing countries to seek to protect their citizens or the economy against the dislocations of inflation with-

Table 2

Chilean Inflation: December-over-December Change in CPI, 1991–1996
(percent)

Date	Central Bank Target	Actual Outcome
1991	15.0-20.0	18.8
1992	13.0-16.0	12.8
1993	10.0-12.0	12.0
1994	9.0-11.0	8.9
1995	9.0	8.2
1996	6.5	6.6

Source: Budnevich Le-Fort and Landerretche Moreno, 1997, p. 118.

out having the political will to bring it down. In some instances, the indexation may be a contractual agreement between private economic agents—such as the linking of wages to inflation in labor contracts—rather than a government mandate. The knowledge that one will be protected against the effects of inflation automatically, if not perfectly, significantly reduces hedging and information costs, helps stabilize real earnings and living standards, and thereby eliminates some of the waste and some of the more glaring inequities caused by inflation (6, pp. 3–4). Many parts of Chile's economy have been indexed. Indeed, Roberto Zahler has called indexation "crucial for the financial system and in developing savings" in Chile's past inflationary milieu (*Financial Times*, February 17, 1994).

While indexing reduces the economic costs borne by an inflationary economy and eases the redistributive burden imposed by inflation, it does not cure these problems. Such a cure can be achieved only through achieving price stability, and indexation may make it more difficult for the monetary authority to eliminate inflation (6, p. 4):

• Indexation helps reduce the urgency of taking measures to control inflation.
• International experience shows that, in indexed economies, when inflation declines to "moderate" levels, people become complacent, and progress toward price stability slows.
• In an indexed economy, a small acceleration of inflation (from,

for example, an adverse external supply shock) can feed on itself, unleashing an inflationary spiral, instead of imparting a one-time blip to the price level as it could more easily in a nonindexed economy. The higher the initial inflation rate, the more likely that such a shock will trigger an inflationary spiral.
• The presence of indexation in an economy, with its ameliorating effects on the economic costs and social dislocations caused by inflation, may lead to the acceptance of incrementally higher inflation, leading to a point at which it is "truly costly" to an economy. The monetary authorities' commitment to stable prices then loses credibility, causing the authorities to introduce stabilization plans, "which normally imply severe economic, social and political costs."

Hence, Dr. Zahler (6, p. 4) maintains:

• In order to avoid this gradual process of "inflationary moral decay," the Central Bank should hold firm in its purpose of bringing inflation down, seeking to take advantage of favourable situations so as to advance more quickly, firmly defending what has already [been] achieved. It should insist on the voluntary deindexation of labor contracts and other prices so as to build in the now falling expectations, instead of past inflation.

Complementing Dr. Zahler's theoretical exposition on the ways indexation of an economy may complicate a monetary authority's efforts to extirpate inflation, in its *Annual Report* for 1993, the Central Bank of Chile (Banco Central de Chile, 1993, p. 20) commented on the economic situation in the country:

Memories of past high inflation rates have marked the institutionality and practices of the Chilean economy and led to generalised indexation as a way of ensuring against sudden bouts of inflation. This is evident in the system of earnings indexation based on past inflation which restricts the speed at which inflation can be reduced since any attempt to go faster would be very costly. In this sense, decreasing target inflation must be more explicitly considered in salary negotiations if the target of one-digit domestic inflation is to be reached.

The Relationship between Monetary and Fiscal Policy

In Dr. Zahler's view, both the government's fiscal policy and private-sector behavior can either help or hinder the monetary authority's efforts to achieve price stability. Specifically (5, p. 3), fiscal policy and private behavior can assist the Central Bank's efforts

> (i) by the government's trying to ensure that public-sector spending grows at a slower rate than the productive capacity of the economy increases;
> (ii) by the government's holding the rate of public-sector wage increases to the sum of the change in productivity in the public sector plus the inflation rate expected by the Central Bank. Such a wage policy both relieves fiscal pressure on the monetary authority and sends a signal to the private-sector labor market to hold wage pressures down; and
> (iii) by the private sector's not spending excessively nor generating protectionist pressures, which tend to increase inflation and hurt medium-term economic growth.

President Zahler calls the coordination of monetary and fiscal policies "essential." If, for example, monetary policy were eased during a recession but the government were running a high budget deficit and had a large outstanding debt, the deficit could lead to expectations of increased inflation. In such a situation, the reduction in short-term interest rates would stimulate consumption, but high-inflation expectations would keep long-term rates high, thereby discouraging investment. With investment depressed, growth cannot be sustained over the long haul (2, pp. 4–5). Further, if monetary and fiscal policies are not in sync, there can be a problem in achieving an exchange-rate target if the target is a fixed exchange rate or a crawling rate within a band. Since small open economies (like Chile's) have very little impact on international interest rates, a small capital flow—by international standards—generated in response to investors' perceptions that monetary and fiscal policies were incompatible, could have a large effect on the exchange rate of the peso and/or the quantity of international reserves held by the Central Bank. During the first half of his tenure, the former president of the Central Bank noted, however, that there was "excellent coordination" of policies between the Central Bank and the Finance Ministry and that the Central Bank monitored economic developments in the private sector and tried to persuade economic agents in the private sector to act responsibly (3, p. 17; 5, p. 4). If private-sector behavior were irresponsible, the Bank would be prepared to use the policy tools at its disposal to compensate for private-sector excesses (5, p. 4). Between 1989 and 1996, the last year for which data are available, Chile's consolidated central-government budget was in surplus (International Monetary Fund, 1998b).

According to Zahler (5, p. 3), "fiscal and monetary policies to restrain inflation should be complemented by an active and modern financial policy, paying attention to the adequate financing, liquidity, and solvency of the banking sector. Such a policy should work towards generating a financial balance in which bank liabilities should closely correspond to the value of assets, both at market prices and in terms of other situations that could emerge from the occurrence of internal or external shocks. Only in this way can one avoid the Central Bank having to intervene as lender of last resort, which, in most cases, ends up compromising overall macroeconomic equilibrium. For this, adequate regulation and supervision of the financial system is the key."

The Central Bank of Chile's Exchange-Rate Policy

In addition to reducing inflation, the other main thrust of policy during Dr. Zahler's term as head of Chile's monetary authority was that *"the current account of the balance of payments matters"* (7, p. 1). As we have noted above, the exchange-rate policy followed by the Central Bank of Chile during Zahler's presidency was to stabilize the trade-weighted exchange rate of the peso within a band extending 10 percent on either side of a central value (4, p. 79). The equilibrium exchange rate is that exchange rate (6, p. 5)

> which is compatible with the full employment of productive resources, in a range which does not introduce extra inflationary pressures, and with a current account deficit in the medium term equivalent to our long-term possibilities of external financing. Such conditions are fully compatible with the maintenance of a controlled and falling inflation scenario. Furthermore, the art of macroeconomic policy design is to seek and to make such compatibility effective. Evaluating the results of recent years it can be

seen that both conditions have been fulfilled; that is, a reduction in the rate of inflation has been achieved while at the same time keeping a deficit on the current account of the balance of payments at a moderate and stable level, in a context of dynamic economic growth and a low rate of unemployment.

In his letter to one of the authors, Dr. Zahler defines the target for Chile's current-account deficit as 2 to 4 percent of GDP (7, p. 2). The Bank opted to set a wide exchange-rate band within which it allows the market to determine the exchange rate because the Central Bank cannot predict the exact equilibrium exchange rate with certainty (3, p. 6). The wide exchange-rate band chosen by the Central Bank may also be viewed as a compromise between fixed-rate and floating-rate regimes in an effort to obtain some of the benefits of both. Absent intervention by the authorities, a wide-band regime is not distinguishable from a floating exchange rate.

The benefits claimed for a floating exchange rate include greater scope for a rapid adjustment of relative prices to supply, demand, or financial shocks; compatibility with national autonomy in the setting of domestic monetary policy; and the absence of incentives for one-way speculation in foreign-exchange markets. (If a government pegs the exchange rate of its currency and the pegged rate becomes inconsistent with economic fundamentals, would-be speculators know in which direction the exchange rate is likely to move and can use that knowledge to amass profits in foreign-exchange markets. The wider the bands within which an exchange rate is permitted to move, the less certain a speculator can be with respect to which way it will move in the future.) Most importantly, floating is continuously compatible with keeping a country's capital account open externally. It also helps discourage unhedged interest-rate quasi-arbitrage between foreign-currency and domestic sources of bank funds that is predicated on the government's pledge of maintaining fixed exchange rates. *Floating* means that the exchange rate is continuously tested in the market and that its stability must be earned, not just legislated, to be credible, although exchange-rate movements tend to be quite "noisy" even under the best of circumstances.

The disadvantages frequently attributed to floating exchange rates include increased exchange-rate volatility, which is said to have deleterious effects on the real economy; the possibility that floating rates may not help insulate the domestic economy from shocks arising from changes in the demand for money; and the possibility that a floating exchange rate will be less effective than a fixed rate in encouraging the monetary authority to maintain a low-inflation monetary policy (Budnevich Le-Fort and Landerretche Moreno, 1997, pp. 119–20). In Chile, however, the position of the exchange rate inside its wide target range is monitored more for any messages it may contain about market expectations and required changes in policy than for the immediate purpose of engaging in frequent intervention. If the exchange rate wanders well away from the central rate, it may prompt substantive policy changes, but does not require them, since changing the width of the target range, or the central rate itself, also remain options that are widely understood to be available. Chile's exchange-rate regime may thus be characterized as a form of managed floating with benign concern for the level and stability of the exchange rate index and with due regard to the sustainability of external price, stock, and flow relations.

In the Central Bank's view, the maximum current-account deficit that is consistent with the country's external-financing ability in the long run is in the range of 3 to 4 percent of Chile's GDP. It is permissible for the deficit to be higher than 4 percent in response to temporary extraordinary circumstances, but as a rule, in order to be consistent with the nation's ability to finance the deficit, it should not exceed 4 percent (3, p. 5). Such a figure may show wise restraint: Several of the five countries most severely affected by the Southeast Asian crisis of 1997 to 1998 had current-account deficits that were more than twice as high in relation to GDP.

The maximum acceptable level of the current-account deficit for Chile was not selected arbitrarily. The Bank selected the 3- to 4-percent range because it felt (5, p. 2):

• Such a level would keep stable—or slightly improve—the usual indicators of external solvency such as the ratios of external debt to GDP or exports.
• The figure was in line with recent historical evidence and prudent projections of the supply of medium- and long-term net foreign investment.
• Systematic and significantly higher deficits would leave Chile "very exposed and vulnerable to sudden changes in liquidity conditions, interest rates, or expectations in financial markets as well as unexpected shocks to the Chilean or Latin American economies."

Again, even though appreciation of the exchange rate could speed progress toward price stability, President Zahler declined to use exchange-rate policy for that purpose because of the dislocations it would bring about in the economy—and the likelihood that it would generate economic and political pressure for a devaluation of the peso, which would increase the inflation rate (3, p. 4). Thus the fact that slow appreciation of the real exchange rate of the peso, which dampens the rate of domestic inflation, is now built into the exchange-rate target band is an expected "equilibrium" consequence of Chile's economic catch-up process and above-average productivity growth in the traded goods sector rather than a deliberate inflation-fighting stratagem of the Central Bank.

Budnevich Le-Fort and Landerretche Moreno (1997, p. 120) conclude that "Chile's unorthodox exchange-rate management and stabilization policy have been effective. International comparisons demonstrate that, in terms of purchasing-power parity, Chile's real exchange rate has been one of the most stable in Latin America, in spite of a high rate of capital inflows."

PRESIDENT ZAHLER'S CONDUCT
OF MONETARY POLICY

True to the monetarist tradition at the University of Chicago, where he studied, President Zahler states, "It is well known that in order to reduce inflation, over the long term it is necessary for the Central Bank to keep the growth of the monetary aggregates under strict control" (1, pp. 157–58). In the Chilean economy, however, instability in the demand for the monetary aggregates militates against focusing on the supply of any of these aggregates as the policy instrument of choice to wield in the fight against inflation. The instability of the demand for money—which has been attributed to such factors as technical innovations in financial markets, deregulation of these markets, and sharp swings in the cost of holding money balances because of "highly volatile" short-term inflation—means that adhering to a rigid money-supply rule would lead to "sharp fluctuations" in interest rates, which would have negative effects on investment and the level of economic activity. Dr. Zahler points out that it is "precisely" this short-term instability in the demand for money that has led to "widespread" interest-rate targeting by practitioners of monetary policy, with the interest-rate target selected in order to achieve domestic macroeconomic stability.

When the monetary authority targets interest rates, it varies the supply of money in the economy in order to achieve its rate target. So the money supply becomes an outcome of the rate-targeting exercise rather than being the economic variable the central bank uses to try to control inflation. As an economist might put it, when interest rates are the central bank's policy instrument, the money supply is "endogenized" (made dependent on the value assumed by at least one other economic variable, in this case, the interest rate) in the short run. Even when the money supply is endogenized in the short run, however, a "sharp spike" in the supply of money "is regarded as an indication, even an alarm bell, that aggregate demand is growing very rapidly and that the economy therefore runs the risk of exceeding the targeted inflation rate." Dr. Zahler notes that whenever the Central Bank of Chile "got a clear conviction" that domestic spending—in terms of both, level and rate of growth—exceeded the corresponding level or rate of growth of potential output, the Bank adjusted the interest rate target. "For this purpose, 'excessive money' was one, but only one, and not the most important, of the indicators we used to develop an understanding of expenditure getting out of hand" (7, p. 2).

Until late May 1995, the Central Bank of Chile targeted the interest rate on 90-day Central Bank Index-Linked Promissory Notes. On May 26, 1995, however, the Central Bank Council decided to focus its policy-making activities on one-day interest rates (5, p. 5). The change was made in order to increase the role played by the market in establishing the term structure of interest rates and "to overcome certain problems which occur with monetary policy based on 90-day interest rates" (5, p. 6):

(i) Changes in interest rates lead to expectations of capital gains or losses as the prices of securities change. Such capital gains or losses are greater the longer the term of the financial instrument;
(ii) expectations of capital gains or losses lead to speculation on the part of people trying to anticipate changes in interest rates; and
(iii) when the Central Bank used the 90-day interest rate as its target variable, these expectations could not be reflected in the price of 90-day paper. Instead they were reflected in "sharp dis-

turbances" in the term structure of financial system portfolios and "abnormal" swings in the yield curve. From the Central Bank's point of view, this factor made liquidity control more difficult and distorted the normal functioning of the financial market.

(iv) Changes in the one-day interest rate cause no capital gains or losses to holders of overnight securities. Focusing monetary policy on such short-term instruments allows the monetary authority greater initiative, flexibility, and frequency in short-term interest-rate movements. Short-term interest rates affect other interest rates "and permit greater control of liquidity conditions for influencing the course of aggregate demand and inflation" (5, p. 6).

Dr. Zahler commented (5, p. 6) on the effects that focusing the Central Bank's operations on one-day interest rates has had on the Chilean economy as follows:

> The greater flexibility in short-term interest rates means that volatility originating in shocks affecting the Chilean economy is more evenly distributed between interest rate movements, portfolio adjustments and variations in the exchange rate, and not only between the latter two mechanisms as has been the case until now. In this respect, the new scheme is making it possible more effectively to absorb part of the volatility observed recently in the foreign exchange market.

Zahler notes that, in addition to the objectives cited above for the Central Bank's widening of the exchange-rate band for the peso and the focusing of interest-rate policy on the overnight rate, both of these policy shifts achieved a second objective: increasing the role of the market in the determination of the exchange rate and interest rates (7, p. 2).

What Economic Indicators Guided the Course
Set for Monetary Policy?

How did the Central Bank of Chile decide what its policy stance should be? One important indicator that the Central Bank has followed since it received its 1989 Charter is the output gap in the Chilean economy, defined as the difference between the actual and potential output of the economy, with the latter estimated to grow by 6 percent per year (2, p. 1; 4, p. 73). President Zahler says that central bankers such as he, whose statutory list of final targets does not include the gap, care about the output gap, *"because we think that inflation depends, among other things, on the output gap"* (2, p. 1). Other things being equal, the wider the gap (i.e., the greater the quantity of unemployed resources), the smaller the amount of inflationary pressure in the economy. Dr. Zahler adds: "It is important to stress, however, that . . . the output gap is *just one* of the determinants of inflation." One of the problems with making monetary policy on the basis of the output gap alone is that there are important lags in economics, among them, the lag between the time a policy is put in place and the time it has its effect and the lag between the time an event occurs and the time that economic data reflecting the event become available. For example, an economic recovery begins before it can be reflected in published GDP data. If the monetary authority based its policy on only the output gap in such a situation, it would likely ease its stance in the early stages of a recovery, thereby sowing the seeds of future inflation. Hence, although the Central Bank should consider the output gap as an important indicator for deciding on the stance of monetary policy, it would not be taken as the only, or the most forward-looking, indicator of the state of the economy it could follow. Rather, "the point here is that the credibility of the Central Bank is at stake here. To maintain it, the Central Bank has to show a strong commitment to its main goal: price stability" (2, p. 3).

Among the other economic indicators that the Central Bank tracked during Roberto Zahler's tenure on its board were labor-market indicators, such as changes in nominal and real wages; the supplies of various monetary aggregates, such as M1 (the sum of currency in circulation and balances in checking or checkable accounts) and M2 (essentially M1 plus balances in savings accounts and small time deposits); credit-market indicators, such as the growth rates of consumer loans, mortgages, and total credit extended to the private sector; indicators of aggregate spending, such as industrial sales, imports, and private consumption; and prices, such as the exchange rate of the peso, inflation as measured by the CPI, and prices in the nontradable-goods sector of the economy (2, p. 2).

As Zahler noted, the policy signals provided by economic data are rarely unambiguous (2, pp. 2–3). He cites one instance in which the Central Bank of Chile chose not to pay attention to the output gap in setting monetary policy. When the Central Bank became independent, its board was confronted with an economy showing clear signs of overheating: real GDP in 1989 was up 10 percent; inflation was rising; growth of the monetary aggregates was above their projected rates; and the demands for money and imports were growing fast. The Bank decided on a "tough" monetary adjustment; interest rates were increased sharply, and by the second and third quarters of 1990, real economic growth in the Chilean economy was close to zero after averaging 6.2 percent annually between 1984 and 1989. Hence, "a rate of 0 percent seemed like an overadjustment." Notwithstanding this opening of a wide output gap and similar slack in the economy in other economic indicators, the Bank decided not to ease monetary policy because the Iraqi invasion of Kuwait precipitated a "sharp rise" in the price of oil, which generated inflationary pressure in the Chilean economy. Hence the Bank did not ease monetary policy until the end of 1990, "when it was totally clear that inflationary pressures had ceased."

Stabilizing the Exchange Rate

President Zahler considers (1, p. 162) several ways in which temporary increases in the real exchange rate of the peso, which arise from an increase in the supply of foreign exchange relative to the demand for foreign currencies, can be offset without compromising inflation-fighting efforts:

• One could boost domestic saving, making it feasible to hold domestic interest rates lower than they otherwise would be, thereby discouraging capital inflows that would boost the exchange rate. But because it is difficult to increase either private-sector or public-sector saving quickly, this remedy may not be feasible. Moreover, it is not clear that it is a good idea to change fiscal policy to accommodate a temporary exchange-rate policy objective.
• One could seek to raise the demand for foreign exchange relative to the temporarily increased supply of foreign currency by reducing import duties—notwithstanding the fact that such a step is the equivalent of an appreciation of the exchange rate by the percentage of the tariff reduction. One possible objection here is that tariff policy should be based on a nation's trade, taxation,

and long-term development policy rather than on cyclical or temporary considerations. Clearly, low import duties are desirable to improve resource allocation in the economy and to contribute to the growth of the economy.

• One could liberalize regulations pertaining to capital outflows, but the scope and speed of liberalization of such regulations should depend on the nation's development strategy and considerations of microeconomic efficiency (e.g., risk diversification) and not on a transitory blip in the exchange rate. In addition, it is not clear which way such a liberalization would move the exchange rate since, if the liberalized regulations facilitated the repatriation of earnings of foreign investors, they could also increase the flow of foreign capital into Chile.

• The Central Bank could sterilize the inflows by issuing domestic debt and invest the foreign-currency proceeds abroad. The flaw in this policy is that the Bank's earnings on the sterilized inflows in the international capital market would be less than it would pay on the bonds it issued to sterilize them; hence, it would lose money, and the public-sector dissaving could add to inflationary pressures in the economy.

Dr. Zahler acknowledges the difficulty of distinguishing between permanent and temporary changes in the factors that affect real exchange rates—and, therefore, between exchange-rate movements the Central Bank should try to offset and those it should not (1, p. 162). At bottom, the Chilean Central Bank is charged by its charter with two objectives, price stability and the normal functioning of the internal and external payments systems. In practice, this situation means that the Central Bank has two targets—an inflation target and a current-account target (7, p. 2).

Zahler emphasizes that the targets are separate, noting that, while the peso's real appreciation—on average 4 to 5 percent per year—helped the Central Bank attain its inflation target, the appreciation "was not welcome and was resisted as much as possible by the Central Bank." The Bank acquired "huge amounts" of international reserves and discouraged short-term capital inflows because of their impact on the exchange rate and hence on the size of the current-account deficit that they "finance." To the extent that it uses the remaining controls on the international movement of capital, identified in the next section, to affect the exchange rate—and, through the exchange rate, the current-account balance—the Bank has separate policy instruments to use in its pursuit of each of its policy targets. However, if Chile's capital controls are phased-out—a goal that Mr. Zahler recognizes would be beneficial to the nation's economy in the long run and most likely a condition for its accession to the North American Free Trade Agreement (NAFTA)—the Central Bank will no longer have two independent policy instruments to pursue the two policy objectives. Rather, when it then tightens monetary conditions and adjusts short-term interest rates to fight inflation, the exchange rate will tend to appreciate in real terms because its level depends, in part, on international interest-rate differentials and can no longer be decoupled from such differentials through capital controls (7, p. 2). Hence, as Roberto Zahler acknowledges, having both inflation-rate and exchange-rate targets would then run afoul of the "Tinbergen Rule." This principle, articulated by the Dutch economist Jan Tinbergen, is that the number of independent policy instruments should be at least as great as the number of policy objectives (1, pp. 160, 162) if internal inconsistencies are to be avoided.

Capital Controls and the Exchange Rate

In practice, the Central Bank of Chile has used two mechanisms to manage the exchange-rate: capital controls and, to a lesser extent, sterilization of investment inflows.

In the standard comparative-static textbook model, an open international-investment regime (i.e., market-determined international capital flows) is a good thing because it will increase expected incomes in both the home and host countries of the investment, reduce expected production costs, and stimulate the international transfer of technology. In addition, efficient management, industrial organization, production networking, and global marketing may be greatly aided by foreign direct investment and the intra-industry trade in intermediate goods, which it tends to stimulate. In short, the arguments for an open investment regime are similar to those favoring free trade.

Zahler explains, however, that there are two important costs of an open investment regime to a small open economy such as Chile's: the monetary authority loses degrees of freedom in managing monetary policy; and capital flows can destabilize the domestic economy (6, p. 10). With respect to the first point, the interest rate that is consistent with domestic price stability in Chile may not be the rate prevailing in international capital markets (1, p. 163). With respect to the second, international capital flows to and from a small open economy can generate a boom-bust cycle, financial bubbles, and external-debt crises (6, p. 11). The sheer size of capital flows, whether short- or long-term, can distort relative prices and valuations in the economy, and the nature of some of these flows, or the extent to which they represent hot money, can add to problems of instability. Correcting a boom involves "a dangerous combination of high domestic interest rates, a fall in asset prices, and a sharp depreciation in the exchange rate, which inevitably leads to significant problems in domestic financial markets and introduces additional inflationary pressures." In addition, frictions introduced in financial markets can cause a significant decrease in the level of real economic activity and a corresponding increase in unemployment (6, p. 11). Hence, Chile's policy relative to its capital account is one of gradual and selective liberalization—gradual liberalization since gradual change eases the adjustment of the economy (5, p. 11).

In approaching the problem posed by foreign-capital-inflow surges to Chile, Dr. Zahler differentiates between long-term inflows, which respond to changes in aggregate demand in Chile and long-term interest rates, on the one hand, and short-term flows that respond to changes in short-term rates, on the other. The objective of measures to restrict the inflow of foreign capital is to attract more long-term capital and less short-term capital since the latter is more volatile—and, therefore, potentially more destabilizing to the domestic economy—than the former. He notes that the Central Bank of Chile could try to steepen the yield curve (i.e., raise long-term rates relative to short-term rates) in order to attract more long-term and less short-term capital, but that is very difficult to do (1, pp. 164–65). Instead, the Central Bank has chosen two other ways of dealing with the potential problem posed by capital imports: imposing a non-interest-bearing reserve deposit requirement on suppliers of short-term foreign currency, and sterilizing some of the inflows (i.e., offsetting the impact of those inflows on the domestic money supply) by purchasing the foreign exchange and issuing bonds against the foreign currency, which it then adds to its international reserves (1, p. 163; 3, p. 9; 7, p. 2). The reserve requirement makes investment in Chile more expensive, the more so the shorter its planned retention in Chile, effectively reducing the first-year rate of return on investment in Chile and tending to close the gap between interest rates in international capital markets and the higher domestic rates for funds temporarily placed in Chile (5, p. 11).

Dr. Zahler admits that imposing a reserve requirement on inflows of short-term foreign investment has both advantages and disadvantages for the Chilean economy. He asserts (1, p. 163) that the policy benefits Chile by

• Raising the cost and hence the required gross rate of return that international investors require on their investments in Chile without the Central Bank's having to buy "huge" quantities of foreign exchange or to allow the peso to appreciate sharply in real terms.

• Helping to reduce aggregate demand so that economic growth will be at a sustainable rate when the foreign gross capital inflows would have been used to finance spending on goods newly produced in Chile or otherwise would have served to stimulate the demand for such goods.

• Giving policy-makers time to decide whether the capital inflow situation is permanent or temporary—and how to react to it.

At the same time, he acknowledges (1, p. 164) two costs of imposing a reserve requirement on capital inflows:

(i) People will tend to find ways around the measure, including trying to disguise a short-term inflow, which is subject to the reserve requirement, as a long-term investment, which is not; and
(ii) there are microeconomic costs to the domestic economy since reserve requirements effectively increase the cost of credit.

On balance, Zahler feels that the benefits arising from the macroeconomic stability that a reserve requirement fosters outweigh the microeconomic costs of the policy (1, p. 164). While all restrictions on capital outflows from Chile by individuals have been removed, some restrictions on outflows by institutions remain. Controls on capital inflows also have been liberalized in recent years, but here too some remain: Foreign investors in Chile must use the formal foreign-exchange market; foreign investments in Chile may not be liquidated and the proceeds repatriated until at least one year after the investment is made; domestic firms must meet certain quality standards before they may seek foreign finance through the issue of internationally traded securities (e.g., American Depository Receipts); and some types of foreign investment in Chile are subject to a non-interest-bearing, 30-percent, one-year "reserve requirement" (i.e., a sum equal to 30 percent of the amount invested must be deposited with the Central Bank of Chile for one year, during which it earns no interest) (Budnevich Le-Fort and Landerretche Moreno, 1997, pp. 126–28).

President Zahler notes that sterilization of the inflow of foreign funds by the Central Bank can be effected on only a limited basis because of the fiscal losses such a policy would entail and the inflationary pressures it tends to generate.

Notwithstanding the net benefit Dr. Zahler sees accruing to Chile from limitations on the free flow of capital, he recognizes (1, p. 160) the desirability of liberalizing those flows:

> It should be emphasized that these arguments do not invalidate the liberalization of the capital account. Rather, they merely point out that, while it is desirable for the country to establish an increasingly solid position for itself in international financial markets, it is crucial for policy-makers to understand that the success of this process depends, to a large extent, on their ability to avoid generating major disruptions in the national economy; consequently, financial liberalization must be carried out both carefully and gradually.

PRESIDENT ZAHLER'S RECORD AT THE CENTRAL BANK

While he did not reduce Chile's inflation rate to his 2-to–3-percent annual goal, Roberto Zahler's record as President of the Central Bank of Chile was, nonetheless, outstanding. As shown in Table 1, during Dr. Zahler's presidency, the year-on-year change in the Chilean CPI was reduced by more than half—to 8.2 percent. At the same time, he helped liberalize regulations pertaining to capital flows to and from Chile while reducing the current-account deficit as a fraction of GDP. Moreover, he achieved both of these goals gradually, thereby sparing Chile the economic—and possible political—dislocations that have accompanied—and derailed—adjustment programs in other developing nations. In many developing nations, the economic changes that have accompanied price-stabilization programs have led to changes of government, with the new regimes undoing the changes—and the progress toward price stability—achieved by their predecessors.

The Record on Price Stability

Whether measured year-on-year or December-over-December, Zahler did a tremendous job of reducing inflation in Chile without subjecting the economy to adjustment costs or disequilibria that were economically or politically unbearable. In 1996, the year Zahler resigned his position, Chile's inflation rate was lower than that of Greece, a member of the European Union. December-over-December inflation fell throughout Zahler's term. It had been 18.8 percent in 1991, the last full year before he became President of the Board of Councillors of the Central Bank of Chile; it was only 8.2 percent in 1995 and fell to 6.6 percent in 1996 (International Monetary Fund, 1998a). Dr. Zahler notes that, between 1991 and 1995, the annual average inflation rate was the lowest in half a century and Chile's rate of economic growth over the five years was exceeded only once during the last fifty years, and then only barely, between 1976 and 1980, when the growth rate was boosted "to a large degree" by the recovery from a recession (6, p. 7). In short, the president achieved his goal of price stability without disequilibria in the economy. When the Bank cut interest rates in November 1994, Zahler stated, "For all practical purposes, the adjustment [his term for the package of austerity measures used to fight inflation] is over" (*Houston Post*, November 12, 1994, p. C2).

The Record on External Balance and Liberalization of the Capital Account

Roberto Zahler's goal was a current-account deficit that runs between 3 and 4 percent of Chile's GDP except when affected by one-time external shocks. Between 1991 and 1995, Dr. Zahler's last full year at the helm of the central bank, the country's current-account deficit exceeded 4 percent of GDP only once, and the country had slight surpluses on current account during two of the five years. The exact current-account balances in percent of GDP for the years 1991 to 1996 were 0.3, –1.6, –4.5, –1.2, 0.2, and –4.1. At the same time, Chile made substantial progress toward liberalizing its regulations pertaining to international capital flows (5, p. 12):

- The minimum period for the repatriation of foreign direct investment was reduced from five years to one year. (Foreign direct

investment is foreign ownership of at least 10 percent or more of the equity of a firm in Chile).
• The minimum sum for floatation of issues of American Depository Receipts (ADRs) was reduced from $50 million to $25 million. (When investment bankers invest in a foreign firm and then issue shares in that investment to the public, those shares are called *depository receipts*).
• Regulations for futures markets were introduced in Chile, banks were granted greater freedom to manage their foreign-exchange position, and exporters were given complete freedom to manage their foreign-exchange receipts.

In the spring of 1995, President Zahler summarized the remaining restrictions on capital flows to and from Chile by saying: "Steps taken so far imply that the capital account today is almost completely open" (4, p. 82). He noted that there were no remaining restrictions on capital outflows on the part of individuals, although some remained for institutional investors and banks (4, p. 82). He anticipated that a new law would decrease restrictions on outflows to "the traditional prudent restrictions used in almost all countries" (4, p. 82). The only major restriction affecting capital flows to Chile by the spring of 1995 was the reserve requirement (4, p. 82).

THE LEGACY

President Zahler's legacy to Chile is profound. Clearly, he slashed inflation, and he made great progress toward achieving normal functioning of both internal and external payments, just what he set out to do. Prior to the rechartering of the Central Bank in 1989, Chile had a history of "stop-go" policies that caused progress toward price stability to be abandoned because disequilibria appeared in the economy. Inflation then quickly regained momentum, and the inflation-fighting credentials of the Central Bank of Chile were damaged. This record corroborates Roberto Zahler's statement that, "having brought down the annual rate of growth of prices to around 9 percent, within a context of a decreasing inflationary time-path, . . . cannot be considered a minor achievement for the Chilean economy" (4, p. 76). Moreover, as President of the Central Bank, Dr. Zahler achieved that reduction in inflation without creating disequilibria elsewhere in the economy, for example in the exchange rate, external balances, or the labor market.

Roberto Zahler's legacy to Chile goes well beyond these substantial achievements, however. By resigning on principle over the incidents that reportedly prompted him to leave office six months before the expiration of his term, he bequeathed to the Central Bank of Chile a legacy of personal integrity, reasoned and principled convictions, and courage in the pursuit of the public good. He emphasized that the official actions of the members of the Bank's governing board must be independent of the government and free of personal conflict of interest. It would be difficult to summarize President Zahler's legacy to the Central Bank and to Chile better than was done in the U. S. State Department cable on his resignation (U.S. Department of State, 1996, p. 2):

> Zahler's departure may have modest effects on Central Bank operations and policy, as he has dominated the Bank's Council. As a member of the Council since the Central Bank became independent in 1989, and President since 1991, Zahler did much to cement the Bank's autonomy from the government. Under Zahler, the Central Bank has raised interest rates whenever inflation has threatened to increase, regardless of pressure from a government sometimes more concerned with short-term political considerations. Zahler's determination to bring down inflation has played an important role in establishing the Central Bank's credibility and affecting market expectations. However, the other members of the Council will feel considerable pressure from the financial community to continue the anti-inflationary effort, and we expect few policy changes. The Frei Administration is under pressure to name rapidly an equally qualified person to replace Zahler in order to maintain the prestige and reputation for independence that the Central Bank has acquired.

The appointment of Dr. Carlos Massad as Zahler's successor promised capable continuation of his policies.

REFERENCES

Banco Central de Chile. 1993. *Annual report 1993*.
_____. 1994. *Economic and Financial Report*, November.
Bundevich Le-Fort, Carlos, and Landerretche Moreno, Oscar M. 1997. "Macroeconomic and Financial Policy in Chile." Pp. 115–38 in George M. von Furstenberg, ed., *The banking and financial structure in the NAFTA countries and Chile*. Boston: Kluwer Academic Publishers.
International Monetary Fund. 1997. *International financial statistics yearbook*.
_____. 1998a. *International Financial Statistics*. CDROM January.
_____. 1998b. *International Financial Statistics Database*. March 25.
U.S. Department of State. Cable (unclassified) Santiago 96 2862, July 1, 1996.
Zahler, Roberto
(1) "Monetary Policy and an Open Capital Account," *CEPAL Review* 1992 (December): 157–66.
(2) "What Stance Should Monetary Policy Adopt in a Recession." Speech published in *Central Bank of Chile Monthly Review* 1994 (May).
(3) "The Economic Policy of the Central Bank of Chile." Presentation at the meeting organized by the Association of Metallurgical and Machinery Industries July 27, 1994.
(4) "Chile: Growth with Stability." *Boletin del Centro de Estudios Monetarios Latinamericanos* 1995 (March-April):72–83.
(5) "Macroeconomic Policy Fundamentals and the Short-Term Outlook for the Chilean Economy." Presentation during the Financial Meeting organized by the ICARE Financial Circle 1995 (July 11).
(6) "70th Anniversary of the Central Bank of Chile." Presentation of the President of the Central Bank of Chile at the inaugural conference of the seminar "70th Anniversary of the Central Bank of Chile." 1995 (August 21).
(7) Letter to G. M. von Furstenberg, Santiago, March 27, 1997.

FORTUNE, MERIT, AND DISTINCTION:
ALAN GREENSPAN

GEORGE M. VON FURSTENBERG
AND MICHAEL K. ULAN

CONTENTS

Dr. Alan Greenspan
Chairman, Board of Governors of the
Federal Reserve System, 1987–(2000)

Alan Greenspan was born in 1926 in New York City. Drawn quickly to business research and entrepreneurship, from 1954 to 1974 and from 1977 to 1987, he was chairman and president of Townsend-Greenspan & Co., Inc., an economic-consulting firm. During this time he held a growing number of corporate directorships and positions in the nonprofit sector. In between he served as Chairman of the President's Council of Economic Advisers, 1974 to 1977, also earning a Ph.D. in Economics from New York University at the age of fifty-one. His noted expertise on economic-data reporting systems and his deep understanding and masterful reading of economic statistics have undergirded his interest in business trends and economic-policy research in a powerful and authentic way.

Dr. Greenspan's career in public service has been extraordinarily varied, fruitful, and distinguished. As Chairman of the National Commission on Social Security Reform from 1981 to 1983, he shored up the foundations of the Social Security System, which will soon need strengthening again, for almost a generation. Earlier he had served as a member of President Reagan's Economic Advisory Board and as a consultant to the Congressional Budget Office. He also had served on the President's Foreign Intelligence Advisory Board, the Commission on Financial Structure and Regulation, the Commission on an All-Volunteer Armed Force, and on the Task Force on Economic Growth.

In August 1987, Greenspan was appointed Chairman of the Board of Governors of the Federal Reserve System, being appointed and then reappointed every four years by a succession of presidents: Reagan, Bush, and Clinton. His current term as Chairman runs through June 20, 2000; his fourteen-year term as a member of the Board of Governors expires in 2006.

In April 1997, Alan Greenspan married Andrea Mitchell, a well-known media (NBC) reporter.

FORTUNE, MERIT, AND DISTINCTION: ALAN GREENSPAN

PREFACE

Alan Greenspan became Chairman of the Board of Governors of the Federal Reserve System in August 1987. He first built on the inflation-fighting foundation put in place by his predecessor, Paul Volcker. But the stock market crash of October 1987 provided an immediate reminder that a central banker's responsibilities encompass not only achieving and maintaining stable prices. They also extend to safeguarding the smooth operation of the payments system and serving as lender of last resort to ward off what might otherwise turn into an intermediation and settlements crisis, adversely affecting the entire economy. Greenspan's inflation objective is not statistical zero but rather a rate of price change sufficiently low that anticipated changes in the general price level are not significant for economic and financial planning. He has also pointed out that the Consumer Price Index (CPI), as composed up to 1996, overstated the rate of inflation by at least one percentage point per annum, and that some overstatement may remain even after statistical procedures were changed in several steps from 1996 to 1998.

Although he is an "inflation hawk," Chairman Greenspan loosened monetary policy in 1990 to accommodate the U.S. economy's adjustment to the dislocations associated with the financial deregulation that occurred earlier in the 1980s. He did not tighten again until well after the economy emerged from the 1990 to 1991 recession. In the absence of factors obviously boosting the demand for money (real balances), "loosening" of monetary policy usually is identified as leading to temporarily higher rates of narrowly defined money supply growth than ultimately consistent with normal rates of growth in real output and the maintenance of an acceptably low level of inflation.

By this standard, average annual growth rates of M1 (an aggregate comprising currency and demand deposits and other checkable deposits) of 11 percent between December 1990 and December 1993 qualify as "loosening," but it left no ill effects.

By 1997, when the year-over-year inflation rate got down to less than 2 percent (1.7 percent), while continuing economic growth brought the unemployment rate to under 5 percent, Greenspan appeared to have provided the framework for the U.S. economy to enter the best of all possible worlds, at least for a long visit. In such a world, stock price valuations may become inflated by "irrational exuberance," he has worried, and the potential harm done by regulatory failure and the unsettled state of banking legislation may be greatly increased. Just as for Governor Brash later in this volume, Greenspan's exceptionally long and distinguished record of public service thus is not yet at an end, and further tests of his leadership lie ahead.

INTRODUCTION

Chairman Alan Greenspan is one of the heads of central banks identified in this study "who showed a disciplined and reflected commitment to the goal of effectively and predictably stable prices." By letter of June 27, 1995, containing this characterization, we asked him to identify those of his statements that he regarded as adding up to a comprehensive exposition of his approach to monetary policy and its guiding rationale. We explained the request by noting, "This is a selection only you can make because of the authentication implied." The response of August 7, 1995, signed by Joseph R. Coyne, Assistant to the Board, noted:

> Chairman Greenspan asked me to respond to your recent request for speeches and testimony on price stability that he regarded as a comprehensive exposition of his approach. . . . The enclosed material is in chronological order, starting with the Chairman's testimony before a House Banking Subcommittee in 1989 on price stability and ending with the Humphrey-Hawkins testimony of last month. . . .

These probably constitute the most important texts available. All but four of the items received involved testimony before congressional committees, most often the U.S. Senate Committee on Banking, Housing, and Urban Affairs. All are referred to by number in the text and fully identified in the reference section. There were two speeches, in 1993 and 1995, before the Economic Club of New York, one at a 1994 Bankers Club banquet in London, and one before the 1995 Annual Monetary Policy Forum in Stockholm. Because these "outside" speeches tended to be less constrained by congressional requirements for information on the near-term economic outlook and planned policy stance, and more concerned with fundamental principles, durable economic links, and longer-term perspectives, they will receive special emphasis in this essay of appreciation.

Alan Greenspan's role in the fight against inflation in the U.S. economy differs qualitatively from that of the two previous central bank governors profiled here. Governors Crow and Zahler *initiated* anti-inflation policies in their nations; Chairman Greenspan built on the efforts of his predecessor, Paul Volcker, and *continued* the anti-inflation fight. Hence, we start by sketching the record of price performance from the appointment of Volcker in 1979 before turning to Greenspan's views of central banking and then to a review of his monetary-policy record. We then proceed to the international implications of U.S. monetary policy, a review of the Greenspan record on inflation, and finally an assessment of his accomplishments.

THE MACROECONOMIC BACKGROUND

Few saw inflation as a major problem in the U.S. economy between the Korean and Vietnam wars. During the period 1953 to 1965, the CPI increased by 2 percent or more in only two years. For the next fifteen years, however, inflation generally kept increasing in the U.S. economy, with the "core" inflation rate (all items less food and energy) peaking at 12.5 percent (year-on-year) in 1980. In October 1979, Federal Reserve Chairman Paul Volcker announced a new monetary policy designed to control the growth of monetary aggregates and set about to wring the historically high inflation out of the U.S. economy. Chairman Volcker's monetary policy contributed to putting the economy through two recessions, one from January to July 1980, during which U.S. real Gross National Product (GNP) fell 2 percent, and the second from July 1981 through November 1982, during which real GNP fell 3 percent.

When the second recession ended in late 1982, the inflation rate had been brought down to about 3 percent, and this level subsequently was maintained as the average inflation rate between 1982 and 1994. Financial investors, however, appeared slow to catch on to the fundamentally changed inflation outlook, with yields on both ten-year and thirty-year Treasuries averaging near 12 percent as late as 1984.

When Alan Greenspan replaced Paul Volcker as Chairman of the Board of Governors of the Federal Reserve System in August 1987, inflation in the United States economy was far lower than it had been at the turn of the decade. In 1987 the CPI rose 4.4 percent December-to-December, or 3.7 percent year-on-year, and the respective "core" rates of inflation were 4.2 and 4.1 percent— measured in terms of the 1967 expenditure weights used in the CPI in 1987. The Federal Funds rate, which had stood at 19 percent in January 1981, was below 7 percent in August 1987, before the October 1987 stock-market crash led to additional easing of monetary policy. This, in spite of a strong economic recovery that brought the civilian unemployment rate from a postwar peak near 11 percent in November 1982 to 6 percent by August 1987. The recent history of inflation is shown in Table 1 below.

CHAIRMAN GREENSPAN'S VIEW OF CENTRAL BANKING

Alan Greenspan notes that the Federal Reserve System has three responsibilities: upholding the purchasing power of the dollar, facilitating the smooth operation of the payments system, and serving as the lender of last resort (1, p. 5). High inflation is associated with financial repression—onerous regulatory or taxation regimes that impede the development of efficient financial systems—and it will interfere with the smooth operation of the payments system. In addition, large deviations of actual from expected inflation may give rise to credit crises and financial panics. Hence price stability helps contribute to the smooth functioning of the payments system as well as to obviating the need for the central bank's becoming a lender of last resort.

In the statements selected for us, Greenspan never explicitly defined "price stability" with a number (2, pp. 11–12), and he publicly has doubted the ability of the CPI, as composed at least up to 1996, to measure inflation without an appreciable upward bias. Price stability is not an end in itself; it is a necessary condition to ensure the

Table 1

U.S. and Industrial-Country-Average Inflation Rates, 1971–1997

(from preceding year in percent)

Date	U.S.	Industrial Countries
1971	4.4	5.3
1972	3.2	4.8
1973	6.2	7.9
1974	11.2	13.4
1975	9.0	11.4
1976	5.8	8.6
1977	6.4	8.8
1978	7.5	7.5
1979	11.4	9.7
1980	13.5	12.4
1981	10.3	10.4
1982	6.2	7.7
1983	3.1	5.2
1984	4.3	5.0
1985	3.6	4.4
1986	1.8	2.6
1987	3.7	3.2
1988	4.0	3.5
1989	4.9	4.6
1990	5.4	5.2
1991	4.2	4.4
1992	3.1	3.2
1993	3.0	2.8
1994	2.5	2.3
1995	2.8	2.5
1996	2.9	2.3
1997	2.5	1.7

Source: International Monetary Fund, *International Financial Statistics Database*, March 25, 1998.

optimal functioning of the economy over the long run since price stability removes the price-level uncertainty that can discourage domestic saving and investment (1, p. 6). It is saving and investment that are the key to raising productivity in the U.S. economy, which, in turn, is the mechanism through which the living standards of the American people rise (1, p. 6). The Fed Chairman notes that, historically, lower inflation has been linked with both higher *levels* of productivity and faster *growth* of productivity (6, p. 4). He hypothesizes that rising productivity may help dampen advances in unit labor costs and hence reduce inflation, with lower inflation, in turn, encouraging productivity-enhancing investment by clarifying the market's price signals (3, p. 12; 6, p. 4). Another deleterious effect of inflation on investment, productivity, and living standards arises from the U.S. tax code's provisions through which inflation raises the effective rate of tax on saving and investment (3, p. 12).

In addition to removing price-level uncertainty, price stability also increases the volume of investment by decreasing long-term real interest rates. Nominal market rates can—and in the late 1980s did—include not only a true real rate and expected inflation, but also an appreciable risk premium as a consequence of the inflationary expectations (1, p. 12). Hence the real interest rate deduced from nominal debt contracts by subtracting the expected inflation rate from the nominal interest rate would be elevated relative to the true (or "truer") hypothetical real yield required on inflation-indexed securities of the same effective maturity and business risk class. Such a type of yield ceased to be hypothetical in the United States, long after it had become common in Chile, when the U.S. Treasury introduced inflation-indexed securities in January 1997.

A Holistic Approach to Price Stability in a Fragile Financial System?

Chairman Greenspan lists controlling inflation first among the Fed's responsibilities. He has treated price stability as the primary long-run policy objective of the Federal Reserve Board, subject to the constraints that the payments system is working smoothly and the Fed is not pressed into service as lender of last resort. Although there can be a conflict between the objectives of maintaining price-level stability and financial stability in the short run if rapid asset-price deflation and widespread loss of asset quality precipitate a financial crisis, in fact, none of the episodes of financial instability encountered during Chairman Greenspan's tenure has significantly detracted from the goal of consistently low inflation rates.

For example, when Dr. Greenspan assumed office in the summer of 1987, he continued his predecessor's tight monetary policy until the worldwide stock-market crashes in October. The Federal Reserve had increased the Federal Funds rate, which averaged 6.1 percent in February of that year, to 7.6 percent just prior to the crash (U.S. Council of Economic Advisers, 1988, p. 331; New York Times,

October 21, 1987, p. D31). On October 20, 1987, the Federal Reserve brought the rate down to 7.0 percent in the wake of the market crash as the contractive effects of asset-price deflation and increased demand for liquidity began to be anticipated (*New York Times*, October 21, 1987, p. D31). Soon afterward, household and bank portfolio imbalances that had grown out of the excessive debt expansion of the 1980s and the subsequent weakness in real estate prices in the early 1990s "put enormous strains on the balance sheets of many households and businesses" (4, p. 1).

These strains also affected financial intermediaries. In response to mounting loan losses and pressure from the markets and regulators to improve their capital ratios, these intermediaries restricted credit supplies to many borrowers (4, p. 1). The Fed then moved to help relax the unusual constraints on loan expansion that had developed from within the banking industry on account of its poor balance-sheet condition. It also helped banks meet new, and otherwise contractive, risk-based capital-adequacy standards. In Chairman Greenspan's view, "the process of easing monetary policy, however, had to be closely controlled and generally gradual, because of the constraint imposed by the marketplace's acute sensitivity to inflation" (3, p. 2). The primacy of the goal of maintaining consistently low inflation remained untouched.

By February 1994, the Federal Reserve concluded that, with the restructuring in the U.S. economy that followed the dislocations associated with the recessions and financial deregulation of the 1980s completed and the recovery from the 1990 to 1991 recession well underway, "a shift in policy stance was clearly indicated" (7, p. 4). Turning its attention more fully to its primary responsibility—price stability—the central bank began to increase interest rates. The Fed moved slowly at first because of its concern about a sharp reaction in markets "that had grown accustomed to an unsustainable combination of high returns and low volatility" (7, pp. 7–8). Altogether, the Federal Funds rate rose 125 basis points (1.25 percentage points) during the first half of 1994, and, in view of the stable inflation rate, real short-term interest rates likely rose a similar amount (8, p. 2). Many economists and financial journalists noted that the 1994 shift in the Fed's monetary policy was unusual in two important respects:

(i) Chairman Greenspan had indicated the likelihood of a tightening of monetary policy before the Open Market Committee met, and

(ii) the U.S. central bank tightened before inflationary pressures became apparent in the economy, i.e., the Federal Reserve Board changed its policy in order to prevent—rather than to counter—inflation (*New York Times*, February 5, 1994, p. 1).

Even when turning his attention to duties other than fighting inflation, Greenspan has remained mindful of the need to achieve price stability and has sought to build upon the disinflationary foundation put in place by his predecessor. In 1989, he said that the disinflation of the 1980s had still left "residual" expectations of 4 to 5 percent inflation in the U.S. economy and characterized the residual expectation as "potentially dangerous in the sense that it could ignite into a much more rapid inflation and clearly one which, in my judgment, would not serve the interests of the American people" (1, p. 12). The following observations may help confirm that the public's expectations of inflation tend to remain fixed for long periods despite sustained change in the inflation rate: At the beginning of 1994, with inflation into its fourth consecutive year of decline (and about one-third lower than it had been in 1989), four out of five new mortgages taken out in the United States were fixed-rate loans—even though the interest rates on these loans were nearly twice as high as those on variable-rate mortgages in their first year. In contrast, during the mid 1980s, when—apart from 1986, the year oil prices plummeted—inflation was substantially higher than in 1993 and 1994 (albeit much lower than at the turn of the decade), two out of three new mortgages were adjustable-rate loans (*New York Times*, February 7, 1994, p. D4). Under these circumstances Greenspan said in 1989 that it would be possible to bring inflation closer to zero over five years without a recession although there might be some modest loss of economic growth on the road to price stability relative to what would otherwise be the case (1, p. 13). The record shows that inflation was brought much closer to zero by 1994 and that there was perhaps less need for gradualism than had previously been thought. Moreover, had it not been for the upward spike in oil prices that accompanied the Iraqi invasion of Kuwait, an event over which the Federal Reserve Board had no control, both the 1990 uptick in inflation and the 1990 to 1991 recession might not have occurred.

Eliminating inflation is not a simple mechanical operation; there are other objectives a central banker must balance with suppressing inflation. In order to minimize the economic costs of reducing inflation and to react to unexpected events, the Federal Reserve System must maintain significant flexibility in its actions (1, p. 6). Once it is achieved, the costs of maintaining price stability—a sense of restraint and budgetary responsibility—"are not very large" (1, p. 13). As we have noted, to Dr. Greenspan, price-level stability does not mean zero inflation as measured by the CPI but rather that inflation be low enough that anticipated changes in the general price level are insignificant for economic and financial planning. In April 1993, he said that, at current inflation rates, we are quite close to attaining this goal (2, pp. 11–12). (The CPI had risen 3.1 percent during the prior twelve months.) Unlike the other risks businesses take—risks that foster economic progress—inflation imposes a "crucial" risk on entrepreneurs that does not contribute to economic advance and should, where feasible, be vanquished (3, p. 14). In addition to containing price pressures, suppressing inflationary instabilities requires diffusing unsustainable asset-price perturbations before they pose systemic risks. The economic consequences of any "inevitable" disruptions in financial markets will be minimized if they are not further compounded by financial instability associated with fluctuations in underlying inflation trends (11, p. 14).

The Federal Reserve tightened monetary policy in several steps beginning in February 1994, before there were widespread indications of acceleration of inflation. Greenspan justified the tightening by referring to the deleterious effects inflation can have on an economy. He said the move was "undertaken to preserve and protect the ongoing economic expansion by forestalling a future destabilizing buildup of inflationary pressures, which in our judgment would eventually surface if the level of policy accommodation that prevailed throughout 1993 were continued indefinitely. We viewed our move as low-cost insurance" (6, pp. 9–10).

It is impossible to know exactly how the U.S. economy would have fared if the Federal Reserve Board had not increased interest rates in 1994, but clearly the economy has functioned well following those rate hikes.

IS THERE A GREENSPAN INFLATION MODEL?

Alan Greenspan does not use a simple model linking the supply of a monetary aggregate to the U.S. price level and hence the inflation rate when he makes decisions about monetary policy. He states that a tight, bivariate link has existed for only about fifteen of the last fifty years. The interaction between monetary growth and inflation was less close during the first twenty or twenty-five years after World War II than thereafter because expectations of inflation's continuing at an appreciable rate did not really take hold until the mid-1960s (2, pp. 7–8). Since inflation of more than 2 percent was rare in the U.S. economy prior to that time, bursts of inflation were seen as temporary—not something that economic agents had to take into account in their long-term decision-making. With expectations initially slow to change, it was not until the 1970s that expectations of inflation became sensitive to the latest developments in monetary policy and Americans started to expect ever-more inflation (2, p. 8). The link between the rate of growth of monetary aggregates and inflation did become established in the U.S. economy once inflationary expectations had taken root during that decade. The embedding of high inflation expectations in the U.S. economy made achieving price stability more difficult for the Federal Reserve. During Greenspan's tenure at the Fed, changes in the velocity of money have made the traditional relationships "between money and national income and money and the price level break down, depriving the aggregates of much usefulness as guides to policy" (3, p. 10). The Chairman attributes the breakdown in the money/income relationship to changes in the pattern of financial intermediation, in particular the flow of funds away from banks toward financial markets—especially to mutual funds—and an increased reliance by banks on nondeposit sources of funds such as equity and nonsubordinated debt (6, p. 12).

P-Star: An Inflation Model for Quiet Times?

Notwithstanding the instability of the velocity of the monetary aggregates and the chairman's keen appreciation of the importance of inflationary expectations, in 1993 he allowed that M2 and P-star—a primitive monetarist model—may reemerge as reliable indicators of income and price over the long term, albeit not in the short run. The P-star model is essentially a variant of the equation of exchange (MV = PQ), which lies at the heart of the quantity theory of money, with an allowance for gradual adjustment of the general price level that is composed of instantly adjusting and only periodically adjusted prices. He indicated that the P-Star model might be of some value for anticipating inflationary pressures once the yield curve becomes normal (less steep), borrowers' balance sheets are restored, traditional credit demands resume, savers have adjusted to the enhanced availability of other investments, and depositories are comfortable with the size and composition of their balance sheets relative to their capital and earnings. Then velocity might be restabilized so that changes in money supply are again a reliable indicator of the future course of inflation (3, p. 10).

Perhaps viewed by Greenspan as no more than an occasionally instructive toy model, the P-star model is designed to answer the question "What long-run price level will current holdings of M2 support?" In the model, P-star, the long-run equilibrium price level, is defined as being consistent with the current value of M2 when velocity is at its long-run level and real Gross National Product (GNP) is at its long-run potential level. Discrepancies between the long-run equilibrium price level, P-star, and the actual price level, P, drive inflation in the model. The relationship is best modeled by an equation in which, with a lag, P-star minus P determines the change in the inflation rate. If P-star is greater than P, the current level of M2, if maintained, will lead to an acceleration of prices, and vice versa. The model permits the forecasting of inflation in the long run on the basis of estimates of the future courses of only M2, real potential GNP, Q^*, and long-run velocity, V^*, given the degree of price stickiness or the speed with which the rate of inflation, P-dot in equation (2), adjusts to the difference of the actual price level, P, from its equilibrium level, P^*, as defined by equation (1) (*Federal Reserve Bulletin*, April 1989, pp. 263–64):

(1) $P^* = (M2)V^*/Q^*$
(2) P-dot = $f(P^* - P)$, $f' > 0$

where V^* = the equilibrium velocity of M2, was defined as the mean of M2 velocity since 1955:Q1 when the model was parameterized in the late 1980s.

Regardless of the policy tool of choice, however, elements of the economic milieu can simplify or complicate the Fed's anti-inflation efforts through their effect(s) on the economic costs of the policy pursued by the central bank. In particular, free and open product and resource markets, reduced unnecessary economic regulation, and smaller federal deficits can facilitate the Fed's efforts to achieve stable prices—the first two by increasing the responsiveness of the economy to price (interest rate) signals and the last by reducing the extent to which private credit demands must be held in check by the Federal Reserve (1, p. 7).

One possible implication of the latter point is that the rate of change in economic activity and prices may be influenced as much by the rate of change in bank assets, primarily domestic credit to the private sector, as by the monetary liabilities of banks. Hence, if the loan assets of banks and their monetary liabilities to depositors do not grow at the same rate, both may be important, and the measured income velocity of money may change. In other words, the behavior of velocity may be affected by a combination of changes in the regulatory regime, the range of products offered in financial markets, and the sophistication of investors and savers, with portfolio considerations and elements of "the new credit view" creeping in (Bernanke and Gertler, 1995, pp. 27–48).

"New-credit" economists hypothesize that, in addition to the traditional monetary channel, there is a "credit channel" through which monetary policy affects the economy. Alan Greenspan's conduct of monetary policy appears to reflect this view. According to the "new-credit" economists, because of information costs, there is an external finance premium—a difference between the cost to firms of externally acquired funds to invest and the opportunity cost of retained earnings. (Learning enough about a firm to evaluate its creditworthiness imposes a cost on a potential outside supplier of investment funds. In addition, there is a cost of enforcing contracts that must be borne by suppliers of outside funds—and passed on to the firms to which financing is provided.) The direct effects of monetary policy on interest rates are amplified by endogenous changes in this premium, which varies with the level of interest rates. The premium rises and falls with the interest rates because of the effects that interest rates have on firms' net worth, cash flow, and liquid assets. Furthermore, the effects that interest-rate-changing open-market operations have on banks' access to loanable funds, on the quality of the assets on their balance sheets, and, therefore, on their willingness to lend, vary with the interest rates themselves (Bernanke and Gertler, 1995, pp. 28–29, 35, 40).

Money Supply Never Was the Only Policy Variable

In 1993, Greenspan said that M2 (essentially the sum of currency in circulation, travelers checks, checking deposits, savings deposits, and time deposits) had been a useful guide for monetary policy in the past, but it had not been the only variable on which monetary policy was based (3, p. 10). Historically, growth of the monetary aggregates, the slope of the yield curve (a geometric representation of the yields on securities of equal risk—generally U.S. government paper—but of different maturities) quality spreads (the difference between the yield on Treasury debt and commercial paper of like maturity), and credit flows had provided the Fed with warnings of inflationary pressures in the U.S. economy. The relationship between inflationary pressures in the U.S. economy and each of these variables was positive; an increase in any one of the indicators signaled rising inflationary pressure in the economy. With the changes in the behavior of the velocity of the monetary aggregates, however, no single variable was identified to take M2's prominent place as a reliable indicator of financial conditions in the economy. With the unusual nature of the most recent business cycle and the financial innovations that have occurred in the U.S. economy, the traditional indicators of inflation have given misleading signals at times. For example, in 1994, the recent pattern of growth of the monetary aggregates suggested disinflation, but by "far more" than had actually occurred (4, p. 6).

How to Get at the Expected Inflation Rate

Inflation expectations, which are forward-looking, could, in principle, be used as a guide for monetary policy, but available surveys of inflationary expectations have limited coverage and are subject to sampling error (6, p. 7). Price-indexed bonds of various maturities [like the Treasury's inflation-indexed securities (up to now five- and ten-year notes) issued since January 1997] would indicate underlying market expectations regarding inflation and would be "a useful adjunct" to the Fed's information base for policy making (6, p. 7). Changes in the price of gold, the term structure of interest rates, and the exchange rate would provide clues about changes in the unobservable market expectations about inflation (6, p. 7). In addition to the difficulty in determining what the market's inflation expectations are, how those expectations form "is not always easy to discern," and expectations concerning inflation can appear to be at variance with underlying forces (6, p. 5).

Even expectations not validated by economic fundamentals can themselves add appreciably to wage and price pressures for a considerable period, potentially derailing the economy from its growth track. For example, despite above-normal unemployment and permanent layoffs, in mid-1993, uncertainties about job security had not led to a moderation in wage increases—presumably because workers "understandably" harbored "deep-seated" expectations that inflation would accelerate (3, p. 4). Nonetheless, "history tells us that it is economic and financial forces and their consequences for realized inflation that ultimately shape inflation expectations" (6, p. 5).

Greenspan's Monetary-Policy Indicators

In the absence of a money-supply aggregate to guide monetary policy and given the unreliability of surveys of inflationary expectations, Dr. Greenspan turned to the set of real interest rates—particularly long-term real rates—as a policy variable with the goal of maintaining the real interest rate around its equilibrium level—defined as the level consistent with keeping the economy at its production potential over time (3, pp. 10–11). Yet the real rate of interest is not directly observable; it must be inferred from the nominal rate and estimates of the expected rate of inflation. Even though the real rate of interest cannot, therefore, be estimated with "a great deal of confidence," it can be estimated with "enough to be useful for monetary policy" (3, p. 11). Similarly, rough judgments can be made about equilibrium real rates of interest, and these judgments can be used in conjunction with other indicators in making and implementing monetary policy (3, pp. 11–12). Long-term interest rates are "almost surely" the ones that affect investment, but the Fed has direct control over only short-term rates (3, p. 11). The success of monetary policy implemented to counter inflationary pressures in a business-cycle expansion can, thus, be measured by the Fed's ability to limit the upward movement of long-term rates relative to short rates, particularly if forward short rates (implied in the term structure of interest rates for longer maturities) could be made to decline. Hence, to implement anti-inflationary monetary policy effectively, the Federal Reserve cannot wait until inflation begins to rise (6, p. 7).

Alan Greenspan brought with him to the Federal Reserve Board a reputation for familiarity with and attention to economic data, particularly an emphasis on looking behind the data to determine whether they represent temporary factors or quirks, on the one hand, or underlying changes in the economy, on the other. His appreciation of data and the economic factors that can affect them are especially valuable in trying to chart a course for monetary policy in an era when the traditional relationships among money, income, and prices are in flux. In judging the risk of inflation, he goes beyond the movements in price indices, which could represent temporary blips or statistical quirks, to determine whether resources are stretched or under pressure, providing a warning of potential future inflation. In this way, Chairman Greenspan has been able to make monetary policy forward-looking without relying completely on economic forecasts. He has avoided tying monetary policy to point estimates of the economy's potential growth or of the lowest unemployment rate that can be maintained without putting upward pressure on production costs and prices—the so-called nonaccelerating-inflation rate of unemployment, or NAIRU. Economic forecasts and estimates of the economy's growth potential or its NAIRU are often very sensitive to the assumptions that underlie the models used to generate them, making the estimates prone to error.

The Relationship between Monetary and Fiscal Policy

For Alan Greenspan, over the long run, the ratio of federal spending to GNP is the crucial variable in sustaining budget balance, and, unless Congress controls spending, whatever the Federal Reserve does will be "incidental." The federal deficit is too large if it crowds out private borrowing. The ability of the Federal Reserve to maintain a noninflationary monetary policy in the face of "very heavy" federal-government borrowing "is limited in the sense that we cannot be perceived to maintain a stable economic environment in that type of context." Moreover,

> If we are confronted with a very large Federal deficit and very large borrowing requirements in the system, and we endeavor to try to constrain the growth of money to noninflationary levels, we will create a major financial crunch, which would be counterproductive to all of the goals that we consider (1, pp. 16, 20–22).

Greenspan has returned to the necessity of a disciplined fiscal policy repeatedly in his testimony to congressional committees, as when he noted that fiscal as well as monetary policy can affect inflationary expectations since markets draw inferences about the degree of competition for funds between the private and public sectors from the budget deficit and, in the extreme, "explosive growth of federal debt makes an eventual resort to the printing press and inflationary finance difficult to resist" (6, p. 5). Notwithstanding his exhortations to restrain federal spending, however, without elaborating on the point, he cautions that not all taxes or government expenditures are equal in their effects on the productive capacity of the economy and that Congress should consider this fact in its budget deliberations (9, p. 6).

INTERNATIONAL IMPLICATIONS OF
U.S. MONETARY POLICY

Chairman Greenspan notes that, in recent years, "central bankers in general" have come to recognize the importance of price stability in achieving maximum sustainable economic growth and in providing the necessary foundation for stable and efficient financial markets (11, pp. 1–2). Central banks have a collective responsibility to maintain the stability of the interdependent international financial system. This responsibility includes—but goes beyond—monetary management and noninflationary growth in their respective nations and extends "to the very health of the international financial system" (11, p. 19). Arguably, this responsibility was shouldered most visibly in the easing of monetary policies in major nations amidst consultations among central bankers when stock markets in major financial centers crashed in October 1987. As in the Southeast Asian crisis of 1997–98, these changes in policy by the central banks, however, may have been primarily the separate rational responses of national institutions to the conditions in their individual domestic economies rather than a concerted arrangement among governors.

Regardless of the degree of coordination among central bankers in the easing of monetary policy, Alan Greenspan's policy actions were consistent with his words: when financial crisis and recession appeared in the offing, he temporarily put the smooth functioning of the domestic and international payments system and staving-off recession ahead of fighting inflation in the Fed's list of priorities. The fall in the Dow-Jones Industrials Average on October 19, 1987, was 22.6 percent, substantially larger than the largest one-day decline in

October 1929, 12.8 percent. The central bankers' joint easing of monetary policy may well have prevented an international financial panic and helped avoid a substantial deflationary shock to the real economy worldwide. (A sub-headline on the front page of *The New York Times* of October 20, 1987, indicated that the previous day's Wall Street crash had generated fears of a recession in the U.S. economy (*New York Times*, October 20, 1987, p. A1).)

The Fed's behavior in October 1987 demonstrates the concern Chairman Greenspan expressed to the Senate Committee on Banking, Housing and Urban Affairs in February 1995, when he said that, with the increased integration of markets of recent years, the failure to control inflation and to maintain confidence in domestic financial markets is likely to have "far greater consequences than might have been the case a generation ago" (10, p. 10). Moreover, the increased speed of transmission of any "mistake" on the part of any actor in the interlinked financial markets increases the potential for systemic risk in those markets (11, pp. 14–15).

The Link between U.S. Domestic and International Economic Policies

Chairman Greenspan recognizes the link between sound domestic economic policies—including monetary policy—and the position of the United States in both the trade and financial spheres of the international economy. For example, in an argument that takes the nominal exchange rate as given, he notes that, with low inflation, the increase in the production costs of traded goods produced in the United States will be subdued so U.S. goods will remain competitive in world markets (6, p. 4). While the Fed is concerned with the exchange rate of the dollar "only to the extent that it is an element affecting domestic policy and the domestic economic outlook of the United States" (1, pp. 16–17), "foreign exchange rates are key prices in the American economy, with significant implications for the volume of exports and imports as well as the prices of imports and import substitutes." Furthermore, exchange-rate movements can provide insights into inflationary expectations with respect to the U.S. economy (8, p. 6). Stable exchange rates contribute to world economic stability, and the best way to achieve this goal is through negligible inflation in the leading industrial economies of the world. Hence, there is no underlying long-term conflict between the Federal Reserve's domestic and international economic policy goals (1, p. 17).

The Fed Chairman linked a major international goal directly to the nation's domestic economic objectives when he testified that, if we conduct an appropriate monetary policy—and appropriate economic policies more generally—we shall achieve our goals of solid economic growth and price stability, and such economic results will ensure that dollar-denominated assets remain attractive to global investors, an outcome that is essential to the dollar's continuing role as the world's principal reserve currency (8, pp. 6–7).

In the writings selected for our consideration, Greenspan does not discuss the appropriate monetary policy for the Fed to pursue if the international economy were jolted by shocks that have implications for the equilibrium level of the real exchange rate and long-term interest rate. Nonetheless, given the general philosophy set forth in his policy-related writings, we can draw some inferences concerning the subject. Suppose, for example, there were a large real depreciation of the dollar. The depreciation could be related to an increase in domestic saving relative to domestic investment, and, in traditional analysis, it would tend to cushion the effect on output and employment by stimulating net exports with a lag. If the fall in the exchange rate of the dollar stemmed from an increase in domestic saving, real interest rates would fall, and inflationary pressures in the United States would abate with the decline in domestic spending. At the same time, the depreciation would tend to put upward pressure on the domestic price level through its effects on the demand for and prices of U.S.-produced import substitutes and U.S. exports, thus countering, at least to some extent, the disinflationary and interest-rate-reducing effects of the increase in domestic saving. Faced with such developments, Greenspan might choose a policy of benign neglect of exchange rate developments rather than promote additional depreciation by easing monetary policy and depressing interest rates further in the short run through faster growth of the money supply.

What about Greenspan's likely reaction to factors that would tend to raise the worldwide level of real interest rates? The opening of new areas of the world to foreign investors, for instance, could have appreciable implications for the worldwide level of real interest rate. It will take a massive amount of investment in the former East Bloc and the developing world to modernize these economies. For example, at the time that the German Democratic Republic was merged into the Federal Republic, some observers estimated that it would require investment in the neighborhood of one trillion DM (then about $600 billion) spread over a decade to bring the productive capacity of the former East German economy up to Western standards. This in spite of the fact that East Germany had only around seventeen million inhabitants and had the most advanced economy in the former East Bloc to start with. If there were to be investment on this scale in the region and in the developing economies, much of the saving likely would come from the industrialized market economies, where investors would be attracted to the higher rates of return expected on investment in the reforming economies than at home. These higher expected rates of return on investment would be reflected in a rise in the real interest rate both in the United States and abroad as the demand for investment funds rose relative to the supply of saving. The structure of output would change under this scenario; there would be more net exports and import-competing goods and services produced and less investment in the U.S. economy. With capital investment in the United States reduced (relative to what it would have been if the marketization of East Bloc and developing economies had not occurred), the nation's future productive capacity would be smaller than it would have been otherwise. Chairman Greenspan would recognize that there is little that monetary policy can do to counter a shock to real interest rates that stems from a change in foreign demands for investment. Rather, he would call on foreign and domestic policy-makers to take steps to increase national saving. He believes that this can be achieved through private savings incentives and through tax and government spending measures, though spending cuts would generally be preferred.

THE RECORD ON INFLATION

In his public statements, Alan Greenspan has emphasized the monetary-policy goal of achieving and maintaining a low inflation rate—a rate sufficiently low for economic agents to leave it out of their decision-making. How does his stewardship of the nation's monetary policy measure up to this standard? There was a noticeable rise in inflation as measured by the CPI in 1990, but, since 1990, there has been a downward trend in inflation as measured by both the All-Items CPI and its core component. In 1997, measured year-on-year, the U.S. inflation rate was more than 60 percent lower than it was during the first full calendar year of Dr. Greenspan's Fed chairmanship; the December-over-December inflation rate was nearly 45 percent lower than the analogous figure for 1988. During the last six years, the year-on-year U.S. inflation rate has not been greater than 3.0 percent, a performance last seen between 1960 and 1965 (U.S. Council of Economic Advisers, 1998).

Since there are lags—frequently estimated at up to two years—in the effects of monetary policy on inflation, one can reasonably assume that 1990 was the first full year during which Chairman Greenspan's monetary policy affected U.S. inflation. Inflation rose during that year, but there were two special circumstances that probably contributed to the price acceleration: the U.S. business-cycle peak and concerns associated with the Iraqi invasion of Kuwait that led to a surge in the price of oil. The core rate of inflation also increased in 1990. The core rate reflects cyclical inflationary pressures in the economy; although it excludes the food and energy components of the All-Items CPI, the prices of the goods and services that comprise the core inflation rate are affected by the prices of petroleum inputs to the production of those goods and provision of those services. Hence, the core rate of inflation does not measure the changes in prices in the economy excluding all the effects of changes in food and energy prices. Notwithstanding these factors, however, the Fed continued the accommodative monetary policy it put in place in 1990 to facilitate the unwinding of the financial problems that households and firms were experiencing as a result of the restructuring of the 1980s.

Since 1990, all of the inflation rates in Table 2 below have trended downward. To some extent, the start of the downtrend was an effect of the 1990 to 1991 recession. Chairman Greenspan, however, has kept inflation on a downward track more than seven years into the current economic expansion, a feat not seen in previous postwar U.S. economic history. In April 1993, with an inflation rate over the preceding twelve months of 3.1 percent and a core inflation rate of 3.4 percent, Dr. Greenspan said that the Fed was "quite close" to achieving its goal of an anticipated rate of inflation that was not significant for purposes of economic planning. Since that time, the annual rate of inflation shown by the CPI (either All-Items or core) has generally been below the respective trailing twelve-month figures for April 1993. By the fairly exacting standard he set, Chairman Greenspan appears to have succeeded in vanquishing inflation.

Table 2

Annual Increases in the U.S. CPI, 1988–1997

(percent)

Year	Overall Rate		Core Rate	
	Dec./Dec.	Yr./Yr.	Dec./Dec.	Yr./Yr.
1988	4.4	4.1	4.7	4.4
1989	4.6	4.8	4.4	4.5
1990	6.1	5.4	5.2	5.0
1991	3.1	4.2	4.4	4.9
1992	2.9	3.0	3.3	3.7
1993	2.7	3.0	3.2	3.3
1994	2.7	2.6	2.6	2.8
1995	2.5	2.8	3.0	3.0
1996	3.3	3.0	2.6	2.7
1997	1.7	2.3	2.2	2.4

Sources: U.S. Council of Economic Advisers, *Economic Report of the President*, 1998, and CEA, *Economic Indicators*, January 1998.

Further, he has expressed the hope that monetary policy could banish the scourge of inflation from the U.S. economy without inducing an increase in long-term real interest rates or causing a recession. Has this proved possible? In February 1994, the Federal Reserve took "preemptive action," raising interest rates before inflation increased. Contrary to Chairman Greenspan's expectations that long-term rates would go "a little higher temporarily" with the tightening of monetary policy, those rates moved up sharply with the Fed's policy change (7, p. 5). Dr. Greenspan attributed the rise in long-term rates that occurred primarily to a "drastic rise" in market expectations of economic growth and associated concerns of possible future inflationary pressures and said that the fact that the interest-rate spreads between Treasury and private debt—the risk premium—did not increase as rates rose suggests that the rise in long rates was seen by the market as a consequence of a strong economy—not the precursor of a weak one in which the default risk associated with private debt would rise (7, p. 6). He asserted that, "given the change in economic conditions, and the market's perception of them, longer term rates eventually would have increased significantly even had the Federal Reserve done nothing" (7, p. 6). Nonetheless, he did note that the increase in long rates reflected an increase in uncertainty in the U.S. economy as well

U.S. Inflation 1971–1997

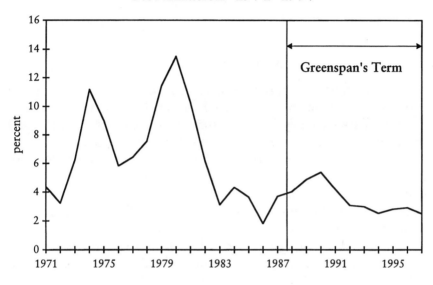

Figure 1

Note: Dr. Alan Greenspan's third full four-year term as Chairman of the Board of Governors of the Federal Reserve System expires in June 2000. He was first appointed Chairman on August 11, 1987, to fill an unexpired term.

Source: International Monetary Fund, *International Financial Statistics Database*, March 25, 1998.

as the strength of the domestic economy. When the Fed tightened, investors reexamined their "overly sanguine assumptions about price risk in longer-term financial assets" and shortened the maturities of their investments, further increasing long-term rates (7, p. 6).

As fears of inflation abated, interest rates fell. By the end of 1995, long-term rates had returned to the levels of early 1994, levels that were the result of the Fed's aggressive easing to accommodate the aftermath of the restructuring of the U.S. economy in the late 1980s and assist the recovery from the 1990 to 1991 recession. The most recent time that interest rates on long-term government and corporate bonds had been as low was the late 1960s—before inflationary expectations took hold in the United States. Nonetheless, interest rates continued to fall in 1996 and 1997. In the closing weeks of 1997, the yield on the thirty-year U.S. Treasury bond fell below 6 percent. In January 1998, it hit an all-time low and fluctuated in the range of 5.7 to 5.9 percent. Figure 1 presents Greenspan's achievements on the inflation front in a longer-term perspective.

Outside Evaluations

Since economists rarely—if ever—speak with one voice, not all economists appreciate the fight Chairman Greenspan has waged against inflation equally. Yet no matter where one looks, there is vastly more praise than reserve. When President Bush appointed Greenspan to serve a second term as Chairman of the Federal Reserve Board, Nobel Laureate and professor *emeritus* at the University of Chicago Milton Friedman, a monetarist who would prefer that the Federal Reserve System be abolished and the U.S. money supply expanded at a fixed rate equal to the long-term growth rate of the economy, said: "As long as it [the Federal Reserve Board] exists, Alan is as good a person as there is" to head the Fed *(New York Times,* July 11, 1991, p. D7).

Speaking about the state of the U.S. economy at the annual meetings of the American Economic Association in January 1994, Harvard professor Robert Barro stated that the economic misery index that he constructs fell during the first year of the Clinton presidency, but he gave most of the credit to Greenspan *(New York Times,* January 5, 1994, p. D2). Another Harvard professor, Martin Feldstein, who chaired the U.S. Council of Economic Advisers under President Reagan and currently heads the National Bureau of Economic Research, agreed that the U.S. economy was doing well and also gave all the credit for the economy's performance to the Fed chairman. "Alan deserves very high marks," he said. "As economists, we are all aware that the economy's performance is not a function of current Administration policy" *(New York Times,* January 5, 1994, p. D2). Allan Meltzer, a frequent critic of the Fed, called Greenspan "the best chairman the Fed has ever had" (Norton, 1996, p. 39). On the other hand, MIT professor and Nobel Laureate Robert Solow took strong exception to the view that the credit for the good performance of the U.S. economy in 1993 should go to Greenspan *(New York Times,* January 5, 1994, p. D2).

What is rarely acknowledged in partisan touts is that neither the U.S. President, the Congress, nor the Federal Reserve can do much more than help provide a framework compatible with a flourishing economy; they cannot produce it.

At the 1995 meeting of the Business Council, apart from the wish for lower interest rates, there was praise for Greenspan's performance at the Fed. The executives attending the meeting called on President Clinton to reappoint Dr. Greenspan as Chairman of the Board of Governors of the Federal Reserve System. John F. Welch Jr., chairman and chief executive of the General Electric Company said, "He has done a first-class job," and Richard M. Rosenberg, chief executive of the Bank-America Corporation stated that, under Chairman Greenspan's leadership, "[t]he Fed has been able to engineer a soft landing for the first time in history" (*New York Times*, October 15, 1995, p. I17). Business support for Greenspan is further indicated by the results of a poll of chief executives of the *Fortune 1000* companies commissioned by *Fortune* magazine. Ninety-six percent of those polled backed his reappointment as Chairman of the Board of Governors, and most gave him high marks for his performance (Norton, 1996, p. 39). Organized labor, on the other hand, has sometimes chafed under his emphasis on wage restraint (e.g., S. Friedman and T. Schlesinger, 1997).

CHAIRMAN GREENSPAN'S STILL INCOMPLETE LEGACY

Chairman Greenspan's oft-stated goal has been to reduce inflation steadily to an economically insignificant phenomenon in the U.S. economy, thereby helping to keep not only nominal but also real interest rates moderate, to facilitate the smooth operation of the domestic and international payments system, and to avoid a recession. He seems to have achieved—or to be well on the way to achieving— this very worthwhile set of objectives, thereby adding to his predecessor's legacy.

There is no question that Greenspan recognizes the economic benefits to be derived from stable prices and has conducted monetary policy with the primary goal of achieving a stable price level. As yet, however, the Federal Reserve Board's devotion to fighting inflation is very much a personalized matter: it depends on the policy inclinations of the members of the Board of Governors; it has not been institutionalized—by either statute or convention. There are Fed governors who favor an easier money policy to stimulate real economic activity in the short-run—despite the likely longer-term inflationary consequences of such a policy (*New York Times*, January 17, 1996, pp. D1, D19). Members of the Federal Reserve Board are nominated by the president and confirmed by the Senate. Despite the empirical evidence to the contrary, some U.S. politicians and economists believe that, through monetary easing, the Fed can raise the real growth rate in the U.S. economy above its long-term trend for an extended period without inflation's eventually becoming high enough to affect the behavior of consumers, savers, and investors. Until the president and a majority of the Senate confirm that the primary job of the Federal Reserve Board is to contain inflation and that there is no long-term stable tradeoff between unemployment and inflation—and act accordingly in nominating and confirming Fed governors—price stability in the U.S. economy cannot be taken for granted.

In the United States, as in the other six democracies whose governors are represented in this volume, politicians are (or are supposed to be) responsive to the wishes of the electorate. Hence, for politicians to act in the long-term interests of the nation where monetary policy is concerned, it will be necessary for the public, much of which believes that monetary ease is a key to economic well-being, to understand that a monetary policy directed toward ensuring price stability in the U.S. economy is in its best interest. The conviction must become ingrained in the electorate (as it is in Switzerland, for example) that the avoidance of inflation is a necessary condition for the efficient operation of the economy and that, historically, productivity growth, the stuff of which rising living standards are made, has been higher when inflation has been lower. To this end, the Federal Reserve System could undertake a concerted effort to educate the American people to the benefits they derive from a stable price level and to the fact that the tradeoff between lower unemployment and a higher inflation rate is a chimera. There is no other possible educator around because the research of academic economists has never spoken with a unified and clear voice on the subject or in a way that connects with an actual economy and its management. This public-relations aspect of the fight against inflation is one area in which Alan Greenspan (like his predecessor) and his colleagues arguably could have been more effective compared, for instance, with the courageous and unremitting public-relations efforts made by Governors Crow and Brash in this regard.

There may be two other areas of particularly unfinished business. In a speech in 1996, Greenspan worried publicly about the possibility of the U.S. stock market's reaching a point where stock price valuations zoom beyond reacting to improving fundamentals, such as lower required real interest rates and improved earnings, and stock prices begin to surge on an unsustainable wave of irrational exuberance by investors. Yet he did nothing publicly to clarify the matter by sharing the Fed's internal analyses or much of his own deep thinking on (1) whether there is indeed a bubble, and if so, (2) what, if anything, could or should be done to keep it from inflating further to its eventual breaking point, and (3) how to prepare for limiting the damage, should a sudden bursting of a bubble occur. For the outside world, at least, there was no organized intellectual follow-up.

Since that warning in December 1996, the stock market has continued to surge, easily getting by a few, and quickly reversed, brief episodes of sharp declines in stock prices, such as occurred in March to April 1997, the second week of August, and again near the end of October 1997. By April 1998, the dividend-price ratio had fallen to half of what it was in 1994 and two-thirds of what it was in 1996 without any striking change in fundamentals. As a result, the equity premium, which may be defined as the excess of the real discount rate applied to expected future inflation-adjusted returns on equity compared with the real interest rate on middle-quality corporate bonds, had become tiny. In dividend valuation models it may even have turned negative, unless real earnings and dividends per share can credibly be projected to grow at an average annual rate considerably above 3 percent per annum from mid-1998 on.

Such a vanishing equity premium is unsustainable in view of the much greater riskiness of equity returns than of bond returns, which have a prior claim on earnings. It is also the type of evidence cited by those who cannot account for the elevated level of stock price valuations without reference to a bubble: this is the phenomenon where stocks keep rising beyond the levels justified by fundamentals because they have been on a rising path for some time and are widely expected to continue along there. "History," Greenspan said, "is somewhat ambiguous on the issue of whether central banks can safely ignore asset markets, except as they affect product prices." He said this at about the time the Southeast Asian crisis was unfolding (*New York Times*, September 6, 1997, p. 24), and he, like history, has remained somewhat ambiguous on the subject.

While a stock market bubble bursting in a robust upswing, as in October 1987, may merely leave a pockmark on the economy, a bubble that has been left to inflate much further and that breaks just when the economy is peaking of its own accord could wreak more havoc. Hence just as with Governor Brash later in this volume, Greenspan's long and distinguished record is not yet quite complete. So far, Yasushi

Mieno is the only governor who has dared confront what he perceived to be a bubble economy to the point of actually puncturing ballooning asset-prices with sharp-edged policy tools in any country. He proved that bubble bursting is no less dangerous than bubble blowing in a poorly regulated financial system that operates under directives and incentives that interfere with efficient risk selection and the write-off of bad debts.

Like Governor Mieno, Greenspan has not visibly tried to establish a unified regulatory and supervisory agency for increasingly universal banks that is independent of both the central bank (Federal Reserve) and the ministry of finance (Department of the Treasury). His attempts to educate the public to impending risks and disconnects in this area and to forestall regulatory failure in anticipating and coping with any foreseeable asset valuation crisis have been quite limited. No independent Federal Banking Commission appears to be on the drawing board. Indeed, part of his efforts with congressional committees appears to be directed at concentrating regulatory and supervisory functions in the central bank in spite of the mutual policy conflicts and conflicts of interest such a structure may invite. The Shadow Financial Regulatory Committee (1996) has drawn attention to such conflicts. Hence Greenspan too has some unfinished business to attend to and he may be tested further before the end of his present term in the year 2000. The first ten years of his chairmanship, however, have been magnificent and beneficial.

One thing can already be said now with complete confidence: Greenspan is much too thoughtful and intellectually disciplined to overstate either what the central bank can guarantee to deliver or the degree of prescience and superiority it can claim for its analyses. The ancient gods' punishment for hubris is not likely to be called down on someone who can volunteer publicly (*New York Times*, July 23, 1997, p. C20):

> We do not know, nor do I suspect can anyone know, whether current developments are part of a once-or-twice-in-a-century phenomenon that will carry productivity trends nationally and globally to a new, higher track, or whether we are merely observing some unusual variations within the context of an otherwise generally conventional business cycle expansion.

There is a pleasing modesty, alertness, and scientific skepticism in these remarks, which must mean that the nation's central bank is in exceptionally good hands.

REFERENCES

Bernanke, Ben S., and Gertler, Mark. 1995. "Inside the Black Box: The Credit Channel of Monetary Policy Transmission," *Journal of Economic Perspectives* 9 (4) Fall:27–48.

Friedman, Sheldon, and Schlesinger, Tom. 1997. "Fed Follies: Why Alan Greenspan Won't Let Workers Get a Raise," *Working USA* 1 (2): July–August.

Greenspan, Alan

(1) "Testimony before the Subcommittee on Domestic Monetary Policy of the Committee on Banking, Finance, and Urban Affairs, United States House of Representatives, October 25, 1989."

(2) "Remarks before The Economics Club of New York, April 19, 1993."

(3) "Testimony before the Committee on Banking, Housing, and Urban Affairs, United States Senate, July 22, 1993."

(4) "Testimony before the Joint Economic Committee, United States Congress, January 31, 1994."

(5) "Remarks at the Bankers Club Banquet, London, United Kingdom, February 1, 1994."

(6) "Testimony before the Subcommittee on Economic Growth and Credit Formation of the Committee on Banking, Finance and Urban Affairs, United States House of Representatives, February 22, 1994."

(7) "Testimony before the Committee on Banking, Housing, and Urban Affairs, United States Senate, May 27, 1994."

(8) "Testimony before the Committee on Banking, Housing, and Urban Affairs, United States Senate, July 20, 1994."

(9) "Testimony before the Committee on the Budget, United States Senate, January 26, 1995."

(10) "Testimony before the Committee on Banking, Housing, and Urban Affairs, United States Senate, February 22, 1995."

(11) "Challenges for Central Banks: Global Finance and Changing Technology," Remarks before the Annual Monetary Policy Forum, Stockholm, Sweden, April 11, 1995.

Norton, Rob. 1996. "In Greenspan We Trust," *Fortune* 133 (March 18): 39–47.

Shadow Financial Regulatory Committee. 1996. Statement No. 103: "Principles of Regulatory Restructuring," issued February 14, 1994. In *Journal of Financial Services Research* 10 (4, Supplement) December: S. 68.

U.S. Council of Economic Advisers. 1998. *Economic Report of the President*. Washington, D.C.: U.S. Government Printing Office.

PART II
EUROPE

SCHLESINGER'S STEADY HONING OF GERMANY'S ANTI-INFLATION RESOLVE

GEORGE M. VON FURSTENBERG AND MICHAEL K. ULAN

CONTENTS

Dr. Helmut Schlesinger
President, Deutsche Bundesbank, 1991–1993

Helmut Schlesinger was born in 1924 in Penzberg, Bavaria. His father, Franz, originally a "German-Bohemian" from what is now the Czech Republic, had built up a small business there. Because his only boy had his mind set on going to university, the family business is now in the hands of one of the founder's granddaughters. But university had to wait because Helmut was called up by the German Army in 1943 to help shore up the crumbling Eastern Front, a dreaded assignment. Severely wounded at the age of twenty, he was withdrawn from the front. At war's end, the youth was fortunate to fall into the hands of the Americans (rather than the Russians), who let him go after a few days.

Schlesinger then attended the University of Munich, first in still war-ravaged premises, obtaining an Economics Ph.D. in 1951. Soon after, Dr. Schlesinger joined the staff of the Bank deutscher Länder, the forerunner of Deutsche Bundesbank. In 1964 he became head of its Research and Statistics Department, his true home in the bank. From there he dominated its research on monetary and economic issues for decades. His career blossomed. He became a Member of the Bundesbank Directorate in 1972, and his first appointment as Deputy President of the Bundesbank, effective 1980, was followed by a second term starting in 1988. From August 1, 1991, to September 30, 1993, he was President of Deutsche Bundesbank, chairing the meetings of both its Central Bank Council (the Bank's supreme policy-making body) and its Directorate (the Bank's executive board).

His presidential term in office, prior to retirement from the Bundesbank— if from little else— near age seventy, was brief. But Dr. Schlesinger was responsible for all articles, of a "principal" nature as he put it, in the official publications of the Bundesbank (Monthly Report, Annual Report) from 1964 to 1991. This gave him a strong, and often decisive, behind-the-scenes influence on the policies of the Bundesbank for almost thirty years.

At last count in 1998, Dr. Schlesinger is a member of the Board of Directors of the Bank for International Settlements in Basle. He is also a member of the supervisory and advisory boards of several multinational corporations. Awarded numerous high honors and Orders of Merit, from both Germany and other European countries, he has remained in the public eye. But whenever possible, he returns to his first loves of research and teaching, having been a professor or visiting professor at a number of distinguished universities for different terms.

Rank order aside, he has at least one other abiding passion. Married to Carola Schlesinger, née Mager, since 1949, the couple have four children and, thus far, eight grandchildren. Carola and Helmut Schlesinger, both actively involved in social affairs, and art and music enthusiasts, have something else in common: Both have been avid mountain climbers since their youth. They have been hiking in many parts of the American Rockies and have explored Alaska, always finding a warm welcome and magnificent vistas in the United States.

SCHLESINGER'S STEADY HONING OF GERMANY'S ANTI-INFLATION RESOLVE

ABSTRACT

Since the currency reform of 1948, Germans have consistently revealed a strong preference for price stability over "inflationary experiments." Until persuaded otherwise, most of them regarded even the European Monetary Union as such an experiment. While the German preoccupation with price-level stability has not always sat well with its neighbors, it has produced profound and internationally open and effective thinking on why and how inflation is to be avoided. At the Bundesbank, Dr. Helmut Schlesinger, one of the best and brightest of the first two postwar generations of leaders, has been at the forefront of this exploration and of drawing its lessons. He is the articulate dean of inflation fighters, and references (in parentheses) in this essay are to those of his writings that he has identified to us as the best expositions of his views as they have evolved since the 1970s.

INTRODUCTION

After losing the value of money and its denomination twice in little more than one generation, Germans have needed no persuading that high inflation is associated with very bad consequences, particularly for the middle class. But what about moderate, single-digit inflation? Is there nothing to be gained from it? As a guiding light in the intellectual vanguard of the Bundesbank, first as Chief of the Department of Economics and Statistics, then as Vice President, and then as President and Chairman of the Central Bank Council (1991 to 1993), Schlesinger's essential contribution has been to argue forcefully over four decades of changing ideologies on the subject that inflation cannot safely be tolerated at any level. Rather, approximate price stability is best for production and investment efficiency, for social balance, and for economic growth. But the central bank needs cooperation from other sectors because actors who set prices outside competitive constraints can otherwise confront it with a cruel dilemma: They can force it to choose between giving up its commitment to price stability and sticking with it and thereby highlighting inconsistencies created by others in a manner that is politically and economically costly to all.

The fear of such inconsistencies' developing from outside pressures or competing commitments may explain the depth of Schlesinger's intellectual engagement and missionary zeal in defending right thinking against all adversaries, political or academic. He has been a champion fighter who has stood his ground tenaciously against every new or warmed-over rationale for accepting inflation and its ultimately corrosive fixes. Following the evolution of his advocacy leads past the wrecks of major doctrines that were very much in vogue not long ago.

DREAM COMBINATIONS AND RUDE AWAKENINGS

For several years in the mid- to late 1990s, the U.S. economy achieved that magic combination of all good things coming together— low inflation, high employment, rapid wealth creation, and consistently satisfactory growth with improved gains in labor productivity and real wages—about which politicians could previously only dream. Adding an external-economy corner to the triangle of economic bliss points legislated in the United States first in the Employment Act of 1946 and later in the Humphrey-Hawkins Act of 1978, Germany's 1967 law for stability and growth (1, p. 6) lists four economic desiderata for the government to pursue: stability of the price level, high employment, external balance, and adequate growth. The Bundesbank, however, is charged directly and preferentially with minding only one of these four goals, safeguarding the currency from erosion by inflation (2, p. 6). For Schlesinger, achieving price-level stability is the only means of having a fighting chance to meet the other three objectives in the "magic quadrangle." There are no sustainable trade-offs: Indeed, without price stability, it is ultimately impossible to uphold any of the other corners of the quadrangle.

His thinking was exceptional in the 1960s and early 1970s, when discretionary demand management was supposed to be the task shared by both monetary and fiscal policy (3, p. 7). According to Keynesian precepts, monetary "ease" could be traded for fiscal "tightness," or vice versa, without the price level and inflation rate needing to be affected. Or, if a stimulus to aggregate demand was desired, policy makers could go "easy" on both monetary and fiscal fronts if they trusted the assurances of the majority of macroeconomists of the time that taking inflation risks for cyclical economic revival would work just fine.

For years, anyone citing the four desiderata, listed at the beginning of this section, in one breath risked being derided as wishful, perhaps even dishonest, in either intentionally masking or stupidly denying the tough choices. Painful choices needed to be made according to accepted professional opinion because several of the four desirable objectives erroneously were thought to be mutually exclusive. Thus, if excess aggregate-demand inflation were indispensable for high levels of employment, by these lights price stability and full employment would not be able to coexist. Followers of the stable Phillips Curve illusion, exposed by Schlesinger (1, pp. 10–13), illogically had deduced such a trade-off from unemployment's often being low when inflation was temporarily above its past average level. Such an association could be observed in the 1950s and early 1960s when the rate of inflation, on a rolling three-year average basis, had, in fact, remained quite steady and low.

Schlesinger refutes the notion of a permanently exploitable trade-off between inflation and unemployment. He notes that the inverse relation between them depicted by the Phillips Curve is based on a cyclical correlation that is predicated on continued constancy of the expected rate of inflation. As soon as systematic attempts to exploit the trade-off through higher inflation set in, that expectation is no longer warranted and higher inflation, and not lower unemployment, is all that results. This conviction, first expressed in 1972 (1, p. 14), needed repeating as late as 1993/1994 (5, pp. 6–7).

There have, of course, been persistent claims that little harm is done in ratcheting up inflation as long as its rate is stabilized eventually. Schlesinger takes aim at such claims by pointing out how extreme and implausible are the prerequisites for such arguments to hold water (1, p. 10): If everyone were to expect firmly the exact same level of inflation well ahead of time even when that level is quite high, and if everyone were equally free and equipped to act on these expectations from the time they were first formed and then possibly modified, and if these expectations turned out to be accurate, the level of inflation might not matter much provided everyone could easily be liquid without holding currency. While knowing all about academic notions of rational-expectations equilibrium out on any limb, in economic experience, he notes dryly (1, p. 11), there never has been such a thing as economic equilibrium with a significant inflation rate. Rather, any appreciable rate of inflation is built on a slippery slope (*auf der schiefen Ebene*, 1972, p. 10) and creates a craving for more inflation (1, p. 15) until, ultimately and inevitably, withdrawal cramps set in.

THE BOTHER WITH THE EXCHANGE-RATE SYSTEM AND EXTERNAL DISTURBANCES

While price stability is no obstacle to high employment, but rather its friend, there is one goal conflict that Schlesinger (1, p. 32) admits but attributes to a system error. That error arises from maintaining a system of fixed exchange rates among the major currencies, with pegs that do not lend themselves to routine and orderly adjustment. In 1993/1994 (5, p. 11) he characterized the former fixed-rate system once again as particularly bitter and frustrating for countries with the hardest currencies. The trouble was that the United States, for decades prior to Greenspan's tenure, had tolerated more inflation than Germany cared to endure. As long as Germany nevertheless remained obligated under the Bretton Woods system to maintain nominally fixed exchange rates between the *deutsche Mark* (DM) and the U.S. dollar, maintaining internal price-level stability was difficult and ultimately impossible without recurring exchange crises followed by re-valuations. For without such revaluations of the DM, Germany's lower inflation would imply continuous depreciation of its currency in real terms and a loss of external balance. Eventually price stability itself would be jeopardized by a combination of rising relative import (and other traded-goods) prices and excessive growth of aggregate demand for German goods (1, pp. 13, 29–30).

Such imported inflation, Schlesinger notes (2, p. 15), could be a problem even after the 1973 demise of the Bretton Woods system to the extent that Germany maintained fixed exchange rates with some of its European partners, as it has, for instance, within the European Monetary System (EMS) since 1979. On the whole, however, he later credits the orientation of EMS currencies on the DM as having made a positive, mutually reinforcing contribution to stability, at least during the period 1987 to mid-1992 (5, p. 11).

While it is quite easy to miss all four corners of the magic quadrangle by a wide margin at once (2, p. 18), it is clear to Schlesinger that price stability, coupled with flexible exchange rates, affords the best chance to come close. As long as flexible exchange rates remained politically taboo, Schlesinger was willing to contemplate capital controls as a second best—even though difficult, and at most partial—solution to the problem of foreign-capital-inflow surges. For, if unchecked, such surges would bring inflation in their wake (1, pp. 19–21). Without capital controls, monetary policy would be preempted by the need to cope with exchange-rate pressures and incapable of focusing on price stability as its goal (1, pp. 26–27). Compared with instability of the price level and imported inflation, capital controls might be a lesser evil. Just like Governor Zahler, the head of Chile's central bank in the first half of the 1990s, Schlesinger did not feel that capital flows on the whole were either stabilizing or allocatively efficient anyway. Translating freely:

> In my estimation, freedom of capital movement has not contributed to the better utilization of the world's resources in years . . . as European countries end up lending to the United States . . . even though capital should flow from highly developed to less developed countries for global efficiency, and not the other way round. (1, p. 21)

What Schlesinger had in mind at the time was that freedom of capital movement and the system of fixed but adjustable exchange rates were becoming impossible to reconcile in the dying days of the Bretton Woods system and that the exchange rate system would need to change. But later on, under floating exchange rates, Schlesinger notes exaggerated exchange rate movements against the U.S. dollar and surges of capital flow, both in and out of Germany, that also are anything but stabilizing (2, pp. 12, 15, 19, 20). Ultimately, therefore, the external sector seems to complicate conducting monetary policy so as to achieve constancy of the domestic price level no matter what the exchange rate regime. Hence some of the conflict between external balance and either price-level stability or economic activity may remain if external balance—and hence interest rates, exchange rates, and domestic economic balance—are upset by international capital-account disturbances. Schlesinger reiterated this concern (3, pp. 3–4) for both Germany and Switzerland:

> If there are any severe difficulties standing in the way of a consistent policy of stability in the monetary area, then external economic influences were, and are, the main cause. . . . Acute global disequilibria which have caused an unusually high degree of volatility in exchange rates, interest rates, and share prices . . . can make it very hard to proceed with implementing well-founded concepts.

Although Schlesinger had looked forward to floating to reduce external constraints on the pursuit of domestic price stability, the transition to floating did not improve Germany's inflation performance. Schlesinger is careful not to plead "special factors" or to give the 1973 and 1978 oil-price shocks much blame for this failure (2, pp. 6–7). Excluding 1951, inflation averaged 1 percent per annum during the 1950s, 2.5 percent during the 1960s, and 5 percent in the 1970s. Clearly the Bundesbank was in danger of being seen as ceasing to practice what it preached. It needed a strong reminder to strengthen its resolve.

WHY PRICE STABILITY?

For years since the mid-1990s, inflation was privately declared dead by purveyors of new paradigms in several of the leading industrial countries. Indeed, looking back over a hundred years, inflation has not always been either a problem or a policy issue. It had not been one during the period of the classical gold standard that had lasted for over four decades before ending in 1914. In Germany, prices were also, on balance, stable from 1925 to 1935, and excepting the Korean War boom, there was little inflation in the 1950s. But it appeared that the core rate of inflation, in Germany as in the United

States, was rising cycle after cycle, almost doubling from 1954–1958 to 1968–1971 (1, pp. 7–8) and then nearly doubling again, to a peak of 6.3 percent, in 1980 to 1981. In more and more sectors, indexation set in, which is itself a fly-wheel and dynamo (*Schwungrad* is the German term used by Schlesinger, 1982, p. 17) of inflation that obstructs adjustment to real shocks. Schlesinger (2, p. 6) found this performance quite unsatisfactory, being convinced that such a permissive attitude toward inflation ultimately could only make all other problems of economic policy worse (2, p. 7).

Higher inflation means a reduction of economic growth while social tensions intensify. Misguided investment, for instance in speculative construction of real estate assets that the market fails to absorb, eventually lowers growth. Japan experienced fallout of this kind during Governor Mieno's tenure in the early 1990s when its land and real estate price-bubble burst. The idea that inflation, either by raising the share of profits in national income or by increasing government saving, would increase total saving and investment in the economy does not square with the facts Schlesinger sees before him (1, pp. 15–17). Rather, inflation is typical of governments heavily involved in deficit financing and in income redistribution (1, p. 14), activities that often discourage private saving. Through tax-collection lags and lower or misdirected economic growth, inflation may well aggravate rather than, through additional seignorage revenues, reduce fiscal deficits and undercut the government's own efforts at infrastructure formation (1, p. 23). Its antisocial effect arises from the systematic redistribution of income and wealth from those, often of modest means, who are net owners of monetary claims to those, often of considerable means, who are the principal owners of real assets or of equity claims to such levered assets (1, p. 25).

MONETARY TARGETS AND OTHER EXPRESSIONS OF RESOLVE

Already in 1972 (1, p. 26) Schlesinger conceded that, in view of the increasing lack of success in stabilizing the price level, it would be proper to ask what stock one should place in monetary policy. In 1972, the obligation to defend fixed exchange rates could still serve as an alibi because it precluded an autonomous monetary policy and gave foreign-exchange rate developments a dominant effect on the rate of growth of the money supply most of the time (2, pp. 26–28). When monetarism came into its own soon after the transition to generalized floating among the major currencies in 1973, performance did not improve, and there was less excuse. Using a difficult image, Schlesinger (2, p. 8) leaves no doubt that, while a particular burst of inflation can have nonmonetary origins, how amply the monetary coat is cut eventually determines the size of the nominal magnitude (Gross National Product or Gross Domestic Product) that is wrapped in it (2, pp. 8–9). As long as the Bundesbank does not let itself be distracted from the pursuit of the goal of price stability by getting too caught up in countercyclical policy, it is quite capable of meeting its price stability mandate in the intermediate run (2, p. 9).

Hence the expectations of monetarists were high toward the end of 1974 when the Bundesbank, soon followed by the U.S. and Swiss central banks and then many others, started announcing money-growth targets for a narrow aggregate, central bank money (M0), which it directly controls. This aggregate is the sum of currency, and of reserves held by banks with the central bank mostly to meet minimum reserve requirements. Schlesinger (2, p. 10) even credits central bank money, also known as the monetary base, with showing a closer relation to spending volume and price developments than the broader and less directly controllable monetary aggregates targeted in the United States. He emphasizes that the steering mechanism by which the central bank influences the quantity of broad money works through the impact of its interest-rate and liquidity policy on the behavior of banks and nonbanks. This impact, while difficult to tie down in the short run, is technically sufficiently dirigible—with suitable error response and error correction—to let the central bank achieve its final goal of low inflation on average, if the averaging period is no less than one year (2, p. 11). Hence having established controllability of the operational instrument (central bank money) and thence of the intermediate target (broad money), and the latter's ultimately close bearing on the final objective, Schlesinger finds the Bundesbank fully capable of achieving its mission of price stability with the monetary instrument available.

Yet he concedes that while there can be no question that the fight against inflation needs to be conducted with monetary policy and means, the proof of the value of proclaiming money-supply growth targets, or of violating them, lies in the extent to which the goal of price stability has been served (2, p. 11). While Schlesinger obviously strains to be positive and to maintain his monetarist leanings, we read his own answer to be that the verdict is mixed (2, pp. 11–12). Such a reading would be consistent with the fact that monetary targeting was de-emphasized in the course of the 1980s by most countries that adopted the practice of advertising preannounced money growth rates in the 1970s and abandoned by several of them in the 1990s (see, for instance, Greenspan quoted in 5, p. 19).

Table 1

Money-Growth Targets and Their Implementation, 1975–1998

(percent of money stock)

	Target: Growth Rate of Central Bank Money (M0) or, since 1988, Broad Money (M3)			Actual Growth Rate		Target Achieved?
	Fourth quarter to fourth quarter of year shown	From preceding year to year shown	Qualification during year of position in range	Fourth quarter to fourth quarter of year shown	Annual average	
1975	8	-	-	10	-	no
1976	-	8	-	-	9	no
1977	-	8	-	-	9	no
1978	-	8	-	-	11	no
1979	6–9	-	Lower limit	6	-	yes
1980	5–8	-	Lower limit	5	-	yes
1981	4–7	-	Lower half	4	-	yes
1982	4–7	-	Upper half	6	-	yes
1983	4–7	-	Upper half	7	-	yes
1984	4–6	-	-	5	-	yes
1985	3–5	-	-	5	-	yes
1986	3^1/2–5^1/2	-	-	8	-	no
1987	3–6	-	-	8	-	no
1988	3–6	-	-	7	-	no
1989	about 5	-	-	5	-	yes
1990	4–6	-	-	6	-	yes
1991	3–5	-	-	5	-	yes
1992	3^1/2–5^1/2	-	-	9	-	no
1993	4^1/2–6^1/2	-	-	7	-	no
1994	4–6	-	-	6	-	yes
1995	4–6	-	-	2	-	no
1996	4–7	-	-	8	-	no
1997	3^1/2–6^1/2	-	-	5	-	(yes)
1998	3–6	-	-			

Source: Tabulation, including rating, by Deutsche Bundesbank with printout dated Sept. 3, 1997.
A two-year M3 growth guideline of 5 percent per annum was also in effect for 1997–1998.

Monetary targeting continued in Germany as long as there was a DM, with the target rate of growth of central bank money fixed as a range of around 3 to 6 percent per annum since the mid-1980s until similar ranges began to be specified for M3. Table 1 presents the entire record. However, as the decade of the 1980s progressed, monetary targeting became increasingly uninformative about both (1) the actual money growth rate, and (2) the inflation rate to expect in view of the targeted money growth rate. Taking the mid-point of the above target range, 4.5 percent, as Schlesinger (3, pp. 18–19) advised, in conjunction with a long-run average rate of growth of output of 2 to 2.5 percent per annum (3, p. 14) would yield an expected inflation rate of 2 to 2.5 percent at unchanged velocity. Such a low rate was, in fact, reached in 1985. Assisted by the strong appreciation of DM from a highly depressed level, from 1985 to 1986 the consumer price level actually declined. In both 1986 and 1987, even before the world-wide stock-market crash of October 1987 induced extra injections of liquidity, money growth exceeded the upper limit of its already very wide target range by one or two percentage points. However, the inflation rate deviated the other way: In fact the price level did not rise above its 1985 annual average level until 1988.

By that time, central bank money, more than two-thirds of which was currency, had ceased to be a viable intermediate target in part because German mark notes, in addition to U.S. dollar bills, were increasingly used as secondary transaction currency in Central and East European countries. The preferred target now shifted from the narrowest, M0, to one of the broadest, M3, in which the weight of currency was only about 12 percent (in 1988). The Bundesbank defines M3 as currency in circulation and sight deposits, M1, plus time deposits for less than four years, yielding M2, plus the savings deposits at statutory notice also owned by domestic nonbanks and held with credit institutions.

Just before the economic, social, and monetary union of Germany created new, internal challenges for monetary policy, price performance had improved, but its predictability with simple monetarist means had declined. The July 1, 1990, monetary union through assumption of the German Democratic Republic into the Federal Republic of Germany then complicated monetary targeting further by leaving the demand for the new money being introduced in the Eastern part, and the production potential of that part, difficult to predict. Nevertheless, against all odds, an attempt was made to retain the concept of a "potential-[output growth]-oriented monetary

German Inflation 1971–1997

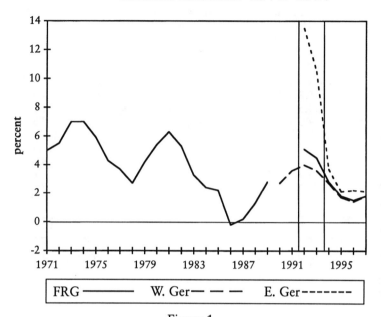

Figure 1

Note: Vertical lines mark Schlesinger's term.

Source: Deutsche Bundesbank, *Monthly Report*, various issues.

management with monetary targets announced in advance" (4, pp. 10–11). Still, partly as a delayed consequence of German unification, money-supply growth rose far above the upper limit, reaching an annual rate of 9.5 percent from 1991 to 1992, the middle year of Schlesinger's presidency. Yet any inflationary consequences, net of price-level catch-up in Eastern Germany, proved rather mild, with inflation in the western part of Germany below 4 percent and falling after 1992. Table 2 and Figure 1 provide the details. Consequences for the price level were especially mild compared with the complaints of Germany's partners about being forced to mimic Germany's high-interest-rate policy or to give up on maintaining fixed nominal exchange rates under the exchange rate mechanism of the EMS.

Unlike other governors represented in this volume, Schlesinger does not discuss fallout for the central bank's credibility directly but concludes (in 5, p. 19) that twenty years of experience with monetary targeting may have been somewhat disappointing. Nevertheless, Schlesinger still feels that, for Germany at least, monetary targeting is

Table 2

Federal German, Western and Eastern German, and
Industrial-Country-Average Inflation Rates, 1971–1997
(change from previous year in percent)

Date	FRG	Western Germany	Eastern Germany	Industrial Countries
1971	5.2			5.3
1972	5.5			4.8
1973	7.0			7.9
1974	7.0			13.4
1975	5.9			11.4
1976	4.3			8.6
1977	3.7			8.8
1978	2.7			7.5
1979	4.2			9.7
1980	5.4			12.4
1981	6.3			10.4
1982	5.3			7.7
1983	3.3			5.2
1984	2.4			5.0
1985	2.2			4.4
1986	-0.2			2.6
1987	0.2			3.2
1988	1.3			3.5
1989	2.8			4.6
1990		2.7		5.2
1991		3.6		4.4
1992	5.1	4.0	13.5	3.2
1993	4.5	3.6	10.5	2.8
1994	2.8	2.7	3.7	2.3
1995	1.8	1.7	2.1	2.5
1996	1.5	1.4	2.2	2.3
1997	1.8	1.8	2.1	1.7

Source: Deutsche Bundesbank, Monthly Report, various issues: Consumer Price Index for All Households. Federal German data 1971–1997, with data for the Western and Eastern parts shown separately after the 1990 unification in the Federal Republic of Germany (FRG), which had previously covered only the Western part. Industrial-country data: See previous chapters.

the best and most timely mechanism of inflation targeting. He does not much discuss other leading indicators of inflation.

Unlike the United Kingdom, Canada, and other countries, including, since 1997, the United States, Germany does not have inflation-protection securities or price-indexed government notes paying a real interest yield. That yield could be compared with the nominal interest yield on conventional, unindexed securities if these two types of instruments had the same effective term-to-maturity.

Such a comparison can give a crude estimate of expected inflation even though changing risk premia also enter the difference between nominal and real yields. Hence money growth remains the most reliable leading indicator of inflation, to be managed, of course, with attention to occasionally shifting velocity trends, in the Bundesbank's view. And indeed, the target rate of money growth announced for 1997 (fourth quarters 1996 to 1997), 3.5 percent to 6.5 percent, or 5 percent per annum on average for two years (fourth quarters 1996 to 1998), showed a steady continuation of the monetary targeting practice beyond Schlesinger's 1993 official retirement from the Bundesbank. His successor as president was Dr. Hans Tietmeyer.

In January 1998, monetary targeting was continued in the run-up to monetary union with the target rate of growth in M3 set at 3 to 6 percent from the fourth quarter 1997 to the fourth quarter of 1998. The Deutsche Bundesbank (1998, p. 22) comments wistfully:

> With its monetary target for 1998, the Bundesbank has set an annual monetary target for the twenty-fourth time in a row and, in all probability, for the last time ever. . . . With its monetary target for 1998, it has created the conditions which allow the European Central Bank (ECB) to carry on smoothly from the tried and tested monetary targeting policy practiced in Germany. In the second half of this year, the ECB Council will take its decision on which monetary policy stance is to be adopted in Stage Three [of European Monetary Union].

Insulation from Political and Cyclical Pressures on the Central Bank

A side benefit that remains from the Bundesbank's attempts to explain its preannounced money supply targets to the public is that their formulation demonstrates both the independence of the Bundesbank and its unwillingness to contribute to the countercyclical political muscle-flexing of the day. What explains this seeming aversion to being drawn into active demand management? Because the lags with which monetary policy affects economic activity are long and variable, monetary policy makers in Germany, as in some other countries, decided not to make ambitious fine-tuning their goal. Otherwise, monetary policy measures could well become effective only when they are no longer needed. The goal of monetary policy should rather be to create general monetary fundamentals that ensure both price stability and adequate economic growth in the medium term. "Or, in other words, German monetary policy is not primarily an anti-cyclical policy, but is geared rather more to longer-term variables such as the growth of the overall economic production potential" (4, pp. 9–10). By preannouncing monetary targets with little or no reference to impending cyclical conditions, the Bundesbank can signal its refusal to be drawn into demand management or to accept short-term stabilization errands that politicians are so eager to have executed for voters thought to be easily impressed by politicians' "taking action" (5, p. 9).

CENTRAL BANK INDEPENDENCE IN LAW AND FACT

The Bundesbank is not subject to orders from the German government. Instead, the sixteen to eighteen independent members of the central bank council (*Zentralbankrat*) set policy. The German government can place issues on the agenda for discussion and disposition, but it does not have a vote in the council and may not offer advice. The most the government could do is to veto immediate implementation of Council decisions for a maximum of fourteen days, asking for reconsideration of the Council's resolutions (3, p. 21). Even this limited, deferral-type veto has never been used.

It took a two-thirds Parliamentary majority under the German constitution to disestablish the Bundesbank as the nation's sovereign central bank in the event of European Monetary Union. However, there have been only hints of a constitutional anchor in the Federal Republic's Basic Law (*Grundgesetz*) of 1949 that would be strong enough also to guarantee the independent position of the Bundesbank (6, p. 8). Even though a simple majority of the lower chamber in parliament (*Bundestag*) could well have been legally sufficient to curtail the independence of the central bank, such a move would have been unthinkable politically. The six amendments to the Bundesbank Act that had been passed by the end of 1997, while dealing mostly with internal organization and governance, have, if anything, tended to strengthen the independence of the Bundesbank over time.

Certainly the Bundesbank relishes every opportunity to assert its independence, knowing that press and the public are behind it. In May 1997 it successfully rejected an attempt by the Federal Minister of Finance to force it not only to revalue its gold reserves, which are kept on its books at a small fraction of their current market price, but to remit the unrealized gains to the Treasury forthwith. These proceeds were to help the government meet deficit-reduction goals, subsequently met by more honorable means, that had become pressing to qualify for leading Europe to monetary union under a strict interpretation of the provisions of the 1992 Maastricht Treaty. While the Deutsche Bundesbank (1997, pp. 4–5) majestically acknowledged that a distribution of hidden reserves would be manageable in monetary-policy terms, it declared, nonetheless, that *prescribing it by law* would constitute interference in the Bundesbank's monetary policy and internal management. The Bundesbank is required to support the government only in so far as it may not go against price-level stability if that is the government's objective. Of course, it is hard to imagine that the Bundesbank would ever err on the inflationary side of the rest of the government, even if it were allowed to do so.

Announcing money-growth targets consistent with inflation of less than 3 percent appears to be one way to ward off inconsistency within the government from the side of the Bundesbank. But accountability goes beyond simply sticking with preannounced rules, if following the rules, no matter what, would not deliver the results originally promised or intended. Table 1 earlier showed that the Bundesbank has missed its money-supply targets half of the time in the twenty-two years since 1975, and when it missed, it missed in all but one year (1995) on the upside. Lags aside, the misses of 1975 to 1978 and 1992 and 1993 were associated with 4 percent average annual rates of inflation in consumer prices, but the year-to-year average annual inflation rate was less than 1 percent 1986 to 1988, and about 1.5 percent 1995–1996 according to Table 2. These were the other two periods when money supply targets failed to be achieved according to the Bundesbank's own rating. The Bundesbank remained faithful to its goal of delivering approximate price level stability even though it eschewed the openly reactive mechanism of inflation targeting.

Schlesinger knows that the independence of a central bank is a necessary—but not sufficient—condition for ensuring the maintenance of the value of money: Not all countries with dependent central banks have had a worse inflation experience than those with independent banks (6, p. 7). Independence of the central bank may strengthen the anti-inflation policy "backbone" of the economy concerned and of its currency (4, p. 19), but it alone cannot determine how much inflation aversion is in the bones in the first place. The decision-makers in independent central banks cannot be completely divorced from their backgrounds, their lives' experiences, professional qualifications, political inclinations, and ambitions for a future in other high positions (5, p. 17). Hence independence must be linked to accountability to the public by means of a clear mandate if it is to yield the benefits of a consistent policy as expected.

Here is an approximation of what Schlesinger himself wrote to one of the authors on the subject of independence in letters dated September 1 and October 7, 1997:

> If one works in a Central Bank, even an independent one such as the Bundesbank, one cannot on every occasion follow the strategic lines one has in mind. There are a number of obstacles: The conflict with external policy requirements, with domestic economic conditions, and—not the least—with the necessity of obtaining a large enough majority in the decision making body, the sixteen to eighteen members of the Central Bank Council. In that Council, the Bundesbank commands only a minority of 8:9 votes currently, up from 7:11 until 1992. In the U.S. Federal Open Market Committee (FOMC) by contrast, the Board normally has a majority of 7:5 over the representatives of the regional Federal Reserve Banks whose German equivalents are the *Landeszentralbanken* (LZB). Unlike the presidents of the Federal Reserve Banks whose appointment is nonpartisan and made with participation by the Board of Governors of the Federal Reserve System in Washington, the LZB presidents are appointed de facto by the state (*Länder*) governments in Germany. The result is that the composition of the Central Bank Council is more "political" and potentially fractious than that of the FOMC, with dissenting votes not uncommon. However, the paramount concern to maintain the purchasing power of the currency ultimately is shared by all the members and has turned Saul into Paul on a number of occasions by the Bundesbank's prayer book.

Dilemmas of Central-Bank Independence

There is a touch of irony in the fact that the "independence" of central banks presumably gives them "discretion," but that any unprincipled exercise of that discretion allows external influences or personal quirks to enter. Any widespread loss of respect for the central bank invites increased oversight and ultimately undermines its independence. In 1998, for instance, the Bank of Japan saw its prestige, and hence its independence, weakened by scandal reaching into its ranks, causing Governor Mieno's successor to resign. Schlesinger continually emphasizes that independence implies an obligation to pursue the goal that is the central bank's primary responsibility in a manner both highly disciplined and transparent (5, pp. 16–17).

As the experience of New Zealand discussed in chapter 7 of this volume shows, there is an attempt to institutionalize this goal so as to make the policy of central banks less dependent on the dominant individuals who have to run them. The problem for all—except for those critics who define themselves as knowing more about future links and relations in the economy than the central bank—is that charters can be written telling the central bank what to achieve. Standing orders can also be issued about what exactly it is to do with its instruments. But the central bank is put into an impossible position when it is given orders about what to achieve at the same time as it is also being told exactly how to achieve it since such orders often turn out to be incompatible after the fact. Such conflicts of overdetermination can arise also when the central bank chooses to task itself with preannounced money-growth targets.

Attempts to automate central banking or to downplay the discernment and exceptional qualities demanded of its leaders are bound to be counterproductive when means-ends relationships with money are tricky and shifting, as they increasingly are. When Chile's Governor Zahler resigned in June 1996 in protest over excessive interference exerted by the government, as well as private bank interests, through his own board, Chile's Finance Minister tried to reassure the world that this was no loss since "no one is indispensable." Finance ministers often may wish secretly for weak personalities at the central bank who would indeed be dispensable, for an independent political weakling is a contradiction in terms.

In Schlesinger's view, independence could also be compromised if the central bank, like the Bank of England before its formal grant of independence in 1997, were charged with the supervision of the very same banks it might choose to bail out as lender of last resort. But in Germany the central bank has not had this supervisory function, at least not since the founding of the Bundesbank in 1948. Of course the Bundesbank cannot completely be excluded from the matter if it is to remain aware of developments and innovations in the banking sector. It therefore acts as an agent for the government agency charged with bank supervision, the *Bundesaufsichtsamt für das Kreditwesen*. But the Bundesbank has no authority to close a bank, to reorganize it, or to order a change in its management. This leaves it largely free of role conflicts between shoring up banks in difficulty and doing what is best for an economy through price stability. In addition, banks are mutually insured through a pool to which they all have contributed. This pool would have to be used before any banks that become illiquid, but not insolvent, may hope for consideration from the central bank. Such attention is limited to cases where there are significant implications for the smooth functioning of the payments system or the state of confidence in banks (5, pp. 13–14). Thus every attempt is made to limit the moral hazard that arises when bank managers and stockholders are tempted to trade on the central bank's residual function as implicit deposit insurer and lender of last resort by taking socially excessive risks.

Schlesinger clearly feels that discretion and confidential deliberation, and the quality of those who engage in the latter, are important even though it should be clear what the object of such discretion and deliberations should be. In his estimation, rapid publication of the minutes of internal policy discussions, including the memoranda of discussions that occur at the Federal Open Market Committee (FOMC) meetings in the United States, is counterproductive. The loud precoloring, put by "Fed-watchers" on central bank actions and utterances, likewise lowers the maximum possible quality of monetary policy and the steadiness of its effects (5, pp. 15, 18). Private lobbyists and publicity agents try to make rules, patterns, and trip wires for central bankers. They build up signal-extraction and early-warning routines, and they fire warning shots that call attention more to those who release them than to the goals that central bankers are to achieve.

THE NEED FOR CONCERTED ACTION
TO SUPPORT STABLE PRICES

Before the transition to widespread floating of exchange rates among the major currencies in 1973, Schlesinger (e.g., 1, p. 5) often warned against overestimating what the central bank can do and the degree to which it can be held responsible for the lack of price stability. By 1982 he no longer allowed most of the excuses once available for the central bank's failing to achieve approximate price stability over the medium term. But there is a difference between technical feasibility of an outcome and assuring its beneficial effect and long-term backing. For the latter the Bundesbank needs political allies. Coordination with the rest of the government and with social partners, as well as order in the public finances, is essential if a policy of price stability is to be not only technically and institutionally feasible but an economic and political success.

Schlesinger's views are pertinent for assessing the credibility of entry conditions negotiated for the European Monetary Union (EMU) and the sustainability of price stability agreed to at Maastricht in 1992. Deeply embedded consent with such goals and with the reforms needed to fortify them, he points out, is the essential societal infrastructure that gives substance to the language of treaties about such goals and induces compliance with formal obligations.

This principle applies widely if costly contradictions are to be avoided. For instance, without mutual understanding and cooperation, organized labor can agitate, with partial success for the organized insiders it represents, for wage increases incompatible with price stability and high employment in the economy. Employment programs that then may be expanded by the German government to bypass the test of markets make this mispricing worse (2, p. 14). The government, particularly when unable to rein in spending and casting about for additional revenue, will raise administered prices and tax and nontax costs of various kinds, including excise and value-added taxes, and user fees. The resulting price increases can quickly add up without ever having been checked by market forces on which the central bank can act. Should the central bank aim for price depression in the competitive sector to offset the price increases in the noncompetitive sector so as to keep the overall price level unchanged? Without a social consensus to limit the contradictions, set up by noncompetitive and nonmarket sectors, pursuit of the goal of price stability can be deprived of many of its benefits and saddled with unnecessary costs that undermine its political legitimacy.

Switzerland's national-bank president Lusser (1996, pp. 201–214), in his sensitive comments on future prospects for EMU, also emphasized the deep political consensus that would be required within and between countries to make such a union work beneficially with price stability, and hence to gain popular acceptance and staying power. Indeed both Schlesinger and Lusser, no matter how apparently monetarist, have a deep understanding that achievement of price stability ultimately is safeguarded not just by technical management that is competent with its monetary instruments. Rather, such a goal is ultimately protected by evoking a supportive consensus that allows the central bank to feel politically secure and widely appreciated in the pursuit of price stability, which is its mandate.

CONCLUSION

Safeguarding price stability beneficially calls for more than a technical fix. It requires wrestling with actual problems and disturbances, foreign and domestic, and teaching and arguing persuasively why price stability is best in the long run. Since academics rightly teach questions, not answers, strong leadership should be expected to come not from universities or economic science but from the central bank and its key figures. Yet that leadership needs to build political, media, and business support and popular alliances. The goal is to have the principle of price stability filter through the spectra of society and gain broad acceptance so that it can induce appropriate behavior in the public and its representatives. Any such conformity would raise the benefits of applying the principle, thereby reinforcing it and strengthening the will to comply.

REFERENCES

Deutsche Bundesbank. 1997. "Revaluation of Gold and Foreign Exchange Reserves," *Monthly Report* 49 (June): 3–5.

_____. 1998. "Review of Monetary Targeting in 1997–8 and More Detailed Definition of the Monetary Target for 1998," *Monthly Report* 50 (January): 17–23.

Lusser, Markus. 1996. *Geldpolitik*. Zürich: Verlag Neue Zürcher Zeitung.

Schlesinger, Helmut
(1) "Geldwertstabilität und Geldpolitik." Address delivered on May 13, 1972 at the "Ottobeurer Wirtschaftstage" of Universität Augsburg. Augsburg: Verlag Die Brigg, 1972.
(2) "Verteidigung des Geldwertes in einer inflatorischen Umwelt." Address to the "Berliner Juristische Gesellschaft," January 27, 1982. Berlin: Walter de Gruyter. Reprinted in *Presseauszüge der deutschen Bundesbank*, 1982 (12): 1.
(3) "Zentralbanken im Spannungsfeld von Geld- und Fiskalpolitik." Address to the annual meeting of the "Schweizerische Vereinigung für Währungsfragen," November 11, 1987. Zurich: *Schriftenreihe der Schweizerischen Vereinigung für Währungsfragen*, No. 5, 1988.
(4) "German Monetary Policy and the Future of European Monetary Inte-

gration." The Inaugural Malcolm Wiener Lecture on the International Political Economy, April 14, 1993. Harvard University: John F. Kennedy School of Government. Reprinted in *Presseauszüge der deutschen Bundesbank*, 1993 (28): 1.

(5) "Zielkonflikte der Geldpolitik." Seminar given on December 16, 1993 at "Hochschule St. Gallen." Hochschule St. Gallen: Aulavorträge No. 57, 1994.

(6) "The Role of the Independence of the Central Bank for the Financial Stability of a Country." Bank of Korea, 1994.7.22. Reprinted in *Presseauszüge der deutschen Bundesbank*, 1994 (56): 4.

(7) Letters to G.M. von Furstenberg, Oberursel, September 1, 1997 and October 7, 1997.

SWITZERLAND'S LUSSER: PRICE STABILITY TO BANK ON

GEORGE M. VON FURSTENBERG AND MICHAEL K. ULAN

CONTENTS

Dr. Markus Lusser
President, Schweizerische Nationalbank, 1988–1996

April 8, 1931–April 21, 1998

M arkus Lusser was born in 1931 into one of Switzerland's oldest titled families. Being a *Häuptergeschlecht*, a head clan, its members have held important offices in ancient Switzerland's *Kanton Uri* since the first half of the thirteenth century, and, after 1848, in the more centralized Swiss confederation we know today. Unlike many such families in which children quickly become the charges of nannies, tutors, fencing and riding instructors, and boarding schools, Markus and his younger sister, Ruth, shared in the cultural life of the family from an early age. Indeed, extremely close and permanent family bonds became a living tradition in this dynasty, as did their keen interest in music, the theater, and the arts, and in public service. For example, his parents were closely involved with *Schauspielhaus Zürich,* which, due in part to mostly Jewish immigrants from Germany, was probably the best German-language stage during, and for a time after, World War II.

The Benedictine monks—renowned for skillfully balancing the needs of mind, body, and soul—took care of schooling Markus in the humanist tradition of ancient Latin and Greek, early philosophy, and history. Yet there was also room for lively training in modern languages, art history, and culture studies, even including going to plays and opera matinees in the company of the novices. To fit all this, his school day extended from 7:20 in the morning to 7:00 in the evening, Monday through Friday, with 4:00 pm dismissal on Saturdays. Many of the refined interests acquired in school, including world history, stayed with Markus Lusser for life.

Proceeding to law studies in Berne in the early 1950s might have seemed almost anticlimactic. But here fortune smiled on him again. At the time Berne had the only faculty of law in Switzerland eschewing the witless rigors of legal formalism that continued to hold in thrall other faculties in Switzerland, as in France and Germany. Lusser's law professors actually had the revolutionary idea that the law should not be designed to make life more difficult for all; rather it should facilitate entrepreneurship and productive innovation. Again Lusser took something important with him: He credits his commitment to deregulation of financial markets and to the abolition of interest-rate and capital-import and -export controls to these formative influences. After studying also in Paris, Lusser obtained his doctorate of law from the University of Berne in 1957, writing on "Civil Suit Procedures in the Canton of Uri," over whose evolution and application, in one capacity or another through the centuries, his ancestors had at times presided.

When head of the Swiss National Bank (SNB), he returned regularly to the University of Berne to confer with Professors Karl Brunner (also of Ohio State University and of the University of Rochester) and Jürg Niehans (also of Johns Hopkins University) on the ins and outs of monetary economics. Brunner and his followers reinforced in him a pragmatic form of monetarism. In 1997, the University of Berne recognized Lusser's long association and distinguished public service by awarding him an honorary doctorate in political science.

Here are some of the highlights of his career: After completing his law studies in Berne and Paris, he began to work for the Swiss Bankers' Association, the *Schweizerische Bankiervereinigung*, in Basle in 1959, becoming its director in 1976. In addition to his responsibilities at this association, he participated in various joint ventures of the Swiss banks, such as Eurocard. Designated by one of Switzerland's political parties, the Christian People's Party, and then appointed by the Federal Council in May 1980, Lusser joined the SNB, Switzerland's central bank. There he became a member of the three-person Governing Board responsible for monetary policy at the start of 1981 and head of Department III (foreign exchange, credits, payment transactions). His painful experiences with monetary policy trying to weaken the external value of the Swiss franc to combat "overvaluation" date back to this time. On being appointed vice-chairman of the Governing Board at the beginning of 1985, he became head of Department II (capital market, bank notes, business transactions with the Federal Government, administration of gold reserves), located in Berne. On May 1, 1988, the Federal Council appointed him chairman of the Governing Board and head of Department I (staff sectors) in Zurich. At that time he also became a member of the administrative council of the Bank for International Settlements (BIS). As head of the SNB, in 1992 he assumed the additional duty of Swiss governor of the International Monetary Fund. The Fund is an over fifty-year-old international financial institution in Washington, D.C., which Switzerland, ever jealous of its independent decision making, had not chosen formally to join until May 29, 1992. While federalist Switzerland's capital is Berne, its central bank is in Zurich and Berne, the BIS in Basle, and the World Trade Organization (WTO) in Geneva.

Upon reaching the age of sixty-five, Lusser retired from the SNB at the end of April 1996 amid some criticism by those who felt that the Central Bank should focus less on price stability and take more responsibility for economic growth and for exchange rates that are "right" for trade. His critics thus ignored that labor market rigidities, high taxation, and overregulation are the main obstacles to job creation and expansion of nonfinancial business, obstacles that monetary policy alone is powerless to remove. Lusser explained that Switzerland, like the United States by and large, follows "republican" traditions (in the sense of public service in the Roman Republic well before Julius Caesar): When you leave public service, all connections to your previous position are cut off: *Servir et disparaître* is the harsh maxim that applies. Six months after leaving public office, Lusser assumed the presidency of J. P. Morgan (Suisse) SA in Geneva.

This biographical note has turned out longer than those for all the other governors because it is based on a letter and detailed comments, dated April 16, 1998, which the governor sent to one of the authors just before his death. His widow, Elisabeth, to whom he was devoted, since added a personal note that this was the last letter Markus Lusser had written before he died suddenly of a heart condition. He also had sent ten pages of comments and elaborations on an earlier draft of the essay that follows. We have used some of these comments simply to correct errors. But in those cases where a great deal of perspective and information was added, we have inserted Dr. Markus Lusser's remarks, translated freely and clearly marked, as a sign of respect.

SWITZERLAND'S LUSSER: PRICE STABILITY TO BANK ON

ABSTRACT

In Switzerland, as for instance in Austria and Poland, the central bank is known as the national bank. When Markus Lusser assumed the presidency of the Governing Board of the Swiss National Bank (SNB) in 1988, Switzerland had already compiled a record of low inflation for decades. However, Dr. Lusser added to the distinguished record of the SNB by further reducing reliance on regulatory and administrative mechanisms and protectionist devices in financial markets. His preference for market solutions and openness led him to confront special-interest arrangements and restrictions on foreign participation and on financial innovation, thereby consolidating Switzerland's special status in the global financial marketplace.

While committed to price stability as the guiding objective of monetary policy, he dealt candidly with the challenges posed for monetary management by any lasting and pronounced aberration of the exchange rate that may be caused by international portfolio and security shocks. Cataloguing the many evils of inflation and stressing the dysfunctionality of attempts to fine-tune monetary policy in response to cyclical disturbances, he lived by high standards of central bank credibility. Contrary to his own monetarist rhetoric, this credibility was based not on the SNB's adherence to very low money-supply growth targets: Its adherence to such targets proved no more strict than that of the Deutsche Bundesbank. Rather it was based on Lusser's demonstrated resolve to make price stability the first order of business of the central bank whenever there appeared to be a conflict between competing objectives.

INTRODUCTION

We close the "European" part of this book with a country that is often described as a geographically and politically small state, a middle-sized industrial power, and a financial superpower: Switzerland. Lusser finds the latter description somewhat exaggerated but notes that Switzerland is indeed special in private banking and in holding out for a stable price level. The Swiss have developed a deep understanding of the reasons to avoid inflation, and how to do it. Only one major issue poses short- and intermediate-term goal conflicts from which it is difficult to escape for this small, mostly open, economy: At certain conjunctures, there may be a dilemma between maintaining stability of the domestic price level and preserving an exchange rate with which Swiss industry can live. Such a conflict becomes pressing at times because Switzerland, as both a major capital importer and even larger exporter, is highly exposed to financial-sector shocks, whether originating at home or abroad, in its exchange relations with the rest of the world. This means that its exchange rate in the short run may be driven not by the requirements of industry or by the current account balance of goods and services transactions, but by the shifting portfolio preferences of large, often institutional, international investors, including the Swiss themselves.

This chapter explains how Lusser has attempted to deal with this dilemma by emphasizing price stability over other desiderata, and how he has defended the credibility of the central bank, tackled financial reforms, and strengthened the role of the Swiss franc and of Switzerland's financial services industry. We close with some comments by the SNB and one of its directors, Georg Rich, on dormant bank deposits and gold purchases dating back to World War II. These unresolved historical issues came to the fore in 1997 to 1998, starting about a year after Lusser had left office in April 1996.

Matters of Reference

Lusser (1996) himself distilled his legacy in a book that was published in German at about the time he left office. He has since explained in correspondence that this book contains edited versions of only a small fraction of his principal addresses. He even wondered whether, during his time in office, he might not have given too many lectures and speeches. This has led him to reflect on the meaning of the central bank's democratic accountability: *I was finally guided by the conviction that an independent central bank in a democratic country is obliged to explain its actions, and what they are meant to accomplish, to the public again and again. The majority of the citizens in our direct-democratic (referendum-based) system after all decide whether the central bank should have its independence and keep it. Hence the SNB is well advised to vie continuously for the trust of the public by making its actions transparent.*

Before his book appeared, President Lusser, like the six other heads of central banks celebrated in this book, had been asked to identify those four (or more) public addresses that best captured his convictions about the importance of price stability and the means to achieve and safeguard this goal. The reference section of this essay identifies and describes these papers, which are cited by number (1 through 4, followed by page number of the original unpublished text) throughout. Page numbers that are not preceded by an item number, by contrast, refer to pages of Lusser's book, with all elements of translation ours. Certain additional materials have been provided by SNB Director Georg Rich, who is its leading English-language communicator and coordinator of research, to shed light on issues, recently raised with renewed intensity, about Swiss banking and gold operations during and after World War II. Comments by Dr. Lusser (5) on an earlier draft, received shortly before his death, appear in italics.

INTERNAL AND EXTERNAL PRICE STABILITY: A TOUGH BALANCING ACT

The problems posed by terms-of-trade shocks and exchange-rate distortions, already severe, are likely to grow in the future because Switzerland, by declining to become a member of the European Union (EU), has excluded itself from the European Monetary Union (EMU) as well. About 80 percent of Switzerland's merchandise imports are from the EU, which also buys 60 percent of Switzerland's exports. The external value of the Swiss franc, whose home base soon will be surrounded by a Euro-area many times its economic size, may well be quite unstable unless monetary policy is tethered to maintaining an approximately fixed exchange rate with Europe's new dominant collective currency. Such an informal tie could, in principle, be acceptable to the Swiss only if the Euro turned out to be a currency quite as hard as the DM used to be. Even then, any costly defense of fixed exchange rates is not credible in a world of free capital flows, making fixed exchange rates a fair-weather standard in open international financial markets. Hence monetary policy unhappily will have to thread its way between the sometimes conflicting objectives of subduing exchange rate aberrations and maintaining the expectation of approximate price level stability, which is the SNB's overriding objective.

Periodic shocks in the Swiss financial sector are attributable not only to international portfolio dynamics but also to the "safe haven" function of Switzerland that is due to the stability of its political, social, and legal systems. In either case, all or most of the shock originates from outside. Lead economists at the central bank (see Rich, 1997a, 1997b) include capital account shocks, expressed as a change in the risk premium on foreign assets (i.e., assets not denominated in Swiss francs), that alter the terms of trade and international interest-rate relations, in their models of the Swiss economy. They then attempt to deduce what the central bank optimally should do about them, but there are no easy choices.

It turns out that in trying to cope with capital surges, both inward and outward, the *Schweizerische Nationalbank*, like, in a different setting, the *Banco Central de Chile,* must perform a difficult balancing act. If, on the one hand, it tries to counteract any real appreciation that seriously disrupts industry and trade by monetary expansion in the short run, it risks jeopardizing price stability in subsequent years when the pressure to get into Swiss-franc assets has passed. If, on the other hand, it fails to react publicly, it will be accused of contributing to deindustrialization of Switzerland, as plants and markets once lost to the country may never be regained. Hence, if the central bank has ever gotten its hands dirty in the past twenty-five years of floating exchange rates, it was in conjunction with trying to control destabilizing exchange rate movements.

At about this point in the earlier draft Lusser commented: *True, the SNB often finds itself caught in a policy dilemma over whether to pursue the goal of price stability consistently or whether also to pay heed to exchange-rate objectives. But when I was president, I never targeted or tried to defend any particular level of the exchange rate, assuming there indeed is a level Swiss industry can live with. To do so would have required me to be able to define the "correct" exchange rate better than the market. I have used the argument of having difficulty improving on the market in this regard to reject demands for exchange-rate management made by Swiss export industries. Switzerland's persistently high current account surpluses make it difficult to speak of chronically overvalued exchange rates. I have always rejected placing monetary policy in the service of exchange-rate objectives, as often urged in France, for instance at the time of the Plaza Agreement of 1985 and the Louvre Accord of 1987 among the Group-of-Seven leading industrial countries. All the SNB can hope to accomplish is to try to counteract any massive and cumulative overshooting of the Swiss franc on either the upside or the downside through temporary measures. When representatives of export industry and of trade unions, as well as certain political groupings, attack the SNB for contributing to the deindustrialization of Switzerland, they tend to forget the exceedingly low interest rates associated with a strong franc. Such rates, by encouraging business investment, lead to rapid growth in productivity and contribute to the international competitiveness of Swiss industry.*

MORE ON THE EXTERNAL CHALLENGE
TO PRICE STABILITY

As the Swiss central bank does not supervise the banks—that function having been entrusted to a separate commission by law—its immediate responsibility for the conduct and risk taking by banks is more limited than, for instance, that of the Federal Reserve in the United States. While not responsible for individual banks, the SNB of course remains responsible for the Swiss banking system as a whole because the welfare of that system is inextricably linked with that of the entire economy. As a result, macroeconomic issues and consequences come close to receiving the SNB's undivided attention.

While often quick to emphasize that the SNB has a money-supply and not an exchange-rate policy, or *Geldmengenpolitik* and not *Wechselkurspolitik* (see Schneider, 1995, p. 65), no governor of a small, open economy has the luxury of being able to ignore the exchange-rate effects of monetary policy or the monetary-policy effects of exchange rates entirely. Canada's monetary-conditions index, which includes a reference to an index of exchange rates, when used as a guide to monetary policy, formalizes such a relationship. Economists generally agree that monetary policy can have little to do with the level of the real exchange rate, or the terms on which countries trade each other's goods, in the long run, but there can be appreciable effects in the short run.

Ever mindful of the only rather fleeting power of "nominal" changes over "real" outcomes (4, p. 14), Lusser also insists that there is nothing the central bank can do about the real exchange rate in the long run. Furthermore, he argues that the relative cost of living in Switzerland may well drift up in view of Switzerland's higher rate of technological progress and growth in labor productivity in the traded-goods sector than competing countries (p. 43). Of course, whether any particular real appreciation, such as the 13 percent export-weighted appreciation of the Swiss franc from the end of 1992 to 1995, is an equilibrium phenomenon or unsustainable is difficult to determine immediately (p. 67). However, there is no doubt that in the short run, for perhaps a year or two (p. 41), monetary factors could "correct" the course of the real exchange rate to some degree, particularly through unsterilized intervention (pp. 44–45).

Unsterilized intervention affects the central bank's balance sheet totals, i.e., its total assets and liabilities. Such intervention is powerful because it induces changes in the Swiss money supply by altering the cost of liquidity and the volume of central-bank reserves of the domestic banking system. Unlike sterilized intervention, it does not just change the composition of the assets of the central bank, and obversely of international investors, between foreign and domestic claims. Such a change in the central bank's portfolio composition is very nearly trivial for the currency composition of the huge volume of liquid private international claims involving a financial center like Switzerland.

Caught between the concerns to maintain Switzerland's competitiveness in goods and services on the one hand and domestic price stability on the other, the Swiss National Bank tried several approaches to reconcile the two objectives before emphasis shifted more clearly to the goal of price stability. During one episode of steep Swiss franc appreciation (1978 to 1981), it had even been drawn into the unsavory business of industrial policy willing to compromise stability of the domestic price level for the sake of defending external competitiveness. This was done first by attempting to block any further appreciation of the Swiss franc or compensating its consequences for industry and then by facilitating its depreciation against other leading currencies in real terms. In the process the SNB invented additional international tax and control instruments and subsidized selected export sectors by absorbing exchange-rate risk on favorable terms. The scheme was designed to allow some Swiss exporters to continue to price to foreign markets so as to keep prices fairly steady and competitive in foreign currency as the exchange value of the Swiss franc soared. For a short time before such measures were lifted in 1980, there was an attempt to discourage continued short-term capital inflows and upward pressure on the Swiss franc by imposing a charge of 10 percent a quarter—tantamount to a steep negative marginal interest rate—on Swiss francs newly deposited by foreigners. The central bank also let the narrow money supply (M1, the sum of currency and transactions as opposed to savings deposits), which had been targeted to increase by 5 percent from 1977 to 1978, grow by *three* times as much, 15 percent, to keep 1 DM from buying any less than 0.8 Swiss franc (80 Rappen). Thus in 1978, as to a lesser extent in subsequent years and again in 1987, the Swiss National Bank allowed the rate of growth of the money supply to be driven by the desire to dampen both the appreciation of the Swiss franc and to cushion any ensuing economic downturn.

Lusser has commented on this portion of the earlier draft by taking, not dodging, full responsibility: *Since 1981 I took part with my two colleagues on the directorate in setting monetary policy for the central bank. The undesired exchange rate appreciation of the Swiss franc in conjunction with the stock-market crash of October 1987 induced us to pursue an expansionary monetary policy. I share responsibility for this easing and the inflation that it brought and do not want to deflect blame by noting that I did not become president of the SNB until the following year.*

Table 1 provides the data record for 1985 to 1997. All but the first three, and last one or two, years of this period are Lusser's term. Achievements on the price front, especially in the second half of this period, can be credited to him to a large degree. The sharp reduction in money growth from a high inherited level of close to 10 percent in 1987 to 1988 to 2 to 3 percent per annum in 1990 to 1993, which earned Lusser the—in soccer terms perhaps not entirely unfriendly—epithet of "stopper," was particularly decisive: The steady decline in inflation and nominal interest rates since 1991 to 1992 is a consequence of this policy. Unexpected monetary tightening may, for a fairly short time, have contributed to exchange-rate appreciation in real terms and a corresponding loss in international competitiveness.

Table 1

Average Annual Percentages, or Percentage Rates of Change,
in Basic Economic Data: Switzerland, 1985–1997

	Growth Rate Real GDP	Unemploy. Rate	M3 Growth Rate	Inflation Rate (CPI)	Treasury Bill Rate	Real Exchange Rate
Column	(1)	(2)	(3)	(4)	(5)	(6)
1985	4.1	1.0	4.8	3.4	4.15	91.3
1986	2.8	0.8	6.7	0.8	3.54	98.9
1987	2.3	0.8	9.5	1.4	3.18	102.0
1988	2.9	0.7	9.8	1.9	3.01	101.2
1989	3.9	0.6	6.2	3.2	6.60	94.1
1990	2.3	0.5	2.4	5.4	8.32	100.0
1991	0.0	1.1	3.2	5.9	7.74	102.7
1992	-0.1	2.6	2.1	4.0	7.76	98.1
1993	-0.5	4.5	3.9	3.3	4.75	98.8
1994	0.5	4.7	5.1	0.9	3.97	106.8
1995	0.8	4.2	2.2	1.8	2.78	112.9
1996	-0.2	4.7	6.9	0.8	1.72	111.8
1997	0.7	5.2	5.2	0.5	1.45	103.0

Sources: Schweizerische Nationalbank, *Geld, Währung und Konjunktur*, various issues, and International Monetary Fund, *International Financial Statistics*, national interest rates: Treasury bill rate; and real effective exchange rate indices: based on relative normalized unit of labor costs (1990=100), with increases indicating appreciation of the Swiss franc in real terms relevant for its competitiveness in international trade. Data for 1997 are preliminary.

Notes: The percentage rates of change shown in columns (1) and (4) are from the preceding year. The rate of growth of the money stock, M3, in column (3), is between yearends. The unemployment rate reported for Switzerland refers to registered unemployment only.

However, the maintained stance of monetary policy can have little to do with Swiss domestic output being flat and unemployment rising persistently over a period of several years, 1991 to 1996, and into 1997. The United States, for instance, has done very well while pursuing a similarly determined monetary policy, with Lusser getting more blame, and Greenspan more credit, than either deserves.

Table 1 covers an instructive episode in which the exchange rate moved first, with monetary policy then activated to dampen this move and its adverse effects on economic activity, but with repercussions for the inflation rate becoming noticeable one or two years later. Specifically, appreciation of the Swiss franc from 1985 to 1987, from an index value of 91 to 102 in the table, was soon opposed by high money growth from 1986 to 1988, which contributed to inflation's

Swiss Inflation 1971–1997

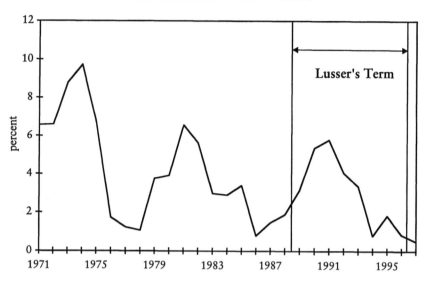

Figure 1
Source: International Monetary Fund,
International Financial Statistics Database, March 25, 1998.

rising from 1.9 percent in 1988 to 5.9 percent in 1991. Similar episodes had occurred earlier. The Swiss inflation experience between
1971 and 1997 is shown in Figure 1.

Lusser rates these stop-go episodes as mistakes because the central bank concerned itself too much with the fortunes of particular
sectors of the private economy and not enough with the public good
represented by price stability (pp. 74, 109–110). For when the rush
into the Swiss franc had stopped, inflation soon reached—for Switzerland—extraordinary levels of 7 percent in 1980/81 and 6 percent
in 1990/91. Then monetary contraction and recession were required
to bring the inflation rate back down to its customary low level since
disinflation is not painless even when it is, in principle, expected. For
the two decades after 1975, without the 1979 to 1982 and 1989 to
1992 episodes of high inflation, the average inflation rate would have
been 2 percent, a rate comfortably close to price stability in view of
"the experience that the consumer price index frequently overesti-
mates the actual increase in the cost of living [by close to 1 percent
annually]" (p. 33).

Lusser has warned repeatedly that inflationary potential may be generated by excessive concern with exchange rate movements (pp. 74, 141). But he also has conceded that a grossly excessive appreciation of the Swiss franc, driven by a wave of speculation, may call for attempts to break this wave when it begins to jeopardize major export sectors (p. 212). At this point of the earlier draft, Lusser added some clarifying provisos: *Not even a short-term deviation from the noninflationary basic course charted for monetary policy can be justified just by one export industry or another's having difficulty maintaining international competitiveness. The industry in trouble would also have to have good long-term prospects of surviving in Switzerland. The shoe and apparel industries would not, I think, fit this bill unless they produce genuine luxury articles or specialty products, because their long-term chances of survival are poor in a high-wage country like Switzerland.*

Swiss Franc and Euro

At the start of the present decade, Lusser anticipated being confronted more frequently with undesirable speculative overshooting in exchange rate movements, making monetary policy harder to conduct (2, p. 17). His discussion of developments in the rest of Europe (p. 213), of the relative exchange-rate stability achieved informally with the D-Mark (pp. 46, 81), of the effects of a loss of confidence in other European currencies (4, p. 12), and of the conditions necessary for a successful monetary union in Europe are all tinged with concern about undesirable fall-out for the real exchange rate of the Swiss franc, particularly against European currencies (pp. 162–63, 212). Most frequently the fear is that the Swiss franc will become overvalued relative to what is good for the country. Central banks that keep their own house "in order" can reduce the danger of exchange rate turbulence and exchange distortions, but they cannot ban it (p. 88). Late in 1997 the SNB (1997b, p. 264), obviously concerned about the prospect of "unexpected and undesirable" fluctuations of the Swiss franc exchange rate, felt obliged to repeat that "it will use the monetary means at its disposal to counter an exchange rate development that is undesirable from the point of view of the economy as a whole" without explaining its tolerances. Thus the issue simply refuses to go away.

While Lusser regards Swiss membership in the European Union as at least debatable (cf. p. 155; 1, p. 3), he also notes pointedly that Switzerland may be more effective in contributing to the improvement of any bad European approaches to regulation and legislation when it provides "system" competition from outside (p. 167). In 1992, a majority of Swiss citizens in a referendum defeated a proposal to join the European Economic Area. This grouping originally contained Austria, Sweden, and Finland as long as they hesitated to become full *political* members of the European Union, but in 1998 contained only Norway and Liechtenstein as countries with such reservations. The list of European countries that have opted out of European Monetary Union (EMU) is longer: Denmark, Sweden, and the United Kingdom. Lusser can conceive of Switzerland's joining EMU eventually if price stability is the Union's overriding and politically accepted objective. Furthermore, EU without EMU may not remain an available option.

Until that distant time, however, exchange rates that are left free to float with only cautious monetary attempts to stabilize their course at the margin are preferable to fixed-rate arrangements on a regional basis (pp. 47, 81–82, 190, 211). Indeed, given the equilibrium tendency for the Swiss franc to appreciate gradually in real terms, nominally fixed exchange rates might require higher domestic inflation rates in Switzerland than in partner countries to produce this real appreciation (4, pp. 13–15).

Asked to help us discern his views more clearly than appeared possible from his public record as head of the SNB, Lusser wrote in April 1998: *In accord with the government of my country—which characterizes membership in the European Union (EU) as a strategic objective—I expect that Switzerland will aim to become a full member of the EU within 10 years. There are few economic obstacles to such a move. Switzerland's trade is already more highly integrated with the EU than that of some of its present members. But I can empathize with the political reservations of my compatriots. The European Union has a "democratic deficit" while Switzerland has the most developed direct democracy in Europe. We are not prepared to sacrifice the right of constitutional initiative, and of putting questions, even fiscal and financial questions, to referenda and plebiscites. So we want fewer "Europe-wide" directives and more systems-competition within Europe before we can feel comfortable with European Union. Because membership in EMU will become inseparably tied to accession to the EU, the performance of the European Central Bank, particularly in avoiding inflation, will also have a major bearing on whether EU membership will become acceptable to the Swiss public. Although Austria has pursued a policy of tying the exchange value of its currency, the Schilling, to the DM for years prior to joining the EU, Switzerland may not be well advised to follow the same strategy with regard to the Euro, at least not until the Euro has proved itself. Furthermore, any kind of exchange-rate pegging would ruin the (real and nominal) interest-rate advantage and the unusually low rates which Switzerland has enjoyed.*

THE SWISS STRICTURES AGAINST INFLATION

When stop-go policies do not themselves contribute to recurring crises (p. 247; 2, p. 3), there are still conflicts and bad breaks that mean that even the most clear-sighted central banking operation cannot safely be put on automatic pilot. Take, for instance, the two faces of flexible exchange rates of which Lusser is so keenly aware. On the one hand, he credits flexible rates with giving monetary policy some autonomy and the country some interest-rate independence, most relevantly from Germany (1, pp. 5–6). On the other hand, he recognizes that monetary policy can find its options curtailed, its intentions temporarily derailed, and its effects crimped by excessive swings in the exchange rate with neighboring countries (1, p. 12).

What then are the benefits of staying on a course very close to price stability? Lusser has provided an impressive canon contrasting the benefits of price stability with the costs of inflation. In the Swiss context, inflation above one or two percentage points per year tends to be unexpected because the central bank's anti-inflationary resolve is entirely credible to the national and international public. The main reasons the president gives for the strict adherence to the principle of price-level stability (pp. 19, 22, 29, 50–51, 55, 62, 72, 83–85, 94–95, 98, 130, 190; 4, p. 13) are that inflation

- reduces economic efficiency by raising transaction, reassessment, and renegotiation costs;
- disturbs relative prices, wage negotiations, and the social climate;
- is antisocial because it lowers the actual below the expected real return on saving, including retirement saving, and represents a hidden form of regressive redistribution;
- distorts resource allocation by favoring temporary diversion to

inflation-hedge investments and hoarding and by encouraging indexation that hinders an economy's ability to adjust to real shocks;

• raises not only nominal but also real interest rates as the prestige and "strategic success position" of the national currency in
international portfolios declines;

• facilitates the financing of budget deficits and the expansion of
the public sector in a way that undercuts economic growth;

• contributes to the wasteful instability of political business cycles
by throwing monetary policy open to manipulation by interests
with short horizons;

• undermines the autonomy and authority of the central bank as
guardian of the public good over the long term; and

• creates a climate of uncertainty about future monetary policy
that harms the domestic economy and disturbs international price
relations.

There is also a remark (p. 62) that even a permanent, and hence expected, inflation trend can detract from long-term growth, in part,
because the variability of the inflation rate may be positively related
to its average level and, in part, because even a constant, but appreciable, inflation rate squanders resources in both the private and public sectors.

While Lusser suspects that periodically elected governments may
be prepared to seek some short-term uplift of the economy, and of
their own ratings, by risking inflation at an opportune time (p. 95),
he can see no possible good coming to the public from taking such a
risk. The fact that the return trip to price stability may well pass
through a dismal valley of stagflation (p. 54) is one more argument
for avoiding inflation in the first place, and not an argument for flinch-
ing from the task of eliminating it once it has happened (p. 51). Learning to live with inflation is not characteristic of Switzerland.

Dissenting Views

While there is a ruling consensus on these matters, even Switzerland has at least some sprinkling of populist politicians and dema-
gogues who love nothing more than blaming the central bank. It is a
depressingly common experience, Lusser notes darkly (p. 241), that
the tried and true generally gets no lasting respect, at least not in
economic policy. Leftists are not alone in assuming that economic

developments are made from the top, and that central bankers personify the economy's command center, which they should take by storm or vitriol. For them it is not fiscal disorder and discouraging tax burdens, excess regulation, and labor market rigidities that are to blame for economic sclerosis. Instead they view the central bank as inflicting gratuitous injury in the interest of capital and high-finance in order to preserve price stability, which is their alleged fetish. Central bankers would be partly to blame for this false presumption of omnipotence if self-importance kept them from acknowledging that they can help provide only a necessary condition, but not the sufficient conditions, for realizing the full potential of sustained economic growth.

Particularly in 1995 and 1996, attacks on Lusser's policies sometimes became both vehement and personal. The inflation-adjusted gross domestic product (real GDP) had not grown in the first half of this decade, being actually slightly lower in 1995 and 1996 than in 1990. Going back to the beginning of Lusser's tenure, the Swiss news magazine *Facts* (Schneider, 1995, p. 62) blamed Lusser for Switzerland's growing less than half as much over the period 1988 to 1995 as either Austria or Germany, with employment falling almost 5 percent in Switzerland while rising 9 percent in Austria. Although Switzerland's economic growth since 1988 has been indisputably paltry, the idea that central bankers should be judged like race car drivers by how much they can rev up the economy is based on illusions about their powers and on reckless disregard for their responsibilities to the future.

CAN THE CENTRAL BANK KEEP ITS EFFICACY?

What about the limits of the central bank's competence and ability to produce desired results when the financial ground keeps shifting, expands globally, and is being leveraged in unforeseen ways? In other words, what is the risk that innovations affecting the provision of financial-service products and their suppliers weaken the ability of the central bank reliably to influence the future price level with the means at its disposal?

Currently the central bank, by being the final source of supply of settlement balances for domestic banks, determines the cost of short-term liquidity in the interbank market. By being either a net purchaser or seller of eligible securities (commonly under repurchase or swap agreements) in the money market, the central bank can actively influence the demand for settlement balances. Because this demand is "inelastic"—meaning rather fixed and insensitive to cost considerations—in the very short run, the central bank has considerable discretion over the terms at which it is met. Any development that would make the demand for settlement balances more elastic with respect to the repurchase rate associated with the provision of short-term liquidity to banks (p. 330) would make the central bank's control over liquidity conditions less powerful. The central bank would have to do more, and do it more precisely, to achieve outcomes with the same error margin as before because greater elasticity enhances the quantity response to changes in interest rate targets and to any errors.

If, for instance, Swiss banks can readily liquidate foreign exchange assets by selling them to foreign holders of Swiss-franc claims booked anywhere in the world, they can generate liquidity on terms that may be more difficult for the central bank to control prospectively. By the same token, if banks operating in Switzerland are fused ever more into multinational or transnational financial conglomerates, their sources of funds could become even more diverse. Their activity levels, risk exposure, and funding costs could be influenced by what is happening on, off, and to the balance sheet, including through their bank and nonbank activities outside Switzerland. There would be ever more need to rely on consolidated and internationally coordinated supervision of financial institutions (pp. 269, 277).

Nevertheless, what is true for individual institutions is not necessarily true in the aggregate. The Swiss National Bank remains the final arbiter of, and lender-of-last-resort to, the Swiss franc business. Of course, the more widely Swiss francs are held internationally, the more any foreign desire to liquidate Swiss franc balances would weigh on the Swiss exchange rate. Thus it would get harder for the SNB to get a firm grasp on what preannounced rate of increase in the monetary base (equal to currency plus deposit balances of banks with the central bank) would keep the economy on the price-level trajectory desired. The unexplained variability of both money demand and supply might increase, and it could become progressively less accurate to associate the provision of liquidity services predominantly with the conventional deposit-taking activities of banks. Lusser mentions other developments, such as interest indexation, i.e., the growing use of instruments with interest rates that float with current short-term rates (p. 19), and the balance-sheet adjustment options represented by securitization (p. 244) as developments that could weaken the squeeze, or relaxation, effect of a given dose of monetary instrument use. Yet he leaves no doubt about the central bank's continuing ability to implement its mandate.

By the same token, while financial derivatives constructed on price-action and pay-out features of the underlying securities have brought expanded opportunities and lowered the cost of hedging a particular exposure, for instance, against interest-rate risk, it is possible only to redistribute that risk among bearers, not to eliminate it for all (p. 283). This redistribution, while undoubtedly affecting the speed of the economy's overall investment response to interest-rate moves in some respects, is not likely to have much effect on the endpoint of adjustment, the point to which the economy and the price level are moving in response to a maintained change in (real) interest rates.

After surveying all this, Lusser (p. 269) concludes that innovations can indeed affect the steering mechanism of monetary policy. The importance of any particular transmission channel as well as the rate of propagation and adjustment to monetary policy impulses may change (p. 283). Hence, the relations between changes in the money supply, even when defined broadly, and economic activity and prices may twist away from past patterns. Yet, with continuous monitoring and analysis by the central bank, the reasons for these deviations generally can be discovered fairly promptly so that suitable calibration adjustments can be made. Since 1991, the SNB's approach to monetary targeting has become much looser than previously. For 1997 to 1998, when it faced serious instability in its main target variable, the monetary base or narrow money M0, it shifted its main focus to M3, a broad aggregate that lies at the other end of the spectrum of money-supply concepts commonly in use. The SNB (1997b, p. 263) has found a fairly close correlation between the development of the money supply M3 and the price level, although such a close relation, even with long and variable lags, is difficult to infer from Table 1. But by experimenting with targets intermediate between instruments that it directly controls and its substantive objectives, the SNB indirectly affirms the primacy of its ultimate target, stability of the price level, over following its preannounced money supply growth rules.

If there is a strong operational concern, it has to do with the adequacy of the measurement and reporting of the risk exposure of financial conglomerates and of their on- and off-balance-sheet activities. If these data are not sufficiently complete and transparent (p. 279), there may be an undue, and unrecognized, risk of financial crisis. Should such a crisis erupt, it could cause a rapid deflation of asset values, disrupt credit supply, and affect the entire economy. Such crises, while popularly associated with Latin America and, more recently, Southeast Asia, could thus erupt elsewhere as well, even if Switzerland is one of the least likely candidates.

Any major crisis could also expose the central bank to undesirable effects on monetary policy if it felt obliged to counteract a developing emergency through the exercise of its lender-of-last-resort function. That function, inherently complicated by border-crossing financial business (p. 277), foreign establishment of banks, and financial conglomeration (p. 243), is to be exercised, at the discretion of the central bank, for the benefit of solvent banks, not to cover for, or subsidize, insolvent institutions (p. 116). But making the relevant determinations is becoming increasingly difficult without prior agreement about such issues as who are to be the lead regulators and examiners in charge of international financial conglomerates. Switzerland is helping to organize such agreements and the institutions that support them in conjunction with the Bank for International Settlements (BIS).

CREDIBILITY OF THE CENTRAL BANK AND OF ITS STATED OBJECTIVES

A central bank's credibility is not established just by getting its formal independence from the rest of the government and from the day-to-day political decision-making process (pp. 207–208). Like any other institution in a democratic society, the central bank must be viewed as legitimate, and its basic mission as worthy, if it is to act decisively in pursuit of its formal mandate and real objective. The central bank too has to court the public, but formal independence allows it to do so in a persistent, true-to-its-word ("time-consistent"), and intellectually refined way (p. 98). It seeks to explain itself mostly to those who form public opinion in both media and financial markets while hoping to become a reassuring and uplifting fixture in the national self-image and collective identity of society as a whole.

Until the practice was discontinued in 1987, Lusser believed that a good way to get the public on the central bank's side would be to publish annual money-growth targets (p. 36). Particularly if these referred to aggregates directly under the control of the monetary authorities, such as the monetary base (M0), defined as the sum of bank deposits with the SNB and currency in circulation, the public would have an easy way of checking whether the central bank had remained true to its word. Bureaucrats, Lusser notes disdainfully (p. 14), normally love to shield themselves from public scrutiny and accountability by surrounding themselves with tools and levers so complicated, numerous, and obscure as to frustrate public monitoring and supervision.

For the sake of credibility—the Swiss would say *honesty*—Lusser is quite prepared to sacrifice action parameters or "degrees of freedom," which he views as illusory and deceptive, such as fine-tuning monetary policy to counter business-cycle fluctuations. Experience has taught him that the relation between the rate of growth of the money supply, the price level, and real economic activity is very loose in the short and even medium run (p. 28), so that there could be no systematic success with fine-tuning. The damage to a central bank's credibility from pretending otherwise is twofold: Not only would it fail to deliver the cyclical stabilization impulses promised reliably, but it would undermine its own ability to deliver the one thing that is in its grasp: a close approximation to price-level stability over time.

Money-growth targets, if kept invariant with respect to shocks to the real economy, would make their contribution as automatic stabilizers (p. 22): interest rates would respond to the ebb and flow of cyclical pressures. Trying to stabilize interest rates—except as a side-benefit of a consistent policy of low inflation that keeps the inflation premium in interest rates low and free from an allowance for inflation instability risk—is not what the president intends (p. 127). Formally using a monetary-conditions index, a weighted average of interest and exchange rate developments, as in Canada, to gauge how the current stance of monetary policy will affect future economic activity and to adjust policy accordingly to aim for the desired effect does not appear very promising for getting a better handle on the future course of the inflation rate. This appears to be the main finding of the SNB's internal investigations (Lengwiler, 1997). Targeting the growth rate of the Gross National (or Domestic, excluding net earnings on factors—mostly capital—employed abroad) Product, nominal GNP or GDP, also would not be appropriate: It would give monetary policy an active, seemingly countercyclical role, which Lusser identifies with false promises (p. 32).

In commenting on the earlier draft, Lusser provided the following, more nuanced, exposition: *Inflationary implications of any particular quantity of money can be affected by market and regulatory innovations. This is why I concluded that it is always necessary to test the likely economic consequences of changes in a particular monetary aggregate by examining additional indicators. Among them are not only movements in other monetary aggregates but also in interest and exchange rates that could shed light on changes in money demand and on prospective economic developments. The difficulty in all this is that monetary policy impulses appear to affect the course of inflation in Switzerland with notably long lags of two-and-a-half to three years. For this reason the central bank needs a compass of the kind which monetary aggregates can provide.*

Ultimately, however, for the Swiss, credibility appears as the reward for the central bank's never giving anyone reason to doubt that, no matter what the disturbance, it will get the economy back on a track of noninflationary growth. It will achieve this within, at most, two to three years. If there ever were cause for such doubt, credibility would be lost quickly. It could be regained only with great pain and difficulty (p. 36). Original credibility would not protect fallen angels from severe punishment.

Credibility without Crutches

In 1988 to 1989 there were large shifts in the demand for central bank money as reserve requirements for banks were, in effect, scuttled, and actual reserve holdings fell by two-thirds between year-end 1987 and 1989 (2, p. 4). The introduction of a real-time gross settlements system for Swiss Interbank Clearing operations as well as the steep reduction in statutory reserve requirements on banks, also at the start of 1988, contributed to this development. By 1990, the central bank had decided to abandon annual money-growth targets in favor of announcing an expected average annual rate of growth of the monetary base or "central bank money" (p. 27; 3, pp. 2–3). The average growth was first to be taken over three to five years and then fixed for five years ahead: It was 1 percent annually for 1990 to 1994 and is the same again for 1995 to 1999.

The growth rate for the first five-year period, while fluctuating in a range of almost +3 to –3 percent from year to year, came in just below the targeted average rate, seemingly without strain. Generally, however, during any of these five-year periods, overshooting or undershooting early on would have to be compensated during the remainder of the averaging period. This would have to be accomplished without "base drift," i.e., without forgiving errors once made and trying again to meet money-growth targets for next year, from the higher or lower base that results from having missed the target, as was the prior practice. But while a case can thus be made that money-growth targets have become stricter in the sense of being more constraining on central bank policy (Rich, 1997a, p. 137), it is doubtful that the SNB would ever allow itself to be put in a bind toward the end of the averaging period if major last-minute efforts still were needed just to meet the average-growth objective. The SNB does not work with five-year plans, and its announcements are communication tools and not collars on the exercise of discretion (p. 27).

Indeed, President Lusser has long found the credibility of the SNB so secure, that it can not be undermined by deviations from intermediate targets relating to central bank money growth, or even final goals relating to keeping inflation down, as long as the reasons for such deviations are adequately explained (p. 29), even to the point of admitting errors. Indeed, he rather seems to relish the opportunity, afforded by deviations from preannounced growth targets, to explain the current stance and rationale of monetary policy (p. 52). Credibility suffers only when the central bank gets lost in a maze of conflicting goals and ceases to focus on price stability above all else (p. 30).

Lusser elaborated on this interpretation in his letter of April 16, 1998, commenting on an earlier draft: *Laying out a one-year or multi-year growth path for this or that aggregate of money is a useful tool but one that is subordinate to the achievement of the main goal, which is stability of the price level. Yet this tool provides an especially useful approach to building confidence in monetary policy: a sense of trust shared by financial markets and the public at large. For the central bank, in announcing money supply targets, reveals to the market and the public what policy it intends to follow. This makes the central bank accountable and its policies transparent: Deviations from the target now have to be justified just as the targets themselves. During my presidency, we used to do so every three months.*

It is clear what would happen if financial innovations, continuing deregulation, cashless settlement and clearance outside the banking system, or other factors were to be perceived as creating a conflict between adhering to preannounced multi-year average money-supply growth targets and adhering to the goal of approximate stability of the price level in the future: This ultimate objective, and not an obsolete intermediate target, would win. The Swiss central bank no longer needs to wave around publicly its instrument crutches to assure the public that it can walk and stay the course to price stability. Once the fruit of its policy is familiar and appreciated, the central bank need not put so much weight on sharing the recipes by which this fruit is prepared and cooked to perfection under changing circumstances.

Central banks with less credibility are not as fortunate as that of Switzerland, where the government has not dared ever to importune or "proposition" the central bank (p. 109). For these others, the mere announcement of inflation-reduction goals could ring hollow (p. 33), particularly if monetary policy is subject to fiscal deficit-financing pressures (p. 130). Without clear indications and checks at each step along the way, of how "lesser" central banks will go about achieving announced disinflation goals—and with what reservations and exceptions, or allowance for special circumstances, for instance, in the external or administered-price sectors—few market participants would place much reliance on their professed intentions. For this reason, Lusser doubts that the rhetoric of inflation targeting can contribute much to achieving price stability or to reducing the cost of disinflation if the target differs from the established pattern. If it does not differ and the pattern fits, such rhetoric becomes a calming mantra designed merely to reinforce a faith long kept. Hence, reflexive avoidance of inflation, deindexation, and preemptive strikes against inflation (p. 55), since made famous by Greenspan, are the key.

When a bout of inflation does break out nevertheless, as not even a Swiss central banker can preclude, it is soon confronted and met by the superior forces at the command of the head of the independent SNB. To reduce the cost of battle and hasten victory, these forces need allies that reduce the sluggishness and unpredictable jerkiness in the adjustment process. Resistance to prompt and smooth adjustment comes especially from sectors with noncompetitively set factor-and-product prices, whether administered by governments, industrial cartels, or trade unions and business or bankers associations (pp. 58, 126–27, 143–44). The central bank needs political allies that will curb these sectors and their ability to delay and obstruct. It also needs cooperation from within the government apparatus because it has not been charged, apparently to its own relief (pp. 118–19), with the administrative supervision of banks. It thus depends on information support from the *Eidgenössische Bankenkommission*, the agency that has been entrusted with this mandate, to be able to discharge its functions as lender of last resort (pp. 331–32).

In other challenges to the conduct of monetary policy, for instance when there is a scramble into Swiss francs as safe haven (4, p. 12), or when a stock-market crash, like that of 1987, poses risks of a contagious liquidity crisis (2, p. 12), the SNB will coordinate its actions with the international network of bank regulators and central banks and do its part. That network has been woven with the help of the BIS on Swiss soil under mandate from the Group-of-Ten (G–10) leading financial countries, a group that Switzerland joined as the eleventh member in 1984. The other members of the G–10 are the United States, Canada, Japan, and seven West European countries who play a significant role in international finance.

Special circumstances can arise at any time in the financial sector. Even at the risk of deviating from approximate price stability for a year or two, the central bank cannot safely ignore them. But the national and international public know that, in Switzerland, "special" circumstances are the exception and not the rule or a routine excuse. Hence surprise deviations of the price level from the desired trajectory, while not entirely symmetric, can occur in both directions, and the inflation rate, averaged over a period of years, remains consistently low.

BANK SECRECY: THE SWISS BANKING ESTABLISHMENT'S CREDIBILITY

While secure in its own macroeconomic credibility, the central bank is inevitably concerned with the soundness and trustworthiness of the financial-service industry, including banks, even though it lacks direct supervisory or prudential control functions over any part of that industry. Lusser long has recognized (p. 224) that bank secrecy can be both an asset and a liability for trustworthiness and the international reputation of Swiss banks. On the one hand, bank secrecy is a normal and valued part of the professional relationship with clients who must entrust confidential information to banks. Violations of this confidence by banks are subject to prosecution under a penal provision of the Swiss Federal Banking Act.

Bank secrecy also prevents disclosure of information to foreign tax and exchange-control authorities, except in cases of tax fraud that are punishable both in Switzerland and in the country seeking its legal assistance. This has led to sensationalized impressions that Swiss bank secrecy is designed for tax evasion, receiving the fruits of capital flight from other countries, and money laundering, as Lusser himself has put it (p. 224). In commenting further on the earlier draft of this chapter, he also explained that these impressions are unjustified: *Swiss laws to counteract money laundering are exemplary and in full accord with international standards. They provide not only for criminal prosecution and penalties, but also for confiscation of the balances in question, with Swiss banks having to report suspicions of money laundering to the authorities.* Swiss banking law thus does not provide for the safe accumulation of the fruits of organized crime. On the other hand, Swiss banks are under no obligation to help other countries enforce their capital controls because Switzerland maintains no such controls itself.

Business motivated by other, perfectly ordinary and proper, professional considerations is likely to dominate. Institutional clients, in particular, are interested in efficient portfolio management rather than anonymity services (p. 249). Furthermore, under pressure of international agreements seeking to equalize competitive conditions and to combat criminal activity, the circumstances under which the protections of Swiss bank secrecy can be asserted are being narrowed progressively. SNB Director Klauser (1995) has provided a description of the changes under way.

Even the business that is primarily due to the facilitation of tax evasion and capital flight cannot necessarily be put down as evil unless one is willing to call all the tax laws and exchange control regulations that produce it worthy of support. For instance, in those years before World War II when Jews could still legally emigrate from Nazi Germany, they had to leave essentially penniless, not being allowed to take more than a pittance with them or to transfer assets abroad. So if some Jews managed to get a few of their mobile assets into Swiss banks anyway without the Germans' being able to find out, no right-thinking person would dare call that desperate capital flight wrong or evil. Quite the contrary. The depositor, not the bank, is the "owner" of the right to bank secrecy, and Swiss banks cannot, of course, assert bank secrecy against any of their depositors who can identify themselves and their claim. To the extent they treated the heirs of victims of the Holocaust like any other bank customer with regard to meeting formal identification requirements, Swiss banks showed an egregious lack of the sensitivity and flexibility called for in such cases.

In a communication to one of the authors dated March 25, 1998, Georg Rich has provided the following clarification:

> The problem of dormant bank deposits is an issue concerning primarily the Swiss banks, rather than the SNB. . . . Bank secrecy is not the main source of the problem, but the lack of Swiss legislation on the treatment of dormant accounts. This means that deposits stay at the banks until they are claimed by the rightful owners or their successors. Many Holocaust victims and their successors found it difficult to claim deposits they owned, or believed they owned, because (i) they did not know at which bank the deposits were booked or (ii) if they knew, they could not prove conclusively that they were the rightful owners. Despite an earlier effort (in 1962) to clear up the issue, the Swiss authorities and the banks handled the problem of unidentified accounts in an inept manner and did not take sufficient account of the special situation of Holocaust victims.

The SNB participates in this debate in a different context, that is, in the context of Swiss gold transactions with the Nazi regime during World War II. In a press release dated March 1997 (SNB, 1997a, p. 5), the SNB addressed this matter forthrightly:

> The SNB finds it difficult to understand why its management of the time did not sufficiently take into account the moral and political implications of their strategy of free convertibility of the Swiss franc in a Europe dominated by Germany. They were aware of the risk that the Reichsbank was supplying Berne with gold looted in the occupied countries. A posteriori, the measures taken to prevent such acquisitions seem to have been altogether too half-hearted in the face of these risks. It must, however, be admitted that it is very difficult to judge their decisions outside the historical context. In particular, we do not know what their perception of the threat of a German invasion was. It is moreover beyond doubt that their legal argumentation was based on an interpretation of neutrality that we no longer subscribe to today.

Monetary gold confiscated by Germany in occupied countries is a well-documented chapter in the history of the Second World War. On the other hand, the question of the origin of non-monetary gold does not appear to have been investigated with the same amount of care. Thus we can no longer rule out today that the SNB may have bought—albeit, unwittingly—gold originating from concentration camps. This, together with the material distress afflicting many survivors of the Holocaust from behind the former "iron curtain" reinforced the SNB's decision to contribute an amount of Sfr 100 million [ca. $70 million] to the fund set up by the Swiss business community for the benefit of victims of the Holocaust.

However one judges the adequacy of the SNB's attempts to contain the damage done by the charges leveled against its earlier omissions and those of the Swiss banking system, it appears to us that a credible attempt has been made to air the issues and to move them closer to resolution.

CONCLUSION: VIRTUE'S REWARDS

Credibility is an outgrowth of institutional mandate and faithful practice, but it is best personified in the reputation that surrounds the heads of the Swiss central bank. Although determined efforts got underway only in 1998 to enshrine the independence of the SNB and the mandate to pursue price stability in the Swiss constitution, its reputation, being secure with the public, has shielded it against interference by the rest of the government. Nevertheless, Lusser, in commenting on this portion of the earlier draft, strongly advocated a constitutional anchor both for the independence of the central bank from the executive branch of government and parliament and for its mandate of defending the stability of the price level. Since constitutional amendments are subject to obligatory referendum in Switzerland, the majority of Swiss voters would thus decide and commit.

Dr. Hans Meyer (1998), Lusser's successor, has again explained that the central bank's credibility is not based on strict adherence to money supply targets of the kind the SNB had announced for high-powered money for many years starting in 1978. Rather, the targets are justified only to the extent they contribute to approximate stability of the price level, which is the intended objective.

Monetary asceticism pays handsome dividends by giving Switzerland lower real interest rates than even Germany, normally up to two percentage points lower (p. 83). In the year in which Lusser left office, 1996, Switzerland's Treasury bill rate averaged 1.72 percent, compared with 3.30 percent in Germany. The Swiss regularly save considerably more than they need or use for investment at home. They keep a wary eye on both the government and the price level, but they are technologically progressive in traded goods and services.

This combination of stability, ingenuity, thrift, and good governance gives Swiss-franc financial instruments high international prestige and a tendency to appreciate in real terms (4, p. 14). While other countries measure the risk premium on their currency against the lead currency in their region in international financial markets, Swiss investors, Lusser notes with obvious satisfaction (p. 72), realistically expect to earn more on investments in other currencies if they are to consider them; in a portfolio sense, the native characteristics of these other assets are inferior.

A *negative* risk premium, particularly if coupled with the prospect of some equilibrium real appreciation, means uncommonly low (real) interest rates. "Real" interest rates are nominal interest rates net of the premium for expected inflation, and they matter for economic activity. Lusser conceives of currency denominations as competing brands (p. 190). One of these, the Swiss franc, is particularly known for quality and hence commands a premium that makes those who save in it, or expect to get paid in it, content with a lower explicit yield. This interest saving, Lusser emphasizes (4, pp. 4–9), contributes to the locational advantage (*Standortvorteil*) of Switzerland: It encourages production that is highly intensive in physical and human capital, and hence in advanced technology that is supported by both of these types of capital. The Swiss franc, in short, is a trump card (1, p. 10) that is not to be thrown lightly into the deck of European common-currency arrangements. It is certain that the Swiss franc will survive the introduction of the Euro and likely that it will prosper alongside it even while Swiss financial institutions assume a major role in the worldwide Euro-financing business. Clearly Switzerland, as a historically grown financial power that has stuck with the right goals for decades, is a very special case and prime exemplar. Its currency and its institutions will not easily be marginalized, not even by a blizzard of euros.

REFERENCES

Klauser, Peter. 1995. "Das Schweizerische Bankgeheimnis und die Bekämpfung der Geldwäscherei," *Geld, Währung und Konjunktur* 13 (4) December: 361–70.

Lengwiler, Yvan. 1997. "Der 'Monetary Conditions Index' für die Schweiz," *Geld, Währung und Konjunktur* 15 (1) March: 61–72.

Lusser, Markus

(1) "Die Schweiz und der EG-Binnenmarkt—Chancen und Risiken des Finanzplatzes," given at Montreux on September 23, 1988, at the "Schweizerische Bankiertag," published in *Geld, Währung und Konjunktur* (Quarterly Review of the Swiss National Bank) 6 (December 1988): 319–28. An English translation of this address has been made available by the Bank for International Settlements, in *BIS Review*, 1988, No. 201 (Basle: BIS, October 12, 1988): 1–9.

Georg Rich (1995), a Director, and Deputy Head of Department I, of the Swiss National Bank, who was President Lusser's principal analytical resource and one of his speech writers, has described this address, like the other addresses, as follows: This paper (1988) constitutes an address to the annual meeting of the Swiss Bankers' Association (SBA). Mr. Lusser became president on May 1, 1988, and was invited to address the SBA, which traditionally invites newly appointed SNB presidents to address its annual meeting, in the autumn of that year. He used this important forum to discuss the implications of the European single market for Swiss monetary policy and regulation of Swiss stock markets.

(2) "Die Geldpolitik der neunziger Jahre-Neue Herausforderungen für die Schweizerische Nationalbank," address before the "Vereinigung Basler Oekonomen" and the "Wirtschaftswissenschaftliches Zentrum" of the University of Basle, January 11, 1990. This paper was published in *Geld, Währung und Konjunktur* 8 (March 1990): 63–72, and is available in English in *BIS Review*, 1990, No. 14 (Basle: BIS, January 19, 1990): 1–11.

Toward the end of 1989, Swiss inflation began to rise, reaching an annual rate of about 6 percent in the fall of 1990 before declining in the subsequent year. Mr. Lusser, still in Rich's words, thought it best if the SNB—as soon as possible—provided its own analysis of what went wrong.

(3) "Die Strategie der Nationalbank," Address to the Annual Shareholders' Meeting ("Generalversammlung") of the Swiss National Bank, April 26, 1991, published in *Geld, Währung und Konjunktur* 9 (June 1991): 167–71.

Each year, at the end of April, the president of the SNB addresses the meeting of shareholders. This address describes the SNB's shift from annual to multi-year targeting.

(4) "Die Schweizerische Wirtschaft im weltweiten strukturellen Anpassungsprozess," delivered at Hochschule St. Gallen, St. Gallen, February 14, 1995.

The speech deals with the structural changes afflicting the Swiss economy and the resulting challenges for Swiss monetary policy; it received considerable attention.

(5) Letter to G. M. von Furstenberg, Zurich, April 16, 1998.

Lusser, Markus. 1996. *Geldpolitik*. Zürich: Verlag Neue Zürcher Zeitung.

Meyer, Hans. 1998. "Grundsätzliche Aspekte der Geldpolitik," Address delivered to the *Vereinigung Basler Ökonomen*, Basle, January 22.

Rich, Georg. Letters to G. M. von Furstenberg, Zurich, November 21, 1995, and March 25, 1998.

_____. 1997a. "Monetary Targets as a Policy Rule: Lessons from the Swiss Experience," *Journal of Monetary Economics* 39 (1) June: 113–41.

_____. 1997b. "European Monetary Integration: A Swiss View," Revised and updated version of paper presented at the European Union Studies Center of the Graduate School and University Center, CCNY, New York, April 10.

Schneider, Markus. 1995. "Markus Lusser/ Der Mann der die Schweiz in die Krise Ritt," *Facts* (37): 61–65.

Schweizerische Nationalbank. 1997a. "The Swiss National Bank's Gold Operations During the Second World War," Press Release, Zurich: SNB, March.

_____. 1997b. *Geld, Währung und Konjunktur* 15 (4) Dezember: 263–64.

PART III

"FAR EAST"

PUNCTURING ASSET-PRICE BUBBLES IN JAPAN: GOVERNOR MIENO

GEORGE M. VON FURSTENBERG AND MICHAEL K. ULAN

CONTENTS

Yasushi Mieno
Governor, Bank of Japan, 1989–1994

Yasushi Mieno was born in 1924. He received an LL.B. degree from the University of Tokyo in 1947 and joined the Bank of Japan later that year. He spent his entire career with the Bank, rising through the ranks to serve as its governor from December 1989 until his retirement in December 1994. At the Bank his career led from Director of Policy Planning, 1973 to 1975, to Director of Market Operations, 1975 to 1978, Executive Director, 1978 to 1984, and Senior Deputy Governor, 1984 to 1989, before being appointed Governor toward the end of 1989.

Born in the same year as Helmut Schlesinger of Germany, he is also a lifelong civil servant in the finest sense whose influence at the central bank antedated his elevation to governor toward the end of his career by several decades. Along the way, he worked in the Bank of Japan's New York office for two years and was also the general manager of the Matsumoto Branch of the Bank of Japan for three years. He married Kazuko Mori in 1951, and they have two sons.

PUNCTURING ASSET-PRICE BUBBLES IN JAPAN: GOVERNOR MIENO

PREFACE

As Governor of the Bank of Japan, Yasushi Mieno had two objectives: to keep inflation in check; and to ensure the health of Japan's financial markets. He saw price stability not as an end in itself but rather as a means of achieving stable, sustainable economic growth. Unlike the other central bankers profiled in this volume, however, keeping inflation in check was not Governor Mieno's major challenge during his term of office. Mieno's main task, to which he turned his attention as soon as he became Governor of the Bank of Japan in December 1989, was deflating the price bubble that had developed in Japanese land and equity markets over the preceding few years. Governor Mieno attacked the asset-price bubble by hiking interest rates, in the process precipitating what has turned out to be a prolonged period of very low economic growth. He won the Bank of Japan an unprecedented degree of independence from the Ministry of Finance, albeit still a smaller degree of independence than that enjoyed by the U.S. Federal Reserve System or even the Reserve Bank of New Zealand.

As the Southeast Asian crisis of 1997 to 1998 has demonstrated once again, asset-price bubbles, if fueled by excessive lending and risk-seeking by banks who have been sheltered under the umbrella of implicit government insurance and directives, are extremely dangerous to economic health. As these bubbles grow and then burst, as they must eventually, they imperil the health of the financial system and the smooth and efficient functioning of the intermediation process, eventually pulling down the entire economy and disturbing its external relations. Six years after Governor Mieno's lancing of the Japanese bubble in 1990 to 1992, major Japanese banks were still mired in bad debt and the economy was still foundering. While Governor Mieno deserves great credit for puncturing the bubble before it got any bigger, neither he nor his successor, who resigned in 1998, was able to complete the successful restructuring and improved supervision of Japan's banking and financial system for which the world has been waiting.

INTRODUCTION

Yasushi Mieno is another of the heads of central banks identified in this study "who showed a disciplined reflected commitment to the goal of effectively and predictably stable prices." As we did with the other central bank heads, we asked him to identify those of his statements that he regarded as adding up to a comprehensive exposition of his approach to monetary policy. In response, we received a letter dated August 10, 1995, from Yasuo Nakayama, Chief Press Officer, Press Division, Policy Planning Department of the Bank of Japan, together with copies of five of the speeches Mr. Mieno delivered during his tenure as Governor of the Bank of Japan. The speeches cover several aspects of Governor Mieno's views of central banking: the history of central banking; the Bank of Japan's conduct of monetary policy; issues facing the Japanese economy and the role of the central bank in confronting these issues; the role of financial and capital markets in Japan; and the role of the Bank of Japan in maintaining financial-system stability.

This chapter first reviews the performance of the Japanese economy in the 1970s and 1980s to establish the setting in which Mr. Mieno assumed the Governorship of the Bank of Japan, then considers the institutional and legal framework within which the Bank of Japan operates. Next we examine Yasushi Mieno's philosophy of central banking, and lay out the operational procedures used by the Bank of Japan during his tenure in the conduct of monetary policy. A later section reviews Governor Mieno's overall record. Finally, this chapter assesses his legacy to the economy of the nation, including the unfinished business of reform that he left behind.

THE ECONOMIC BACKGROUND

Macroeconomic Performance of the Japanese Economy

Compared with the first quarter century after the end of World War II, the 1970s—particularly the years after 1973, the time of the first OPEC oil shock—and the early 1980s were years of lower rates of economic growth and higher rates of inflation in most developed countries. Nevertheless, Japan's rate of economic growth tended to be higher and, as shown in Table 1, its rate of inflation lower than the average for the International Monetary Fund's Industrial-Country aggregate (International Monetary Fund, 1998). Between 1973 and 1996, Japanese economic growth averaged 3.4 percent per year, more than 40 percent higher than the 2.4 percent annual rate of the industrial countries as a whole (in which Japan has a substantial weight). Between 1973 and 1997, Japanese inflation averaged 4.0 percent per year, about two-thirds of the rate of the industrial countries taken together, 5.8 percent. In short, from a macroeconomic point of view, the Japanese economy has performed comparatively well since 1973, but not since 1989 if one looks more closely. The measure of inflation cited here is the year-on-year change in the Consumer Price Index (CPI).

Prices in the Stock and Real Estate Markets

While inflation in the prices of goods and services in Japan—the prices tracked in conventional price indices—was low relative to that in other industrial countries during the late 1980s, a bubble developed in the prices of Japanese equities and land. While the precise definition of *bubble* differs among economic models, an asset is said to be *on a bubble* when its price rises not in a manner that appropriately reflects improving fundamentals but solely because economic agents expect it to rise (Folkerts-Landau et al., 1995, p. 177). When he assumed office, Governor Mieno faced the challenge of deflating the asset-price bubble and dealing with the consequences. The alternative of letting the bubble expand further would only have magnified the risk to the financial system and the exposure of government that was supposed to be standing behind the financial institutions that had been subject to its guidance.

The governor cites achieving and maintaining financial-market stability as an objective of monetary policy. Financial and capital

Table 1

Japan and Industrial-Country-Average Inflation Rates, 1971–1997
(percent)

Date	Japan	Industrial Countries
1971	6.4	5.3
1972	4.6	4.8
1973	11.7	7.9
1974	23.3	13.4
1975	11.7	11.4
1976	9.5	8.6
1977	8.2	8.8
1978	4.1	7.5
1979	3.7	9.7
1980	7.8	12.4
1981	4.9 (4.3)	10.4
1982	2.8 (2.1)	7.7
1983	1.9 (1.7)	5.2
1984	2.2 (2.7)	5.0
1985	2.0 (1.4)	4.4
1986	0.6 (-0.3)	2.6
1987	0.1 (0.8)	3.2
1988	0.7 (1.0)	3.5
1989	2.2 (2.6)	4.6
1990	3.1 (3.8)	5.2
1991	3.3 (2.7)	4.4
1992	1.7 (1.2)	3.2
1993	1.2 (1.0)	2.8
1994	0.7 (0.7)	2.3
1995	-0.1 (-0.3)	2.5
1996	0.2	2.3
1997	1.9	1.7

Note: All rates of price change shown are from the preceding year except that the figures given in parentheses for Japan are from December of the preceding year so as to show *within* year, rather than *year-over-year*, inflation rates in the years surrounding Governor Mieno's tenure.

Sources: International Monetary Fund, 1996; 1998.

markets are important to the functioning of the economy since they provide a market for transactions in financial products and supply intermediary services in the transfer of funds from lenders to borrowers and from capital-surplus to capital-deficit entities. When financial markets fail to identify and to price risks efficiently, they misdirect saving and investment, often with great harm to the entire economy. On the one hand, Governor Mieno (1, p. 9) has suggested that it is not appropriate to treat asset-price stability as a target of monetary policy in the same way as stability of the general price level: Asset prices depend largely on expectations of private economic agents that fluctuate from day to day and cannot be controlled by monetary policy alone. But he also has emphasized, on the other hand, that the Bank of Japan must pay close attention to asset prices, as large fluctuations of asset prices during the 1980s were accompanied by major fluctuations in the economy and sustainable growth was undermined. With large asset-price fluctuations both a cause and a symptom of economic instability, the Bank of Japan has no choice but to monitor asset prices and to assess what is going on in financial markets (2, p. 9).

The "bubble economy" was a time when the prices of Japanese land and equities soared without an accompanying underlying increase in the productivity of these assets. It was also a period during which many businesses and households leveraged major expenditures on the basis of these inflated asset prices. The bubble and the economic activity founded on it were not sustainable; sooner or later, the bubble had to collapse, exposing the fragility of the economy built upon it. Ostrom (1993, pp. 3, 8), of the Japan Economic Institute, puts the period of the bubble economy at 1987 to 1989. He asserts that the reduction of the Bank of Japan's discount rate from 3.0 percent to a then–record low of 2.5 percent and margin purchases "created ripe conditions for an inflationary bubble in asset prices." Wood (1992, p. 20) agrees with Ostrom about the period of and the proximate cause of the bubble (the February 1987 reduction in the Bank of Japan's discount rate to 2.5 percent). Wood goes on to attribute the Bank's cut in the discount rate to the 1987 Louvre Accord, under the terms of which the central banks of many other major economic powers also loosened their monetary policies to support the value of the U.S. dollar on foreign-exchange markets. He notes, however, that Japan had a domestic motivation for cutting interest rates as well: the Japanese economy had experienced a growth recession in 1986, and

Table 2
Percent Changes in Japanese GNP, Stock Prices, and Land Prices, 1980–1994

	Nominal GNP	Stock Prices	Land Prices
1980	7.3	8.8	13.4
1981	9.4	10.0	8.6
1982	5.0	- 1.0	6.8
1983	4.4	16.8	4.6
1984	5.9	28.9	5.4
1985	6.6	15.1	7.3
1986	4.7	26.1	14.3
1987	4.7	36.0	25.8
1988	6.7	21.7	28.0
1989	5.9	25.1	24.4
1990	6.9	- 8.7	30.0
1991	7.6	-12.6	3.0
1992	4.1	-26.7	-15.5
1993	3.0	- 3.9	-17.9
1994	0.8	2.8	-11.5

Note: Annual percentage changes are to the first quarter (GNP) or to the end of March (the two price series) of the year shown.
Sources: Nominal GNP — International Monetary Fund, International Financial Statistics Yearbook, 1995; Stock Prices — New York Times; Land Prices — Bank of Japan, Economic Statistics Annual 1994, 1995.

the Japanese thought a loosening of monetary policy would contribute to a recovery.

The Bank of Japan did not realize that the recovery from the 1986 growth recession was already under way by the time the discount rate was reduced. Wood reports: "The result was a boom to beat all booms, but one distorted fatally by the peculiarities of Japan's banking system and the archaic laws governing the country's property market" (1992, p. 20). Between the end of December 1986 and its peak three years later, the Nikkei average of stock prices doubled (New York Times, January 1, 1987, p. 52; New York Times, December 30, 1989, p. 42). Between March 1987 and March 1990, average land prices in Japan's six largest cities more than doubled (Bank of Japan, 1995, p. 331). The data on annual percentage changes in the Nikkei 225 stock-market index and an index of land prices in the country's six largest cities are presented in Table 2. The land and share price changes are derived from end-March data. The interest-rate series of Table 3 are also end-March figures (New York Times,

April 1, 1993, p. D16; Institute of Fiscal and Monetary Policy, 1, p. 63; 2, p. 65). Since the end of March, which is the end of the Japanese fiscal year, is the time of the land-price series, the authors chose stock-price and interest-rate observations that most closely conform to that date.

In portfolio equilibrium, one can reasonably expect raw land prices to rise at a rate equal to the nominal interest rate on government paper plus a portfolio risk premium, which may be negative if there are no other widely available inflation hedges. An equally primitive benchmark for sustainable stock price movements might be that domestic stock prices may rise at the same rate as nominal Gross National Product (GNP) if there are few new issues and the shares of heavily multinational or transnational corporations are excluded. Apart from the effects of normal economic growth, asset prices also tend to be affected by changes in real interest rates, in part because the asset price is the capitalized value of the income stream expected to be generated by the asset and a change in interest rates changes the capitalization rate, and, in part, because, for equity securities and

Table 3

Selected Japanese Interest Rates, 1980–1994
(percent)

	Discount Rate	Long-Term Prime Rate	Fixed-Rate Mortgage
1980	9.00	8.8	8.22
1981	6.25	8.8	8.52
1982	5.50	8.4	8.34
1983	5.50	8.4	8.34
1984	5.00	7.9	8.10
1985	5.00	7.4	7.62
1986	4.00	6.4	7.50
1987	2.50	5.2	6.66
1988	2.50	5.5	6.60
1989	2.50	5.7	6.60
1990	5.25	7.5	7.68
1991	6.00	7.5	7.86
1992	4.50	6.0	6.78
1993	2.50	4.9	6.30
1994	1.75	4.4	5.46

Note: All interest rates are for the end of March of the year shown.
Sources: Institute of Fiscal and Monetary Policy, Ministry of Finance, *Financial Statistics of Japan 1989* and *1995*.

land, changes in interest rates also affect the net returns realized on these heavily leveraged assets—at least in the short run. The relationship between interest rates and asset prices is inverse: a fall in interest rates raises asset prices and vice versa. The October 1983 cut in the discount rate from 5.50 percent to 5.00 percent may have contributed to the 1983 to 1984 rise in stock prices but does not seem to have affected land prices. The further halving of the discount rate to 2.50 percent over two years is clearly associated with surges in stock *and* land prices. Their elevated level and continued rise may have been sustained by the continuing low interest rates and the expectation that the Bank of Japan would reduce interest rates when necessary to prevent a recession. Such a stance might be expected to maintain the inflated asset prices on which much real and financial activity in the Japanese economy had come to be based.

When Governor Mieno assumed office on December 17, 1989, this expectation could have changed. His quick tightening of policy little more than a week after assuming office could have been read by stock-market participants as an indication of his determination to end stock speculation. The land-price bubble, however, proved initially still thick-skinned and continued to expand. Between May 1989 and March 1990, the discount rate was raised four times—more than doubling in the process—but land prices continued to climb steeply. As shown in Table 3, long-term interest rates tended to move in the same direction as the discount rate, although not always simultaneously or to the same extent.

With land prices continuing to rise in the face of interest-rate hikes, in March 1990 the Ministry of Finance told banks not to increase lending to property companies by more than the rate of increase in their total loans. Six months later, the Bank of Japan ordered city banks (corresponding to money-center banks in the United States) to limit their lending for the last quarter of 1990 to 70 percent of the level of a year earlier (Wood, 1992, p. 29).

While associating the timing of the rise in asset prices with elements of the Japanese macroeconomic milieu may be difficult, in 1993, the International Monetary Fund (1993) offered the following list of possible reasons for prices of Japanese assets to increase by far more than the rise in the overall CPI:

(1) Deregulation of the financial system and other structural changes left excess liquidity in the economy, and this credit was

taken up quickly by specific groups active in asset markets pumping up asset prices.

(2) Changes in the Japanese tax regime encouraged real-estate investments and borrowing for business investment, home construction, and the purchase of consumer durables.

(3) While greater competition in a liberalized and externally more open financial sector may have increased the appetite for high-risk loans by banks, greater international competition and structural changes in the domestic economy made markets for goods and services more competitive, restraining inflation in those markets.

(4) Adding to the asymmetry of price movements, asset prices, which are set in auction markets, can respond more quickly to changes in monetary policy than can the prices of goods and services.

IMF staff members Hargraves, Schinasi, and Weisbrod (1993, pp. 5, 8, 12) have added the following explanations for rational bubbles by focusing on the inappropriate incentive structure of financial institutions:

• When restrictions on the outflow of capital were removed in 1980, banks had to raise interest rates to retain deposits. Thus, they had to make investments that had higher expected rewards. Those investments were riskier than those in which banks had invested theretofore.

• When the dollar began to decline in value on foreign-exchange markets, those Japanese who had made dollar-denominated investments took large losses in yen terms. These losses induced more Japanese investment at home, boosting asset prices.

• With deposit insurance in place, the Government of Japan—rather than bank depositors—assumed the risk of bank failure. Hence, there was no depositor pressure to ensure that the banks were lending money for sound investments.

The Changing Structure of Japanese Capital Markets

Japanese firms tend to have higher debt-to-equity ratios than companies in many other countries, such as the United States. In the absence of a well-developed domestic capital market, these firms traditionally obtained their financing through bank loans. Many Japanese firms are members of a *keiretsu*, a group of related companies that includes a bank. Firms that were not part of a *keiretsu* that includes a bank tended to maintain close working relationships with a bank and obtained the bulk of their financing from that institution. In 1970, banks held about 97 percent of Japanese corporate debt. Japanese financial markets, particularly the market for debt securities, expanded greatly between 1970 and 1989. Economic growth in Japan, globalization of financial markets, and deregulation contributed to this process. The markets for the various types of short-term debt increased in size by 11.8 percent per year between 1975 and 1985 and by 29.5 percent per year between 1985 and 1989. By 1990, the share of corporate debt held by banks had fallen to 60 percent.

Regulatory reform was promoted by both market participants and the Bank of Japan; in some cases, the Bank of Japan took steps to liberalize financial markets in order to facilitate the implementation of monetary policy in the increasingly fragmented global financial marketplace (Okina, 1993, p. 33; Singleton, 1993, p. 1). The main changes in the financial-market regulatory regime during the late 1980s were (i) reduction of the minimum size of certificates of deposit from 500 million yen to 50 million yen and allowing maturities to extend from two weeks to two years instead of just from three to six months, and (ii) reduction of the minimum transaction for Treasury Bills from 100 million yen to 10 million yen, and introduction of three-month Treasury bills in addition to the six-month bills already issued. In addition to these changes in the regulatory regime within which Japanese short-term money markets operated, the range of securities traded on these markets widened between 1985 and 1987 to include uncollateralized calls, Treasury and financial bills, and commercial paper.

Notwithstanding the growth in Japanese money markets during the late 1970s and the 1980s, by the late 1980s, they were still smaller in terms of the value of financial instruments relative to GNP than those in the United States, the United Kingdom, and Germany, but the gaps were closing. The fraction of the short-term securities market represented by government paper was smaller than in the U.S. market but similar to those of the German and U.K. markets (Okina, 1993, pp. 33, 35).

Japanese equity markets were and remain thin. While hundreds of millions of shares of listed securities change hands each trading day in Tokyo, a large fraction of the shares in Japanese corporations are held by other corporations and are not traded. In the early 1990s, these cross-holdings of shares accounted for more than 60 percent of the capitalization of the Tokyo stock market (Wood, 1992, p. 24).

THE LEGAL FRAMEWORK: HOW INDEPENDENT
IS THE BANK OF JAPAN?

By law, the Bank of Japan is subordinate to the Ministry of Finance (Ostrom, 1993, pp. 10–11). In 1942, when, at the height of World War II, the government of Japan took measures to centralize control over the economy, the Bank of Japan Law was revised. That act is still in force today. Article 43 of the law states that a competent minister can order the Bank of Japan to carry out particular tasks when the minister finds them necessary for the Bank to achieve its mission (Ostrom, 1993, p. 11). Wood notes that the Bank of Japan Law was modeled on the Nazi Reichsbank Law and that "the Nazis did not believe in independent central banks" (1994, p. 96). Article 47 gives cabinet officials the authority to dismiss the governor and vice governor of the Bank. While this power has never been used, in 1949 a standoff arose between the governor and the Minister of Finance in which the dismissal of the governor was raised as a possibility. The dispute ended only with the resignation of the entire cabinet. In 1949, the occupation authorities added a Policy Board composed of members from the public and private sectors and chaired by the governor to the structure of the Bank. This group meets semi-weekly to discuss monetary policy (Ostrom, 1993, p. 11).

Governor Mieno has asserted that, with the introduction of the Policy Board, the Bank of Japan was given the sole authority to set interest rates (4, p. 19). Mr. Mieno's interpretation of the 1949 change in the structure of the bank is erroneous, however, according to Hisayochi Katsumata of Tokai University. Expressed more positively, this interpretation does not furnish a credible base on which to stake the laudable claim of central-bank independence. According to Katsumata, in proclaiming the independence of the Bank of Japan, Governor Mieno misreads or ignores language in the 1949 statute leading to the creation of the Policy Board, which "specifically kept intact the spirit of Article 43, for example" (Ostrom , 1993, p. 11). If there are inconsistencies between the 1942 Law and the 1949 Policy Board system, precedence suggests that it is the Policy Board system that is inconsistent with the statute (rather than the other way around) and that the Policy Board system should yield to the statute.

It appears that, according to both the spirit and letter of the law, Governor Mieno did not yet have the independence of a Chairman of the Federal Reserve Board to set monetary policy or even that of the Governor of the Reserve Bank of New Zealand to pursue independently a monetary policy that is consistent with an inflation target agreed to with the Minister of Finance. Under these circumstances, it is remarkable that Mr. Mieno fought for, and achieved, the degree of independence from the Ministry of Finance that he exercised as Governor of the Bank of Japan. Having already retouched the law through the force of his personality de facto, about a month before leaving office, Governor Mieno (4, p. 19) suggested openly that the 1942 Bank of Japan Law may not be an appropriate governing statute for the Bank in today's situation. He pointed out that some of the definitions of the Bank's mission contained in the law reflect the wartime situation of the Japanese economy while others are not consistent with the Policy Board system introduced in 1949. He also noted that the 1942 statute gives the Government of Japan "broad authority" over the Bank of Japan, including the authority to issue orders concerning the administration of the Bank, and he implied that such "broad authority" is no longer appropriate. Nonetheless, in the same address delivered close to the end of his term of office, he said he did not intend to press for a review of the law although he believed that a time for the thorough review of the law would come (4, p. 19).

GOVERNOR MIENO'S VIEWS ON MONETARY POLICY

Governor Mieno indicates that monetary policy should have two objectives: (1) stabilizing the value of money, and (2) maintaining and fostering the financial system (2, p. 6). He notes (4, p. 16) that the two objectives are complementary rather than competing:

> Of course, a currency can serve as the real infrastructure for the economy and society only when appropriate monetary policy is securing its value and settlement and financial systems are operating smoothly and with stability. In this sense, the two objectives we constantly emphasize, those of stabilizing the "value of the currency" and of stabilizing the "financial system," reinforce each other to achieve the ultimate goal.

Moreover, to Mr. Mieno, "price stability" does not mean merely stability of current price indices. He says (2, p. 6):

> There can be stability of prices in the medium to long run only
> when the economy is on a well-balanced and sustainable growth
> path. Therefore, one of the objectives of monetary policy should
> be to realize non-inflationary sustainable economic growth from
> the medium- to long-term perspective.

He prefers not to specify exactly what he means by "price stability."
He maintains that zero change in the price level, however defined,
may be too exacting an objective for monetary policy, particularly in
recessions, but views it as the appropriate objective on average for
the medium to long run. He also cites both price stability and sustainable growth as goals of monetary policy. But, clearly, in the
governor's view, price stability is key since it provides the basis for
"reliable economic calculations" that are the foundation for efficient
economic conduct in the household and business sectors of the
economy. Conversely, unstable price levels, whether marked by
inflation or deflation, make economic calculations difficult and increase uncertainty, thereby impeding stable economic development
(2, p. 7). He maintains that price fluctuations also "undermine the
foundation for economic growth" by causing "inequities in income
and asset distributions" and by "threatening the stability of daily
life" (2, p. 7). His mission statement (4, p. 16) is

> First and foremost, the mission of central banks is widely recog-
> nized and established in the major industrial world as being the
> "maintenance of the value of the currency," or in other words,
> "to provide the basis for economic growth through the sound
> supply of money."

Nonetheless, for Governor Mieno, price stability is not the only
appropriate policy objective for a central bank in the short run. It is
not clear whether he intends simply to allow the type of automatic
monetary "easing" that is afforded by real interest rates falling of
their own accord in recessions, or whether he advocates intentionally
taking inflation risks for the sake of short-term stimulation. The fact
is that he has never taken such risks, so his actions may speak more
clearly than his words. This is what he wrote (4, p. 17):

> I myself have never limited the roles of the Bank of Japan solely
> to the maintenance of price stability. In the midst of a recession,

I judged it appropriate that the short-term priority should be placed on economic recovery. However, it is important to bear in mind that monetary policy should never digress from the medium-term target of stable prices even when paying attention to short-term goals. As I have often stated, monetary policy should be measured with a "yardstick" against the time scale of a central bank, which means that the ultimate and consistent goal of monetary policy is economic stability from the medium- to long-term perspective.

While Governor Mieno states clearly that price stability should be the prime objective of monetary policy, he is less clear about how to judge whether the central bank is achieving that objective. Aside from the ever-present problems associated with measuring any economic variable, he questions whether the monetary authority should focus on the Consumer Price Index, which affects consumers now (and, in effect, reflects how well the central bank did its job in the past), or the Wholesale Price Index and the corporate-service price indices, movements in which may well affect consumers later. In addition, in order to judge future price movements, the Bank of Japan must monitor conditions in the product and labor markets, exchange-rate movements, and the monetary situation in general (e.g., money supply and lending activity). Monitoring the factors that will affect prices in the future is important. Once inflation sets in, the public will expect further inflation and act accordingly, thereby making it more difficult to extirpate inflation from the economy through monetary policy. In addition, the lag between the time at which policy decisions are taken and the time they affect the economy allows inflationary expectations to become more deeply embedded in the economy (2, p. 8). Governor Mieno notes that a democratic society may easily have an inflationary bias and that the threat of inflation is manifested differently every time it appears in the economy, a fact that complicates the central bank's task of countering that threat (3, p. 4).

In addition to the effects of asset prices on the macroeconomy, the Bank of Japan is concerned about the health and stability of financial markets since the Bank implements monetary policy through buying or selling government securities in the financial markets. Thus, the stability of a currency's value depends on the central bank's ability to use the financial markets as media between itself and securities traders (2, p. 9).

The International Monetary Fund (1993) has advised that, although asset prices are volatile and determined by many factors other than monetary policy, they should not be ignored when there is reason to believe that excess liquidity is being channeled into asset markets rather than flow markets. The price indices that are used to monitor inflation in most countries do not cover financial asset prices, although they may contain or reflect certain real asset prices such as

Table 4

Margin Requirements on the Tokyo Stock Exchange, 1980–1991
(percent)

Date	Margin Rate
January 16, 1980	60
April 2, 1980	50
April 26, 1980	60
June 11, 1980	50
December 17, 1980	40
March 14, 1981	30
March 26, 1981	40
April 2, 1981	50
April 15, 1981	60
June 9, 1981	50
July 3, 1981	60
September 9, 1981	50
September 24, 1981	40
September 29, 1981	30
November 26, 1981	40
February 18, 1982	30
December 3, 1982	40
July 8, 1983	50
March 24, 1984	60
May 19, 1984	50
January 17, 1985	60
November 6, 1985	50
March 13, 1986	60
February 27, 1987	70
October 21, 1987	50
March 17, 1988	60
June 3, 1988	70
June 30, 1990	60
February 21, 1991	50
February 27, 1991	40
September 6, 1991	30

consumer durables and the (user or rental) cost of homes. Broader indices could be constructed, but traditional macroeconomic relationships that apply to the goods-and-services economy may not apply to asset markets; it may be necessary to use a microeconomic approach, evaluating the effects of monetary policy in individual asset markets. Moreover, not all increases in asset prices ought to be viewed as inflationary by any definition. For example, one would not want to use monetary policy to eliminate asset-price increases that reflect expectations of higher real returns or lower real interest rates. Trying to counterbalance asset-price inflation with deflation in the price of goods and services can also be problematic because it is likely to destabilize the demand for money.

One microeconomic policy instrument that can be used to target speculation in securities markets is a margin requirement—a requirement that a purchaser of securities must pay at least a specified fraction of the price of securities in cash. In Japan, margin requirements are set by each stock exchange with the guidance of the Ministry of Finance. Other Japanese stock markets tend to follow the lead of the Tokyo Stock Exchange in setting margin requirements. As shown in Table 4, the margin requirement on the Tokyo Exchange fluctuated between 30 and 60 percent during the first half of the 1980s. In the run-up to the bubble and during the period of the bubble itself, the margin requirement was raised to 60 percent in March of 1986 and to 70 percent in February of the following year. Except for a few months in the wake of the worldwide crash of October 1987, the margin requirement for purchasing stocks remained at 70 percent through mid-1990. While the margin requirement for purchasing stocks was increased as the bubble inflated share prices, at 70 percent, there remained substantial scope for raising the margin requirement further had the Ministry of Finance wished to do so in order to dampen stock-market speculation.

Except perhaps when discussing the side-effects of capital-inflow surges to developing countries, economists have done very little work on the question of how to deal with asset-price inflation. The Bank for International Settlements, the central banks' central bank, has paid the question some attention since 1992, noting that, in Japan and several other countries, deregulation of financial markets was accompanied by rapid rises in asset prices. Kindleberger (1995, p. 35) has concluded that "when speculation threatens substantial rises in asset prices, with a possible collapse in asset markets later, and harm to the financial system . . . monetary authorities confront a dilemma calling for judgement, not cookbook rules of the game. Such a conclusion may be uncomfortable. It is, I believe, realistic." Commenting on the policies that the Bank of Japan was following in deflating the asset-market bubble in the autumn of 1992, U.S. Federal Reserve Chairman Alan Greenspan said that "we have not seen this phenomenon before in its current form. Reliance on the old models clearly has been inadequate." He added that the Bank of Japan was responding to the situation in "an appropriate manner" (*Institutional Investor*, June 1993, p. 92).

THE EXECUTION OF MONETARY POLICY

Since the recent history of financial markets in Japan differs greatly from those in the other economies surveyed in this volume, we begin this section with a short review of the evolution of monetary policy over the last quarter century. The Bank of Japan's conduct of monetary policy has changed dramatically since the 1970s. Until the early 1980s, the Bank's principal means of affecting the supply of money and credit were (1) "window guidance," which is "advice" given to major banks concerning to whom and how much the banks should lend, and (2) control of interest rates (International Monetary Fund, 1993). In the absence of well-developed interbank credit markets, if commercial banks sought funds to lend to would-be borrowers in excess of their deposits, the banks tended to borrow directly from the central bank. Although financial-market reform, with its widening and deepening of these markets, began during the 1980s, when window guidance was terminated around the middle of 1991, loans to other financial institutions still comprised 20.7 percent of the Bank of Japan's assets. By the end of 1993, these loans accounted for only 12.1 percent of the Bank's assets (Ostrom, 1993, p. 5). Window guidance amounted to credit rationing. There is evidence that, given the Bank's window guidance, firms that were members of a *keiretsu* that included banks had easier access to credit than other firms, however. For example, during 1979 to 1980, when window guidance was restrictive, firms whose *keiretsu* included a bank invested more than other firms, other things equal (Hoshi, Scharfstein, and Singleton, 1993, p. 65).

This pattern of investment appears to lend support to the "new-credit" view of monetary policy, which holds that, since there are information costs in an economy, there is a difference between the cost to firms of externally and internally obtained funds. These information costs, along with a cost of enforcing contracts, are reflected in an external-finance premium in interest rates (Bernanke and Gertler, 1995, pp. 28, 35). If the "new-credit" view applies in Japan, banks know more about and provide more funds to related than to nonrelated firms and, presumably, have less trouble enforcing contracts against related than unrelated companies. In the event, however, it appears that the close relationship between banks and other firms in the *keiretsu* may simply have made it easier for the nonfinancial firms to leverage their investments—as it turned out, often imprudently. Sometimes the same assets were used by related companies as collateral for several loans, thereby helping to inflate the bubble economy (Wood, 1992, p. 55).

Reforms that led to the broadening and deepening of financial markets made it necessary for the Bank of Japan to change the tools it used to control the volume of money and credit in the economy. The changes in financial markets that were "particularly significant" in the evolution of the Bank's operating procedures were (1) the fall in the importance of bank lending as a source of funds in the economy, (2) the "dramatic expansion" of the range of instruments used by banks to raise funds, and (3) the rise to predominance of assets with market-determined prices in portfolios in all sectors of the Japanese economy (Kasman and Rodrieguiez, 1991, p. 31).

Increased borrowing by the Government of Japan after 1975 led to the liberalization of the nation's financial markets since the Government of Japan's need to sell securities made it difficult for the Bank of Japan to keep in place limits on bank interest rates. Pressure from commercial banks led the central bank to authorize the commercial banks to issue certificates of deposit in 1979. The increased supply of government debt instruments "threatened to undermine" the Bank of Japan's control of the money supply since the Bank was pledged to repurchase the securities from private-sector owners. The Bank forced private banks to increase the proportion of government bonds in their portfolios even though more attractive investments were becoming available. The glut of government paper induced the liberalizing of controls on bond interest rates, the removal of restrictions on sales of bonds in the secondary market, and the expanding of the maturity range of the bonds (Kasman and Rodriguiez, 1991, p. 30).

With the development of financial markets in Japan and the shift of investment financing from bank loans to securities, the Bank of

Japan's controls on bank lending (window guidance) became less effective as a tool of monetary policy, and the Bank stopped using the reserve requirement as an active tool of monetary policy. Over the decade before the Bank stopped using window guidance in 1991, several economic variables, including the exchange rate, asset prices, and broad money supply, were used for monetary-policy operations with market interest rates becoming "increasingly central" to those policy operations (Kasman and Rodrieguiez, 1991, pp. 33–35). As was the case in other countries, including the United States, deregulation and the resulting structural change in financial markets changed the relationships among monetary variables and between those variables and real output in the Japanese economy (International Monetary Fund, 1993).

In January 1996, the Bank of Japan decided, in principle, to cease using lending through its discount window as a tool of monetary policy (Wada, 1996, p. 2). The Bank says it watches a variety of economic indicators—e.g., interest rates, price indices, corporate liquidity conditions, and the general business outlook—in setting its monetary policy, but Japanese monetary policy *always* starts with acting on, and reacting to market pressures on, interest rates in the short-term money market (Okina, 1993, p. 32).

The Bank of Japan targets call rates and other interbank interest rates rather than bank reserves (Ueda, 1993, p. 8). By making interest rates its target variables, the Bank of Japan makes the Japanese money supply dependent on interest rates: In the very short run the Bank thus adjusts the supply of money to the level needed to achieve its interest-rate targets and to this extent the money supply is not an independent variable in the setting or execution of the Bank's policy. However, beyond the very short run, the Bank can, of course, adjust the interest rate objective as needed to affect money growth. While the monetarist tradition has focused on stable growth of the money supply as the appropriate target of monetary policy, Milton Friedman has said: "My impression is that Japan illustrates a policy that is less monetarist in rhetoric than the policies followed by the United States and Great Britain, but far more monetarist in practice" (Ostrom, 1993, p. 6).

Monetary Policy During and After the Bubble

During 1986 and the first part of 1987, in order to counter the deflationary effects of the appreciation of the yen on the economy, the Bank of Japan cut its discount rate five times to a (then) record low of 2.50 percent by late February 1987 (*New York Times*, February 21, 1987, p. 37). In addition to stimulating the economy, other things being equal, a reduction in interest rates encourages savers to buy equities. Tending to offset the incentive to invest in Japanese stocks represented by the cuts in interest rates, in March 1986 and again in February 1987, the margin required to purchase shares on the Tokyo Stock Exchange was increased by ten percentage points on each of the two occasions to a total of 70 percent. Notwithstanding the increases in the margin requirement, these reductions in the Bank's discount rate probably contributed to the bubble in asset prices. By 1989, both Governor Satoshi Sumita and then–Deputy Governor Mieno repeatedly warned of the danger of inflationary pressures in the economy (Henning, 1994, p. 61). In May 1989 Governor Sumita increased the discount rate to 3.25 percent, and in October of that year, he hiked it a further half percentage point (IMF, 1996).

Within fifty hours of taking office in December 1989, Governor Mieno moved to raise interest rates even more. Although a consensus that an increase in interest rates was needed at the time was "nearly achieved," the Bank's intent was leaked to the press before Finance Minister (and future Prime Minister) Ryutaro Hashimoto had approved the move. Mr. Mieno's intent to raise interest rates angered the Finance Minister, who insisted on a one-week delay; the governor waited eight days (*Institutional Investor*, June 1993, p. 92; Henning, 1994, p. 163). At the time, the Mieno- Hashimoto conflict was widely viewed as a contest of wills between the men, with the Finance Minister openly questioning the Bank of Japan's institutional authority to set rates, "badly flouting the public fiction that such matters were the province of the Bank of Japan alone" (Henning, 1994, p. 163). The intervention of former Prime Minister Keichi Miyazawa and Noboru Takeshita, the leader of Mr. Hashimoto's faction of the governing Liberal Democratic Party in the Japanese Diet (and a future Prime Minister), may have been required to settle the dispute (Henning, 1994, p. 165), but Wada (1996, pp. 2–3) doubts that there was any such intervention.

Over the following eight months, Governor Mieno increased rates two more times, bringing the Bank of Japan's discount rate to 6.00 percent in August 1990. This instance of monetary tightening marked the first time the Bank of Japan had increased interest rates primarily to check rising land and stock prices rather than widespread inflation as reflected in the CPI (*New York Times*, May 30, 1994, p. A33).

With the change in the Bank's policy, the bubble on the Tokyo Stock Exchange burst. The Nikkei-Dow index of the prices of 225 stocks peaked at 38,916 on December 29, 1989; it fell to 14,309 by August 1992. Part of the decline in share prices was probably linked to the recessions that affected many of Japan's trading partners and, later, Japan itself. The recession in Japan reduced the profits of most Japanese firms listed on the Tokyo Stock Exchange, though not necessarily on their frequently vast foreign operations. Land prices continued to rise into 1991 but, as already shown in Table 2, fell precipitously thereafter. At the end of 1989, people in Japan's Management and Coordination Agency put the value of Japanese real property at four times that of U.S. real property, and, at the peak of land prices, the land on which the imperial palace in Tokyo is situated was said to be worth more than all the real estate in California or as much as all the real estate in Canada (Wood, 1992, p. 50; *New York Times*, May 30, 1994, p. A33).

In most industrial economies, tightening monetary policy tends to dampen economic activity because it discourages consumption financed with credit and investment, which is usually financed with borrowed money, and because it adversely affects the cash flow of firms and consumers. In the Japanese economy the deflationary effect of tighter money on real output was magnified because of the bursting of the financial bubble. By the summer of 1990, speculators began to miss margin calls on securities and mortgage payments on real property (*Institutional Investor*, June 1993, p. 92). Many loans had been secured by land or stocks, the prices of which had been inflated to levels not supported by the underlying value of the real assets. Asset values fell more than $6 trillion, and, in April 1991, the Japanese economy tumbled into recession (*New York Times*, May 30, 1994, p. A33; 1, p. 2). Governor Mieno received death threats as a result of his interest-rate hikes, and at least one mock bomb was mailed to the Bank of Japan because of the higher rates (*Institutional Investor*, June 1993, p. 92). Shin Kanemaru, at that time "the country's most powerful politician," said that someone should behead Governor Mieno (*New York Times*, May 30, 1994, p. A33).

In trying to account for the animus directed toward Governor Mieno, Wood (1994, p. 94) notes that the Bank of Japan was too slow to cut interest rates after the bubble burst. According to Wood,

Governor Mieno engaged in "monetary overkill," either because he wanted to make up for what he rightly saw as "excessive laxity" in the monetary policy of his predecessor, Satoshi Sumita, or because he "totally failed to comprehend" the debt deflation of the 1990s and what that means for money supply, the financial system, and the economy. Some people in Japan thought that Mr. Mieno was pursuing a sociopolitical as well as a monetary agenda; they thought he wanted to use monetary policy to promote political reform and to end fincial speculation (Wood, 1994, p. 95). Wada, on the other hand, maintains that the Bank of Japan tightened its monetary policy stance to restrain the overheated economy and that, if the Bank had not tightened its policy, the bubble would have been larger than it was. In addition, Wada (1996, p. 3) finds that, while the Bank eased its policy stance beginning in 1991 to boost the Japanese economy, since the bubble was so large, "even prompt monetary easing could not stop the deterioration of the economy" that accompanied the bursting of the bubble.

As already shown in Tables 1 and 3, with recession came a dramatic fall in the inflation rate in Japan, allowing the Bank of Japan to reduce interest rates without stoking inflationary fires. The Bank began to reduce its discount rate during the summer of 1991; by September 1993, the discount rate had fallen to another record-low level of 1.75 percent. Speaking in December 1993, Governor Mieno said that the proper role of Japanese monetary policy in the then-stagnant economy was to reduce interest rates in order to improve corporate profits and cash flow. He noted that monetary easing reduces the pain of adjustment in the aftermath of the bubble, promotes that adjustment, and helps prepare the groundwork for future economic recovery (1, p. 7).

The Bank of Japan and the Exchange Rate

Governor Mieno spoke frequently about the level of the exchange rate of the yen, its effects on the Japanese economy, and the need for international coordination to move exchange rates *(Report from Japan, Inc.,* June 24, 1994; *Financial Times,* June 21, 1993, p. 16; *Japan Economic Newswire*, March 26, 1990; *Japan Economic Newswire*, December 18, 1989). Japan also has been badgered frequently by the other Group-of-Seven (G–7) major industrial countries to do this or that to influence the real exchange rate of the yen as though this rate were largely policy-determined. After the beginning of the recession in 1991, in the aftermath of a substantial rise in the foreign-exchange value of the currency the previous year, Mieno was concerned about the effect of yen appreciation on domestic output and employment (International Monetary Fund, 1996). Nonetheless, until March 1995, the Bank of Japan engaged in only sterilized intervention in the foreign-exchange market; only after that date did it engage in unsterilized transactions (Ostrom, 1993, p. 10).

Sterilized intervention in foreign-exchange markets is intervention in which the effect on the domestic money supply is offset in domestic financial markets; unsterilized intervention is intervention that is not offset in domestic financial markets and, therefore, leads to expansion (contraction) of the money supply when the central bank buys (sells) foreign exchange. If the Bank were to engage in sterilized intervention to appreciate the yen, it would buy yen for foreign currency while simultaneously buying financial instruments, such as Japanese Treasury bills, for yen, leaving the total supply of yen outside the Bank unchanged. One should not be surprised that sterilized intervention in the foreign-exchange market has little—if any—effect on the exchange rate. The world's central banks and finance ministries do not have the ability to move the foreign-exchange market very far or for very long in open financial markets unless they credibly signal a change in policy, including monetary policy. Even then the question remains whether they can have much lasting effect on the *real* exchange rate, adjusted for the changed international differentials in expected inflation, in well-functioning and open international financial markets.

What Governor Mieno meant by "international policy coordination" among central banks is limited in scope. He maintains (2, p. 12) that each central bank's primary responsibility is the stability and growth of its domestic economy:

> Policy coordination does not mean that all major countries fall into step and pursue policy in one specific direction. The common understanding among G–7 countries [the United States, the United Kingdom, Canada, France, Germany, Italy, and Japan] in terms of policy coordination is that the countries concerned should have a policy properly in accordance with their respective circumstances in order to achieve non-inflationary sustainable economic growth as a medium- to long-term goal. In doing so, the more the world economy becomes borderless and markets integrate, the more emphasis is placed on the responsibility of achiev-

Japanese Inflation 1971–1997

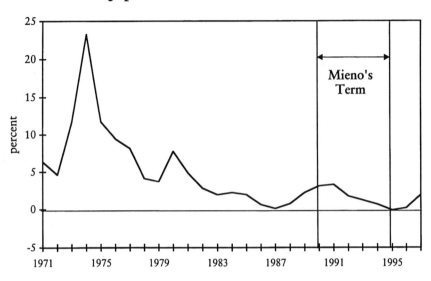

Figure 1
Source: International Monetary Fund,
International Financial Statistics Database, March 25, 1998.

ing one's own stable economic growth. This is all the more so
with a country with a large-sized economy like Japan.

In the governor's opinion, the appropriate purposes of international
economic meetings are the candid discussion of the policies each country plans to pursue to achieve stable growth domestically and the
sharing of accurate understandings with respect to the effects such
policies would have on the world economy or global financial markets (2, pp. 11–12).

THE GOVERNOR'S RECORD
Subduing Inflation

Yasushi Mieno took charge of Japan's monetary policy in December 1989. Hence, it is appropriate to evaluate his record with
respect to price stability on a December-to-December basis. Data on

December-to-December changes in the Japanese Consumer Price Index since 1981 were added in parentheses to Table 1. They show a striking decline from year to year throughout the period for which Governor Mieno's policies could affect them. Figure 1 places this record in a longer-term perspective. Monetary policy affects prices only with a lag, which Milton Friedman has called "long and variable" and estimated to be as long as two years. Hence, it is clear that, taking charge in December 1989, the governor was not in a position to affect the 1990 inflation rate very much. His policy decisions may have affected price changes beginning in 1991 and running through 1995, even though he left office in December 1994. Some of the decline in inflation, however, may be attributable to the weak state of demand in the Japanese economy rather than to Mr. Mieno's skill as a practitioner of monetary policy. Over the period 1991 to 1995, the Japanese Consumer Price Index rose at a compound annual rate of 1.1 percent per year.

The Bubble and Its Aftermath

Inflation in the prices of goods and services has not been a major problem in the Japanese economy in the 1980s or 1990s; the emergence of a speculative bubble in asset prices and the consequences of that bubble for the Japanese economy have been the major problem Mr. Mieno faced during his term as Governor of the Bank of Japan. Bubbles are not, however, scourges that befall countries entirely spontaneously but developments that often feast off market and regulatory imperfections and off incentive distortions and thrive on mechanisms for shifting losses to taxpayers. With the rapid rise of asset prices and the leveraging of collateral in investment schemes during the bubble years, the governor saw that the bursting of the bubble was inevitable. Its consequences for the Japanese economy would be both severe and difficult to arrest because of a buildup of unneeded capital equipment, household durables, and commercial buildings, and a marked weakening of balance sheets of both financial and nonfinancial firms (1, pp. 3, 8). When Governor Mieno pricked the bubble and hastened its end, he took the necessary first step to restoring the health of the Japanese economy even if it did not turn out to be sufficient.

Among the major problems in assessing—let alone dealing with—the adjustments necessary to restore health to the Japanese economy are the dearth of relevant information on the financial situations of companies and perhaps an unwillingness of top managers to get on top of major developing problems. On the latter point, Takeshi Hosomi, former vice finance minister and at the time the head of the NLI Research Institute, said during the spring of 1994: "Japanese are happy if problems are cured while they remain unaware of them existing. Basically, Japanese like being deceived. Right now, the authorities are busy deceiving them" (*Los Angeles Times*, September 4, 1994, p. D3). Near the end of his term, Governor Mieno himself said that full disclosure of the scope of bad debts could damage public trust in banks and should not occur until measures to enable the public to accept the disclosures calmly are taken (*Los Angeles Times*, December 12, 1994, p. D4).

There were lots of bad debts about which to deceive the public—and the authorities. Only Japan's twenty-one largest banks, which provide 45 percent of outstanding loans, must furnish data on loans that are in delinquency or default, not having paid interest for six months or more. During Governor Mieno's term in office, banks were not required to report on the volume of rescheduled loans or loans on which interest-rate concessions had been made to stave off delinquency of the borrower (*Los Angeles Times*, December 12, 1994, p. D4). In the United States, loans on which debt service has not been paid for ninety days are deemed to be in "non-accrual" status. Japanese bank reports do not cover loans—estimated to be $130 billion at the close of 1994—to nonbank financial institutions, which, themselves, were "inundated under a mass of their own real estate loans that have gone sour" (*Los Angeles Times*, December 12, 1994, p. D4). Although seven of Japan's eight housing-loan institutions were "teetering on the edge of bankruptcy" in 1994, their problem loans were not classified as bad debts according to Japanese accounting and reporting standards (*Los Angeles Times*, September 4, 1994, p. D3). Between April and September 1994, the twenty-one banks required to report bad debts wrote off a record $20 billion, but their total bad debts fell only $2 billion—to $133.3 billion—over the six-month period, and even these data, which show a 1.8-percent fall in bad debts, are "cooked." If the loans the banks sold to the Cooperative Credit Purchasing Company, very roughly the Japanese equivalent of the U.S. Reconstruction Finance Corporation, are included in the total, their bad debts rose 3.1 percent over the half year (*Los Angeles Times*, December 12, 1994, p. D4).

Confusion and denial continued to reign. In June 1994, Mr. Hosomi said he did not think there was "any person, including any person at the Bank of Japan or the Finance Ministry" who had any real grasp of the magnitude of the problem, "even within several trillions of yen." At the time 1 trillion yen was approximately $10 billion (*Los Angeles Times*, September 4, 1994, p. D3). According to the Ministry of Finance, at the end of March 1996, problem loans held by Japanese deposit-taking financial institutions (i.e., banks) came to 35 trillion yen, equal to about 7 percent of the country's Gross Domestic Product (International Monetary Fund, 1996). This figure is consistent with Takeshi Hosomi's estimate that the total of bad loans held by the entire Japanese banking system was $700 billion in June 1994, roughly one-seventh of Japan's GDP in that year if Mr. Hosomi's figure includes institutions, such as insurance companies, that do not take deposits but make loans (*Los Angeles Times*, December 12, 1994, p. D4; International Monetary Fund, 1996). We illustrate the difference between U.S. and Japanese reporting standards with Mitsubishi, which is the only Japanese bank listed on the New York Stock Exchange (and, therefore, required to meet the standards of disclosure set by the U.S. Securities and Exchange Commission). It told the Commission that, in 1993, 36 percent of the bad loans it reported to American authorities were not reported in Japan (*Los Angeles Times*, September 4, 1994, p. D3).

The problem of the asset-price bubble was not amenable to "solution" with the tools at the Bank of Japan's disposal. As we have indicated above, greater disclosure of the true financial states of both financial and nonfinancial firms in Japan might have prevented the emergence of the bubble (or at least stopped it before it grew as large as it did) and certainly would have clarified the extent of the adjustment problem when the bubble burst. It would, however, take changes in Japanese law—and rigorous enforcement of the new statutes—to effect the increased disclosure of companies' financial situations and to reform regulatory and supervisory practices: No change in monetary policy alone can achieve these ends. Margin requirements are the one tool that can be targeted directly to discourage the emergence of a speculative bubble in share prices, though raising them does not preclude the use of borrowed funds secured in other ways to purchase stocks. Margin requirements are set by stock exchanges on the advice of the Ministry of Finance; unlike the situation in the United States, they are not under the control of the central bank.

Countering Economic Stagnation

While the post-bubble period has been marked by low inflation in Japan, it has also been one of anemic economic growth. The overspending on consumer durables, producer durables, and office buildings during the bubble-economy boom pushed the expansion of production capacity in the manufacturing sector of the Japanese economy to the neighborhood of 8 percent per year, well beyond the economy's assumed long-term sustainable annual growth rate of 3 to 4 percent (1, p. 3). Many consumers and producers found themselves with more of these long-lasting assets than they wanted, and demand for them fell precipitously.

Governor Mieno noted that one of the "major negative consequences for the future of the Japanese economy" arising from the excessive financial and economic activities of the bubble years was the necessity of "a very deep destocking phase" (1, p. 3). The large erosion of people's wealth resulting from the declines in stock and land prices may also have restrained consumer demand, further depressing the Japanese economy. On the supply side of the market, nonfinancial firms with weak balance sheets (i.e., with assets the values of which had plummeted after 1989) were not seen as good risks by potential lenders, and the potential lenders themselves, burdened with bad debts on their books, were not in a position to supply liquidity to potential customers—hence the very slow economic growth of the last several years.

While initially resisting pressure to reduce interest rates, a few months after the economy entered a recession, Governor Mieno began to try to revive the economy by either cutting them actively or at least letting the poor state of the economy pull them down (Henning, 1994, p. 169). The Bank of Japan cut its discount rate from 6.00 percent to 5.50 percent in July 1991. Twenty-seven months and five cuts later, the discount rate stood at 1.75 percent, a record-low figure (1, p. 6). In December 1993, Governor Mieno said he believed that current interest rates were sufficiently low to support the corporate sector "when companies begin to make forward-looking business decisions and fixed business investments" (1, p. 7). He explained that the Bank of Japan had reduced interest rates "with a clear awareness of the positive impact on improving corporate cash flows" (1, p. 7). Nonetheless, the governor recognized that the low corporate demand for funds, which was the result of the inventory overhang, balance-sheet and economic restructuring, and consumer pessimism, meant that, unlike the situation during earlier periods of slow economic growth, even historically low interest rates were not accompanied by faster growth in the monetary aggregates or in economic activity (1, pp. 4–6). In addition, between mid-1991 and the end of 1993, the Government of Japan pumped about 30 trillion yen of fiscal stimulus into the economy (equal to roughly 2.5 percent of the nation's GDP). Despite this stimulative policy mix, which Mr. Mieno called "one of the most sizable counter-cyclical actions in Japanese history," there was no improvement in the nation's economic outlook (1, pp. 2, 7).

UNFINISHED BUSINESS

Yasushi Mieno assumed the Governorship of the Bank of Japan with two objectives: to maintain stable prices in the context of achieving sustainable economic growth and to ensure the stability of the financial system. He came into office recognizing that the bubble economy of the late 1980s imperiled these goals. Showing the courage of his convictions, despite political opposition, he hiked interest rates and broke the bubble. In the aftermath of the crash that he precipitated, Mr. Mieno's record on price stability was outstanding. As economic growth continued to be anemic, episodes of actual deflation in the price level of goods and services indicated that he may even have overdone a good thing. Disruptions in the intermediation process and the loss of net worth by financial and nonfinancial businesses and consumers alike precluded resumption of satisfactory growth until pervasive reforms of the financial sector and resolution of its bad debt problems had been put in place. Such reforms have, however, been slow in coming as almost another four years were wasted *after* Governor Mieno left office before decisive steps began to be taken. Clearly it is difficult to blame Governor Mieno for failing to achieve in a hurry what entirely eluded his successor.

One of the problems Governor Mieno faced from the beginning of his term is that the Bank of Japan is not independent of political control in either the letter or the spirit of Japanese law. It also has only limited authority for restructuring even the banking part of Japan's conglomerated financial business because the banking system's regulatory and supervisory agency is in the Ministry of Finance. Nonetheless, as the mock bombs and implied threats on his life demonstrate, Mr. Mieno exerted exceptional leadership at the Bank and functioned more independently than did his predecessors. Perhaps even more important than the Bank of Japan's lack of independence, however, is the lack of adequate reporting on the balance sheets of Japan's businesses, particularly its financial institutions. Without accurate information on the financial situations of the nation's businesses, it is virtually impossible to formulate and implement policies that will ensure stable, noninflationary economic growth and the health of the financial sector. Changing all this and restructuring the Japanese financial system with the correct incentives for efficient risk selection, risk pricing, and prudent lending has remained Japan's unfinished business.

The reviews that the governor earned in office are mixed. Some observers praised his integrity, independence, and determination to implement an appropriate monetary policy; others faulted him for various reasons. Yasushi Mieno was named "Central Banker of the Year" by *Euromoney* (see below) in 1991 for raising the Bank of Japan's discount rate despite the opposition of the Finance Minister and foreign governments and for his refusal to compromise on his monetary policy, which restored the Bank of Japan's credibility. *Euromoney* says that, among Japan's financial and bureaucratic elite, Governor Mieno alone was aware of the inherent danger the asset-price inflation posed to the nation's economy. According to Russell Jones, assistant director of research at UBS Phillips & Drew International, who calls Yasushi Mieno "the central banker's central banker," Mr. Mieno's concern with inflation dates from the oil shock of 1973 to 1974, which led Japanese inflation to top 20 percent. Jones states that, as a result of the inflationary burst of the mid-1970s, "Mienomics has been all about keeping inflation down" (*Euromoney*, September 1991, pp. 109–112). An unidentified banker observed that "trying to avoid his predecessor's mistakes, he [Mieno] made the opposite mistakes" (*Institutional Investor*, June 1993, p. 92). In 1993, *The Financial Times* (June 21, p. 16) offered the following characterization:

> He is a fiercely, skillfully independent figure who inspires loyalty among his staff, commands respect from his peers and provokes anger among many politicians who believe he should be their servant. The Bank of Japan's formal independence from the finance ministry and its political masters is limited, but Mr. Mieno has won more autonomy for the bank than any recent governor.

Global Finance (September 1994, p. 120) gave Governor Mieno a grade of "A" for his conduct of monetary policy and noted that, while the Bank of Japan is not formally independent of the government, Mr. Mieno "epitomizes that class of career civil servant in Japan who acts independently anyway."

Yoshio Suzuki, chairman of the advisory board at Nomura Research Institute and a former executive at the Bank of Japan, concurs: "My view is that nobody could have behaved better during such an unlucky period" (*New York Times*, May 30, 1994, p. A33). Robert Alan Feldman, senior economist at Salomon Brothers Tokyo, said, "I think he has done brilliantly," and Yukio Noguchi, an economist at Hitosubashi University, calls Mr. Mieno "one of the greatest governors in Bank of Japan history (*Institutional Investor*, June 1993, p. 92; *Wall Street Journal*, June 15, 1993, p. A1). Discussing Governor Mieno's early days in office, an unidentified official in the international department of the Ministry of Finance said, "Drastically raising interest rates may have been overkill, but that was inevitable because of the magnitude of the crisis" (*Institutional Investor*, June 1993, p. 92).

On the other hand, commenting on the interest-rate increases of 1989 to 1990, Makoto Utsumi, at the time the Vice Minister of Finance and later a professor at Keio University, said: "The point all along was to avoid a hard landing. I think if we had tightened more slowly we could have had a soft landing" (*New York Times*, May 30, 1994, p. A33). Yokio Yashimura, the director of the Ministry of Finance's international banking division, said that, after Mr. Mieno, "management of monetary policy will be very delicate" because of the fragile state of the banks, and there will be a potential for excessive monetary ease (*Institutional Investor*, June 1993, p. 92). While concern over infringement of monetary policy is a good reason for avoiding financial fragility in the first place, the macroeconomic objective of price stability was certainly not compromised in Japan. Furthermore, Governor Mieno's policies exposed, but did not create, the unsound practices and positions of banks. All in all, the consensus of most Japanese economists seems to be that Governor Mieno will be remembered as "better than average" in a country where the average tends to be high (*Institutional Investor*, June 1993, p. 92).

REFERENCES

Bernanke, Ben S., and Gertler, Mark. 1995. "Inside the Black Box: The Credit Channel of Monetary Policy Transmission," *Journal of Economic Perspectives* 9 (Fall): 27–48.

Folkerts-Landau, David, et al. 1995. *International Capital Markets Developments, Prospects, and Policy Issues.* Washington, D.C.: International Monetary Fund.

Hargraves, Marcia, Schinasi, Garry J., and Weisbrod, Steven R. 1993. "Asset Price Inflation in the 1980s: A Flow of Funds Perspective." *IMF Working Paper WP/93/77*, Washington, D.C.: International Monetary Fund.

Henning, C. Randall. 1994. *Currencies and politics in the United States, Germany, and Japan.* Washington, D.C.: Institute for International Economics.

Hoshi, Takeo, Scharfstein, David, and Singleton, Kenneth J. 1993. "Japanese Corporate Investment and Bank of Japan Guidance of Commercial Bank Lending." Pp. 63–94 in Kenneth J. Singleton, ed., *Japanese monetary policy.* Chicago: University of Chicago Press.

Institute of Fiscal and Monetary Policy (1). Ministry of Finance, *Financial Statistics of Japan 1989*, Tokyo, n.d.

_____ (2). Ministry of Finance, *Financial Statistics of Japan 1995*, Tokyo, n.d.

International Monetary Fund. 1993. "Monetary Policy, Financial Liabilities, and Asset-Price Inflation." Pp. 81–95 in *World Economic Outlook*, Annex I. Washington, D.C.: May.

_____. 1996. *International Financial Statistics,* CD-ROM last updated April.

_____. 1997. *International financial statistics yearbook.* Washington, D.C.: International Monetary Fund.

_____. 1998. *International Financial Statistics* Database. March 25.

Kasman, Bruce, and Rodrieguiez, Anthony P. 1991. "Financial Liabilities and Monetary Policy in Japan," *Federal Reserve Bank of New York Quarterly Review* 16 (Autumn): 28–46.

Kindleberger, Charles P. 1995. "Asset Inflation and Monetary Policy," *Banca Nazionale del Lavoro Quarterly Review* No. 192 (March): 17–37.

Mieno, Yasushi

(1) "Roles of Financial and Capital Markets Under Current Japanese Monetary and Economic Conditions." Article abstracted and translated from a speech given to the Capital Markets Research Institute, Tokyo, December 7, 1993.

(2) "The Conduct of Monetary Policy by the Bank of Japan." Article excerpted from a speech given to a Kisaragi-kai meeting, Tokyo, May 27, 1994.

(3) "The Development of Central Banking." Speech given at the Bank of England's Tercentennial Anniversary Symposium, London, June 9, 1994.

(4) "Issues Facing the Japanese Economy and the Roles of Central Banks." Speech given at the Research Institute of Japan, November 15, 1994.

Okina, Kunio. 1993. "Market Operations in Japan: Theory and Practice."
Pp. 31–62 in Kenneth J. Singleton, ed.

Ostrom, Douglas. 1993. "New Directions in Japanese Monetary Policy,"
JEI Report (April 28): 1–13.

Singleton, Kenneth J. 1993. "Introduction." Pp. 1–6 in Kenneth J. Singleton, ed.

Ueda, Kazuo. 1993. "A Comparative Perspective on Japanese Monetary
Policy: Short-Run Monetary Control and the Transmission Mechanism."
Pp. 7–29 in Kenneth J. Singleton, ed.

Wada, Tetsuro. 1996. Letter to G. M. von Furstenberg, Tokyo, November
29, 1996. Wada then was the Chief Press Officer, Press Division, Policy
Planning Department, Bank of Japan, responding to correspondence originally addressed to Governor Mieno.

Wood, Christopher. 1992. *The bubble economy*. Tokyo: Charles E. Tuttle
Co.

____. 1994. *The end of Japan Inc*. New York: Simon and Schuster.

A SEA CHANGE FOR NEW ZEALAND: GOVERNOR BRASH

GEORGE M. VON FURSTENBERG AND MICHAEL K. ULAN

CONTENTS

Dr. Donald T. Brash
Governor, Reserve Bank of New Zealand, 1988–(2003)

Donald T. Brash was born in Wanganui, a small town in New Zealand, in 1940. His father was a pacifist clergyman. Between his family background and his undergraduate study at the University of Canterbury in New Zealand, the early influences on him were all Keynesian in economics and Fabian socialist in politics. In the course of advanced studies abroad, his views continued to evolve. Brash received his Ph.D. from the Australian National University in 1966 with a dissertation on the impact of American corporate investment on the Australian manufacturing sector. It was published by Harvard University Press.

Brash began his professional career at the World Bank, where he worked from 1966 to 1968 and again between 1969 and 1971. Between 1968 and 1969, he was one of twelve staff members of a commission headed by the former Prime Minister of Canada, Lester Pearson, which wrote a report on the problems impeding economic development for World Bank president Robert McNamara. In 1971, he returned to New Zealand to be chief executive of Broadbank, a merchant bank, where he was involved in developing the emerging commercial bill market and the nonbank foreign exchange market. In 1980, he was an unsuccessful candidate of the then-governing Nationalist Party for Parliament at a by-election. He ran as a Nationalist not so much because he supported the policies of the government but rather because he wanted the corporatist policies of the time changed and saw the National Party as the only party that might achieve his goal. Two years later, he left merchant banking to become chief executive of the New Zealand Kiwifruit Authority, a quasi public-sector organization that promotes the international sale of kiwifruit. In 1986, he returned to banking, becoming chief executive of the Trust Bank Group, a company set up to merge the interests of nine of the twelve trustee savings banks. He is a strong supporter of the market-oriented economic reforms that have been implemented in New Zealand since the early 1980s. Between 1985 and 1988, despite his membership in the National Party, at the request of the Labour Government, he chaired several committees charged with reforming the goods and services tax and different aspects of the tax system.

Donald Brash was appointed Governor of the Reserve Bank of New Zealand in September 1988. At age forty-seven, he was the youngest governor in the history of the Bank. He participated in the design and implementation of the new monetary policy framework established by the Reserve Bank of New Zealand Act of 1989, introduced an internationally unique approach to banking supervision, and greatly improved the operating efficiency of the Bank. He acquired wide acclaim, at home and abroad, as a sterling inflation fighter and courageous economic renewer, and was reappointed for a third five-year term ending August 31, 2003. If he stays the course, he will likely be the longest-serving of the distinguished heads of central banks represented in this volume.

A SEA CHANGE
FOR NEW ZEALAND:
GOVERNOR BRASH

PREFACE

When Donald T. Brash became governor of the Reserve Bank of New Zealand in 1988, the economy's inflation rate was twice the industrial-country average. With his support, the following year Parliament passed a law making price stability the sole objective of the Bank's monetary policy and holding the governor personally responsible for achieving an inflation target publicly agreed upon between the governor and the minister of finance. Brash brought "underlying inflation" (the change in the Consumer Price Index less the direct effects of changes in interest rates and of supply shocks to the economy that have a significant effect on the Index) down from 4.9 percent in the year ending December 1988 to 1.7 percent for the year ending December 1991. This was a year ahead of the schedule agreed upon with the minister of finance for bringing inflation down to the range of zero to 2 percent per year. With rare exceptions, Brash has kept underlying inflation within that target. Following the 1996 general election, the new government widened the target zone for inflation to zero to 3 percent per year (*Financial Times,* December 20, 1996, p. 20).

Probably more important for the long-term economic health of the nation, Governor Brash has led the Reserve Bank's intensive efforts to explain to the public that monetary policy cannot have more than one objective at a time, that inflation is the only economic variable monetary policy can sustainably affect, and that inflation is a deterrent to economic growth and efficiency.

INTRODUCTION

Donald T. Brash is the last but by no means least of the heads of central banks identified in this study "who showed a disciplined reflected commitment to the goal of effectively and predictably stable prices." As we did with the other central bank heads, we asked him to identify those of his statements that he regarded as adding up to a comprehensive exposition of his approach to monetary policy. In his response, dated July 6, 1995, he noted:

> We share your view . . . that building a public constituency in support of price stability is of fundamental importance. Indeed, I would probably spend more of my time doing this than anything else on my programme. I probably average two or three speeches a week, and in addition spend a considerable amount of time providing background off-the-record briefings for media. In April/ May of this year I actually did 43 speeches over the two months, quite my most active speaking programme ever.

> To avoid creating undesirable financial market turbulence, more than 90 percent of these speeches are made on condition that media are not present. This is not, of course, because what I am saying is confidential but rather because whenever I speak on the record the media are looking for some financial market "angle." . . .

Consistent with the emphasis that Governor Brash places on public speaking, all of the statements that he sent us are public addresses rather than testimony offered before the Parliament of New Zealand or one of its committees. The speeches enclosed for our consideration included addresses delivered both in New Zealand and abroad. In a letter to one of the authors dated June 12, 1996, Governor Brash provided detailed comments on and corrections to an earlier draft of this chapter along with further background materials. All materials provided by Governor Brash are identified in the reference section and cited simply by number throughout this essay.

Unlike the situation faced by other central bankers whose anti-inflation efforts are portrayed in this book, the monetary policy administered by Donald Brash in New Zealand was embedded in an overall market-oriented structural reform of the economy of the island nation. We first recall the poor performance of the New Zealand economy in the 1970s and up to the mid-1980s that gave rise to the structural reforms and helped promote price stability as the sole objective of monetary policy. Next we consider the Policy Target Agreement as the governor's employment contract. We then discuss Donald Brash's philosophy of central banking and review the operational procedures used in the conduct of monetary policy. Following that, we review Governor Brash's overall record as he has sought to reduce both inflation and inflationary expectations in New Zealand. Finally, we assess his legacy to the economy of the nation.

THE MACROECONOMIC BACKGROUND AND THE STRUCTURAL REFORMS

The Macroeconomic Background

During the 1970s and early 1980s output growth was lower and inflation higher in most developed countries than during the preceding quarter century, 1945 to 1970. As shown in the year-on-year data of Table 1, New Zealand's rate of inflation in the CPI was higher than the average for the International Monetary Fund's Industrial-Country aggregate.

Between 1982 and 1984, New Zealand had wage and price controls in place. The controls probably contributed to the nation's beating the industrial-country-average inflation rate during 1983 and 1984 (Walsh, 1995, p. 156). Over the period 1971 to 1988 (including the two years of price controls), however, the compound average annual inflation rate was 12 percent while the average rate in the industrial countries taken as a whole was only 7 percent. Over the same period, the average annual rate of growth of New Zealand's real Gross Domestic Product (GDP) was 2.4 percent, 20 percent lower than the industrial-country average of 3.0 percent. New Zealand's rate of economic growth was below the OECD average despite the pursuit of expansionary fiscal and monetary policies in the 1970s and the early 1980s. Because of the loose monetary policy, and notwithstanding two years of price and wage controls, New Zealand's CPI quintupled while the average OECD CPI "merely" tripled from 1970 to 1984. Inflation, combined with overregulation, made the New Zealand economy weak and unresponsive to economic signals during that period (4, p. 4).

The combination of slow economic growth, persistent balance-

Table 1

New Zealand and Industrial-Country-Average Inflation Rates, 1971–1997
(change from previous year in percent)

Date	New Zealand	Industrial Countries
1971	10.7	5.3
1972	6.5	4.8
1973	8.3	7.9
1974	11.2	13.4
1975	14.5	11.4
1976	17.0	8.6
1977	14.6	8.8
1978	11.5	7.5
1979	14.0	9.7
1980	17.1	12.4
1981	15.2	10.4
1982	16.3	7.7
1983	7.4	5.2
1984	6.1	5.0
1985	15.5	4.4
1986	13.1	2.6
1987	15.7	3.2
1988	6.4	3.5
1989	5.7	4.6
1990	6.0	5.2
1991	2.6	4.4
1992	1.0	3.2
1993	1.4	2.8
1994	1.7	2.3
1995	3.7	2.5
1996	2.3	2.3
1997	1.8	1.7

Source: International Monetary Fund (1998b).

of-payments and fiscal deficits, rapidly rising external debt, rising unemployment, and "a seemingly entrenched tendency towards high and increasing inflation" prompted pervasive free-market-oriented structural reform of both the private and public sectors of the New Zealand economy during the mid-1980s (2, pp. 1–2).

The Reforms

Dissatisfaction with New Zealand's relatively poor economic performance and with its large government sector led to a series of privatizations of government enterprises and policy reforms. Privatization is often part and parcel of fiscal consolidation and market-oriented reforms that are propitious for granting independence in the pursuit of price stability to the central bank. Under the terms of the State Owned Enterprises Act of 1986, enterprises were "corporatized." This process involved managing enterprises on a commercial basis, freeing them from government red tape, putting a private sector board in charge, removing political interference, and requiring enterprises to reorganize and to become profitable so that they could be sold to private investors. The list of industries fully or partially privatized in New Zealand includes forestry, oil, steel, printing, rail, telecommunications, airlines, shipping, and insurance.

Many subsidies were slashed—farm subsidies were eliminated—and controls on interest rates and capital flows were removed while foreign trade was liberalized and the central-government deficit eliminated. In fiscal year 1983, the central government ran a deficit of over 9 percent of GDP; in contrast, from 1987 through 1996, the central government ran budget surpluses during all of the fiscal years but one (International Monetary Fund, 1997, pp. 636–37; 1998a, p. 512). Governor Brash attributes the high and variable inflation of the 1970s and early 1980s to the expansionary macroeconomic policy of that period (4, p. 4).

Market-oriented structural reform of the New Zealand economy has continued in the 1990s. With Governor Brash's support, significant changes in the regulation of commercial banks were introduced in January 1996. Under the new regulatory regime, it is up to the directors of a bank rather than officials of the Reserve Bank of New Zealand to ensure the soundness of their financial institution. Instead of reporting to the Reserve Bank in confidence, bankers must now issue "detailed quarterly public disclosure statements" in which they provide information on the quantities of risky assets on their balance sheets at the end of each calendar quarter and their intra-quarter peak holdings of such assets. These quarterly statements must be audited semi-annually by independent auditors (9, p. 13). Potential depositors are to use the information in these statements when deciding where to place their savings. As Governor Brash put it, instead of complying with detailed central bank guidelines on the management of their institutions, directors of commercial banks "must simply attest, in public disclosure statements, that the internal controls are appropriate to the nature of their banking business" (9, p. 13). Directors must confirm publicly that a bank has adequate systems to monitor and control risk. Directors of a failed institution who are shown to have been negligent in ensuring that their bank has adequate risk-control systems in place may be sued by aggrieved creditors.

There are questions about the practicability of the new system of bank regulation. Some bankers ask how well directors can understand and monitor risks. Others are concerned that it will be difficult to provide meaningful information about a bank's balance sheet without compromising the institution's competitive standing. The ability of the average citizen to understand the risk information contained in the banks' quarterly statements, which is fundamental to imposing the market's discipline on bank behavior, has also been questioned. Yet Governor Brash has reaffirmed his belief in market-based regulation of banks in the aftermath of the financial crisis that struck many Asian economies during 1997 (13, p. 6).

Late in 1984, the incoming government directed the Reserve Bank of New Zealand to begin reducing inflation. During that year, the Reserve Bank gave monetary policy a medium-term focus and directed policy toward the single goal of price stability. In addition, regulations and controls on New Zealand's financial system were removed so that monetary policy since has been implemented through market-based instruments. From that time on, interest rates and the floating exchange rate of the New Zealand dollar "have become the key transmission channels for monetary policy in New Zealand" (2, p. 3). A decade later, Governor Brash said that, since 1984, although "the temptation must have been strong, . . . there has been no attempt by any government to influence the implementation of monetary policy" (4, pp. 5–6, 8).

Although piecemeal reforms had given the Bank the tools to achieve price stability as early as 1985, the Bank at first still lacked the credibility needed to minimize the output costs of disinflation and the resolve to maintain a low rate of inflation under these conditions. In fact, from 1985 to 1987 annual inflation climbed well into double digits (Fischer, 1995, p. 67; Walsh, 1995, p. 156). This spike in the inflation rate, however, was caused in large part by the introduction of a 10-percent value-added tax, the Goods and Services Tax, in 1986 (10). Thereafter, attention in New Zealand turned to the idea of *institutionalizing* the new approach to the objectives and conduct of monetary policy (2, p. 3).

A New Act for the Reserve Bank

Donald Brash became the Governor of the Reserve Bank in September 1988, at a time when inflation was declining but was still nearly twice as high as the average for all developed nations. In December 1989, a new Reserve Bank of New Zealand Act, which Dr. Brash favored, was passed by Parliament with the support of the two major parties and signed into law. The act went into effect February 1, 1990. Section 8 of the act reads: "The primary function of the Bank is to formulate and implement monetary policy directed to the economic objective of achieving and maintaining stability in the general level of prices" (Walsh, 1995, p. 156). While the legislation cites the achievement and maintenance of stable prices as the "primary function" (rather than the only function) of the Bank, the statute mentions no conflicting policy objectives. Governor Brash clarifies this point:

> The *primary function of the Bank* is the implementation of monetary policy aimed at "achieving and maintaining stability in the general level of prices." There is no other objective mentioned for *monetary policy*, and therefore we see monetary policy as being required to give sole attention to "achieving and maintaining" price stability. But of course the *Bank* has some other functions, specified in the Act, the most important of which is to register and supervise commercial banks with the objective of maintaining the stability of the financial system. (10)

In contrast, Section 8 of the 1964 act that the 1989 law replaced required that monetary policy be directed to the maintenance and promotion of economic growth and social welfare in New Zealand, having regard to the desirability of promoting the highest level of production and trade and full employment, and of maintaining a stable internal price level (Walsh, 1995, p. 156). Brash saw several problems with the Bank's implementation of monetary policy under the 1964 Act: First, the act contained no definition of the objectives so it was not possible to ascertain whether they were being achieved. Second, the Reserve Bank had "little operational independence" to achieve presumed objectives of the law. Third, legal responsibility for monetary policy "rested almost entirely" upon the Minister of Finance (4, p. 3).

In view of this, "multiple objectives give the Reserve Bank multiple excuses for failing to meet any of the targets" (quoted in 7, p. 8). Fischer (1995, p. 67), an economist on the staff of the Swiss National Bank, has noted that, since the mid-1970s, both economic circumstances and developments in economic theory "have brought into sharper relief the difficulty of pursuing multiple mandates with the limited tools at a central bank's disposal." Fischer's observation is essentially a restatement of the "Tinbergen Rule," articulated by the Dutch economist Jan Tinbergen: For each policy objective, there needs to be a separate policy variable. With only one policy variable—the money supply—at its disposal, over time, the central bank can effectively pursue only one objective.

The 1989 Act requires that the governor of the Reserve Bank and the Minister of Finance agree on a definition of "price stability" (i.e., on the Bank's target inflation rate) (Fischer, 1995, p. 77). Further, in line with the general movement toward personal accountability in the public sector in New Zealand, the 1989 Act provides that, on the initiative of either the Minister of Finance or the nonexecutive directors of the Bank, the governor can be discharged for "inadequate performance." "Inadequate performance," however, is not defined in either the act or the Policy Target Agreement (PTA), a document that we discuss later in this chapter (10; Fischer, 1995, p. 77; Walsh, 1995, pp. 156–57). Neither the historical record nor tradition has helped clarify the standard, but it may be exacting. Thus, though certainly not charged with inadequacy, Governor Brash was called to account by the Finance Minister for the Reserve Bank's missing its inflation target for the year ending March 1996, notwithstanding the facts that the target was missed by only 0.1 percentage point and that there was a special circumstance—an increase in government charges—that boosted inflation during the year.

It was originally proposed that the salaries of the governor and other top officials of the Reserve Bank be keyed to the inflation rate, but that idea was rejected as "politically inflammatory" since it would have increased central bankers' incomes as a reward for policies that, at least initially, would be deflationary, causing an increase in unemployment in the short run (*Financial Times,* September 25, 1992, p. 16).

The 1989 Act also changed the way the Reserve Bank was funded. Prior to the passage of the act, the Bank kept the revenue it received from seigniorage, effectively permitting it to establish its own budget. Under the terms of the 1989 Act, however, the receipts from seigniorage go to the government's coffers. The new funding arrangement is reflected in a five-year agreement, signed in April 1991, between the Minister of Finance and the governor. This agreement caps operating expenses at the 1990/1991 level of N.Z. $56.7 million for five years. The governor and his staff were able to function well within this constraint: five years later, the Bank's operating expenses were 38 percent below the agreed funding cap—about 40 percent below the level of expenditures during the 1987/1988 fiscal year. In addition, between 1987/1988 and 1995/1996, the Bank's staff was cut nearly 50 percent to just under 300 full-time equivalents (2, p. 13–14; 10).

This, then, is the legal and institutional framework within which Governor Brash has functioned for the better part of his tenure at the Reserve Bank.

THE PTA AS AN EMPLOYMENT CONTRACT

In effect, the Policy Target Agreement between the governor and the Minister of Finance (i.e., the government) is an employment contract for the governor. It states the objectives of monetary policy and a measure by which the Bank's (i.e., the governor's) performance can be evaluated; if the governor fails to meet the inflation target specified in the agreement, he can be fired. Given the target, however, the governor is free to conduct monetary policy with discretion and without direct interference from the government. Walsh (1995, pp. 157–58) has demonstrated that a simple contract making the reward to a central banker a linear function of the rate of inflation could eliminate the inflationary bias of discretionary policy while ensuring an optimal policy response to aggregate supply shocks. While the Reserve Bank Act permits the dismissal of the Governor of the Bank for failing to meet an inflation target, for domestic political reasons, neither the Reserve Bank Act of 1989 nor the PTA makes his salary a function of the inflation rate.

Professor Walsh (1995, pp. 157–60) analyzes the "employment contract" of the Governor of the Reserve Bank of New Zealand from the standpoint of its social optimality as a document to ensure price stability. He calls the attempt to make the governor accountable for achieving price stability found in the 1989 Reserve Act part of "the unique institutional structure set out in the Act." Walsh develops a model to determine the socially optimal commitment of policy to stable prices. He finds that an optimal monetary policy directed toward price stability can be sustained by a dismissal policy based on the measured rate of inflation (with some allowances for measurement error), with the target rate adjusted for supply—but not demand shocks to the economy. The features of the optimal contract derived by Walsh appear close to the framework established by the 1989 Act.

There could be some upward bias in the Reserve Bank's accountability structure since the target inflation rate *can* be adjusted for supply disturbances but the PTAs do not specify, *a priori*, the explicit reaction function to the supply disturbance before the disturbance occurs (Walsh, 1995, pp. 161–62). In addition, if the government and the central bank renegotiate an inflation target after observing a supply disturbance, the government will have an incentive to set the probability of reappointment of the central banker in such a way as to achieve the inflation rate that minimizes the social costs of monetary policy, taking the revised target as given. The socially optimal policy formed before the revised target is set is not the same as the optimal policy once it is set, and, if there is nominal-wage rigidity in the economy, a time-inconsistency problem could arise.

Time inconsistency is the term economists apply to a situation in which, for short-term benefit, policy makers change a policy that has gained credibility, and in credence of which private-sector economic agents have made financial commitments, in an effort to exploit those commitments. Time-inconsistent behavior destroys the credibility of economic policy. Nevertheless, Walsh (1995, p. 160) concludes with only two qualifications that "the Reserve Act of 1989 seems to mimic quite well the firing rule designed to sustain the socially optimal commitment policy (to price stability)."

THE GOVERNOR'S VIEW OF CENTRAL BANKING

Central Bank Responsibilities

For Donald Brash, the one responsibility of a central bank with respect to monetary policy is to achieve and maintain stable prices:

> I believe it is not only *appropriate* that price stability is the only objective of monetary policy—on the grounds that the rate of inflation is the *only* thing which monetary policy can sustainably affect—it would be *damaging to growth and employment* (in New Zealand at least, given where we start from) to widen the objectives. (7, p. 8)

He explains that price stability is not really "an end in itself but simply a means to other ends" (e.g., employment and economic growth) (7, p. 3). While calling growth and employment "more important" objectives than the inflation rate, he maintains:

> If it were possible to achieve a lasting increase in the rate of economic growth, or a lasting reduction in unemployment, in return for a bit more inflation, then I for one would be awfully tempted. But it is not possible. (6, p. 2)

He adds, "It is worth recalling that Bill Phillips (Phillips, 1958), a fellow New Zealander [who was teaching at the London School of Economics in 1958 when he discovered the downward-sloping curve relating the unemployment rate and the rate of change in money wages that now bears his name], never claimed that there was an exploitable policy trade-off when he originally uncovered the unemployment/wage relationship" (4, p. 4).

The Reserve Bank governor maintains that there is no exploitable tradeoff between unemployment and inflation because it is not possible to "purchase" a permanently higher level of economic activity by accepting more inflation. Instead he holds that inflation tends to reduce the long-term rate of growth in an economy for the following reasons (5, p. 4):

- Inflation in an economy that has a tax system that is not designed for an economy with inflation induces too much real-estate investment and too little investment in the production of goods and services.
- High inflation tends to be variable inflation, generating uncertainty about the future and making investment decisions more difficult.
- High inflation causes nominal interest rates to rise. Even if the real rate of interest (the nominal interest rate minus the expected rate of inflation) is unaffected by the inflation, the increase in the nominal rates causes cash-flow problems for businesses and discourages investment—particularly investment with long payback periods.
- In an economy like New Zealand's, where the tax system is not designed to take inflation into account, high inflation discourages saving because the after-tax return to savers is often negative.

• High inflation "almost invariably" leads to policy instability (i.e., "stop-go" policy alternation), which tends to increase potential investors' uncertainty about expected returns on investment.

Estimates of the economic damage of inflation vary, but Stanley Fischer, formerly of MIT and now with the IMF—as distinct from Andreas Fischer cited everywhere else in this chapter—has estimated that reducing inflation from 10 percent per year to zero increases an economy's long-term annual growth rate by about one percentage point (5, p. 4).

How Are New Zealand's Inflation Targets Set?

The most salient features of the institutional procedure through which the nation's inflation target is set were indicated earlier in this chapter: an inflation target is publicly agreed upon between the Minister of Finance and the governor of the Reserve Bank of New Zealand, and the governor is charged with achieving that target rate of inflation.

Decisions about the objectives of monetary policy are the prerogative of the government rather than the central bank (7, p. 4). It was the government of the day that passed the Reserve Act of 1989, and a future government could amend or replace it. The Minister of Finance must negotiate targets for monetary policy with a potential appointee as governor of the Reserve Bank *before* appointing or reappointing the governor. The targets may be revised by mutual agreement between the two parties, with the revisions recorded in writing and published in the *Gazette* of the House of Representatives (Walsh, 1995, p. 157). While the Policy Targets Agreements are negotiated by the governor (or would-be governor) of the Reserve Bank and the finance minister, the governor alone is responsible for achieving the targets specified in the PTAs.

The Reserve Bank Act provides several mechanisms through which the Reserve Bank of New Zealand—and its governor—are held accountable for achieving and maintaining price stability (2, pp. 9–11):

• There is a single objective (price stability) by which to judge the success of monetary policy.
• The PTA is an explicit statement of a transparent policy target, thereby increasing the probability and ease of holding the Bank to account.

• The PTA holds the governor personally responsible for achieving the inflation target specified in the document. The 1989 Act provides that, on the advice of the finance minister "that the performance of the Governor in ensuring that the Bank achieves the policy targets fixed under section 9 or section 12(7)(b) of this Act has been inadequate," the Governor-General may, by Order in Council, remove the RBNZ governor from office.

• At least semi-annually, the Bank must publish and table in Parliament a *Monetary Policy Statement*, which reviews the Bank's conduct of monetary policy for the six months just past and details the policies and procedures through which monetary policy will be directed toward price stability in future periods. In addition, after each *Monetary Policy Statement* is published, the governor testifies before, and is questioned by, the Finance and Expenditure Select Committee of the New Zealand Parliament about the *Statement*. (2, p. 11)

Nonetheless, neither the PTA itself nor the inflation target it contains is carved in stone. Each PTA explicitly contains a set of conditions under which the Reserve Bank need not achieve its stated inflation target (2, p. 11). These caveats are based on the premise that the benefits of maintaining price stability in the short run "may, in some limited circumstances, be far outweighed by the output and employment costs of doing so" and that "there are situations in which a departure from the rules, as long as it is carefully defined and limited, makes sense" (2, p. 12).

The conditions under which PTAs permit the Reserve Bank to deviate from the price-stability targets they contain involve supply shocks to the New Zealand economy, such as changes in the external terms of trade, changes in indirect tax rates, natural disasters, or major declines in livestock numbers due to disease, and changes in the price level arising from government levies when the effects of these shocks on the CPI are "significant." While the PTA does not define "significant," the Reserve Bank defines the term as involving an impact of at least 0.25 percent on the CPI over a twelve-month period. In addition, the direct impact of interest rates on the CPI is excluded from the Reserve Bank's definition of "underlying inflation" (Walsh, 1995, pp. 157; 10). In New Zealand, interest rates on home mortgages are included in the CPI so that, other things being equal, when monetary policy is tightened to combat inflation, measured inflation actually rises (10). While the Bank will accommodate a one-time adjustment of the domestic price level arising from the initial supply shock, it will counteract second-round adjustments to such shocks that can result in wage-price spirals (2, p. 12). The PTAs do not permit the Bank to accommodate demand shocks.

More fundamentally, under the terms of the 1989 Act, it is the government that determines the objective of monetary policy. To change the inflation target, it can invoke a formal and public "override" provision of the act. Governor Brash stresses the words "formal and public." A government that wishes to override the Reserve Bank's price-stability objective "could not do so very easily, or furtively" (2, pp. 5–6). In order to alter the objective of monetary policy stated in a PTA, the government must promulgate an Order in Council, which is valid for only one year, after which new Orders in Council are needed if the government wishes to plead for continuing the release from the statutory monetary-policy objective of stable prices. If the change in policy target that is occasioned by the override conflicts with the current PTA, a new agreement must be negotiated between the minister of finance and the governor of the Bank and tabled in Parliament (2, p. 6).

Although devoted to price stability as the only appropriate goal of monetary policy, Donald Brash says he is "not at all perturbed" by the override provision of the 1989 act; in his view, the override provision is "neither a weakness nor a negation of the value of central bank independence" (2, p. 7). He asserts:

> On the contrary, I regard the override as a strength. Where trade-offs are to be made between or among political objectives, it is vital for good economic management that the nature of the choices being made is well understood by all. Provision for making trade-offs, through the override facility, forces transparency on that process. (2, p. 7)

He goes on to quote John Crow, the former Governor of the Bank of Canada, who is the subject of the first chapter in this volume, on the subject:

> Simply put, in a democratic society, a central bank has to be accountable in some way to the elected representatives of the people—the government and/or parliament—for some reasonably clear responsibilities. (2, p. 7)

Governor Brash points out that, under the terms of the override procedure, if, for example, the government thinks that monetary policy should be changed because of a structural shock, such as a change in the real exchange rate of the New Zealand dollar, and that the shock can best be offset through a change in the nominal exchange rate and a one-off change in the price level, the whole process will take place in the open (2, p. 8). A change in the real exchange rate of the country's currency changes the prices of tradable goods and services relative to those of nontradables, thereby affecting supply and demand conditions in the nation's economy.

In his view, the governor's job during the renegotiation of the PTA necessitated by the government's decision is to ensure that the full implications of the trade-off choice made by the government are spelled out as accurately and publicly as possible. Yet, the very public character of the override reduces the probability that it will be invoked and enhances the credibility of the Bank's commitment to price stability (2, p. 8).

GOVERNOR BRASH'S CONDUCT OF MONETARY POLICY

The Basic Approach

Donald Brash has said repeatedly that the Reserve Bank of New Zealand has only one monetary-policy objective—the achievement and maintenance of price stability. The monetary-policy instrument through which it tries to limit inflation is the quantity of interbank settlement cash. It varies this component of the money supply to influence interest rates (its operational or intermediate target) in order, ultimately, to control inflation. More indirectly, the Bank is also interested in affecting the effective exchange rate—an index number tracking the weighted average exchange rate of a currency against a basket of other currencies—of the Kiwi or New Zealand dollar (Fischer and Orr, 1994, p. 10). Governor Brash notes that settlement cash is a "minuscule" part of the monetary base and indicates that the changes in the targets for settlement cash are "essentially signaling devices rather than anything else." He goes on to say:

> When our target for aggregate settlement cash is reduced, . . . the market knows that we are deadly serious about wanting conditions to tighten because the risk of their being forced to discount

> Reserve Bank bills at a penal rate (currently 90 basis points [i.e., nine-tenths of a percentage point] above the market rate) is sharply increased. (10)

While settlement cash is the only monetary-policy instrument the Bank has used since the beginning of 1991 and there have been only three changes in the target for settlement cash since that time (one of which was effected "in four quick steps"), monetary conditions in New Zealand have moved through a complete cycle since that time (10). In principle, the Bank uses changes in the target for settlement cash as a way to articulate the Bank's concerns about the inflation outlook. In practice, such changes in the settlement cash target are rarely required (12):

> Normally, it is sufficient to publish our inflation forecast, which we do quarterly, with appropriate comments, for the market to adjust monetary conditions very promptly in the desired direction. (10)

As discussed later, during Governor Brash's tenure at the Bank, generally the market's adjustment of monetary conditions has been not only in the desired direction but also to the extent necessary to bring and keep underlying inflation within the PTA target range. This fact might give the appearance that the Bank has been successfully following a "monetarist" model of price level determination. Such a model, at its most basic, is characterized by the equation of exchange, $MV = PQ$, but with predictable trends in V and Q, where:

> M = the quantity of money,
> V = the velocity with which it circulates,
> P = the price level, and
> Q = the volume of real output.

However, the governor does not believe in the existence of such a simple bivariate control relationship between M and P. He has stated that he and his colleagues are not "monetarists" in the "narrow sense" of that word:

> We are skeptical of our ability to control growth in the money and credit aggregates in any very precise manner, and in any case

the relationship between the quantity of money (no matter how defined) and subsequent inflation appears to have been so elastic over the last decade as to be devoid of any policy value. (10)

However, while New Zealand's financial institutions can make credit less available to would-be borrowers in response to the Reserve Bank's "signal," the Bank can and must validate that signal if it wishes to see tighter monetary conditions maintained in the New Zealand economy. Thus, the governor is far from abdicating monetary responsibility and competence for the achievement of inflation goals. Other things being equal, changing the rate of growth of liquidity in the New Zealand economy will affect the inflation rate in that economy. Since other things rarely remain equal, the Bank will just have to figure how to take them into account and still achieve its inflation goals unless exceptions are warranted by the nature of a particular disturbance.

Does the Reserve Bank Have an Exchange-Rate Policy?

In a small, open economy such as New Zealand's, sustained movements in nominal exchange rates can affect inflation directly and relatively quickly through the prices of traded goods. Hence, the Bank monitors the exchange rate of the New Zealand dollar through the trade-weighted (exports plus imports) index of the exchange rates of the currency against the Australian and U.S. dollars, the yen, the pound sterling, and the mark. The weights of the currencies in the index are revised from time to time as the relative importance of New Zealand's trading partners changes; the weights are public information (1, pp. 328–29; 2, p. 17). Despite the importance of the exchange rate for the nation's price level and the fact that tightening or loosening of monetary policy raises or lowers the nominal exchange rate of the Kiwi in the short run, the Reserve Bank has no exchange-rate target—only an inflation target (5, p. 5).

Governor Brash distinguishes between the nominal and the real exchange rates in discussing the importance of the exchange rate to the New Zealand economy and what the Bank can do to influence the exchange rate. The nominal exchange rate is the price of one unit of foreign currency expressed in terms of domestic currency; the real exchange rate is the price of one unit of foreign goods and services expressed in terms of one unit of domestic goods or services. The latter concept encompasses both the nominal exchange rate and the levels of the price indices at home and abroad. These price indices are used, in effect, to deflate the foreign and domestic currency amounts in the nominal exchange rate to obtain the real rate index, the movements of which can be tracked over time.

Governor Brash (1, pp. 328–32) makes several points about the exchange rate of the Kiwi as it relates to the Reserve Bank's monetary policy in addition to the obvious fact that in a quintessential small open economy like today's New Zealand, the exchange rate has an important influence on local prices. They are:

- In an open economy (such as New Zealand's), the exchange rate has an important influence on local prices: a sharp depreciation could raise inflation above 2 percent per year, and a sharp appreciation could cause inflation to fall below zero percent.

- The Reserve Bank uses a trade-weighted (exports plus imports) index of the exchange rate of the New Zealand dollar against the U.S. dollar, Australian dollar, pound sterling, mark, and yen to judge the appropriateness of the Kiwi's foreign-exchange value.

- Over the long term, New Zealand's currency is likely to appreciate in nominal terms because the nation's inflation rate is lower than those of its trading partners. Exporters will not be placed at a competitive disadvantage by nominal appreciation that is equal to the inflation differential.

- The Reserve Bank does not have a fixed target for the exchange rate and sees the "correct" level of the rate as a range rather than a point estimate. In any event, the real exchange rate cannot be influenced *sustainably* by monetary policy. In the short run, a change in the nominal exchange rate is a change in the real exchange rate. However, other things remaining equal, the real depreciation initially produced by the nominal depreciation precipitated by an expansionary monetary policy will, before long, be undone through higher inflation in New Zealand.

- While the Reserve Bank cannot make New Zealand's products more competitive by engineering a real depreciation of the nation's currency collectively, private producers can do so individually: "Competitiveness comes from real cost structures that compare well with those abroad; from quality of design, product, and service and from adaptability, to keep in touch with ever-changing market conditions." The best thing the Reserve Bank can do to help exporters (and import competitors) "is not to confuse the picture by allowing inflation to wobble away from price stability."

While recognizing that the Reserve Bank cannot sustainably affect the real exchange rate of the nation's currency, Governor Brash calls the real exchange rate "one of the most important price signals in the economy" and one that need not always signal perfectly. Normatively, the rate may be higher than one would wish if local producers' competitive position is hurt and investment in export and import–competing sectors of the economy is discouraged. If, on the other hand, the rate is too low for comfort, living standards are depressed since the exchange rate would make many consumption goods (including imported food) "artificially expensive" and discourage investment in the nontradables sector of the economy, including infrastructure (1, p. 331). Nonetheless, the Reserve Bank of New Zealand has not intervened in the foreign-exchange market since the nation's currency was floated in March 1985 (7, pp. 5–6).

Getting to Price Stability

Prior to the 1996 election, all of the PTAs between the governor of the Reserve Bank and the Minister of Finance defined zero to 2 percent inflation as "price stability" (Walsh, 1995, p. 157). This figure takes into account an estimated upward bias in price-change measures in the New Zealand economy of one percentage point per year (4, p. 14). While the aggregate CPI is perhaps the most visible measure of the price level, the Bank has focused on eliminating "underlying inflation," the CPI minus the effects of significant supply shocks and the direct effects of interest rates on the index. Following the Iraqi invasion of Kuwait, when oil prices surged, the price of oil was temporarily removed from the index that the Bank followed in assessing underlying inflation in the economy. In the first PTA, which was signed March 2, 1990, the governor and finance minister agreed that price stability should be achieved by the end of 1992 (10; Fischer, 1995, pp. 75–77). As shown in Table 2, in the year to March 1990, the underlying inflation rate in New Zealand was 3.5 percent (11).

In December of that year, after a change in government from the Labor Party to the more conservative National Party, and in the face of criticism that the December 1992 target date for achieving price

Table 2

12-Month Inflation Rates in New Zealand, 1988–1996
(percent)

Year Ending	CPI Change	Underlying Inflation
Dec. 1988	4.7	4.9
Mar. 1989	4.0	3.8
Jun. 1989	4.4	3.6
Sep. 1989	7.2	3.9
Dec. 1989	7.2	3.4
Mar. 1990	7.0	3.5
Jun. 1990	7.6	4.0
Sep. 1990	5.0	3.7
Dec. 1990	4.9	3.4
Mar. 1991	4.5	3.5
Jun. 1991	2.8	2.6
Sep. 1991	2.2	2.1
Dec. 1991	1.0	1.7
Mar. 1992	0.8	1.3
Jun. 1992	1.0	1.4
Sep. 1992	1.0	1.5
Dec. 1992	1.3	1.8
Mar. 1993	1.0	1.8
Jun. 1993	1.3	1.6
Sep. 1993	1.5	1.5
Dec. 1993	1.4	1.3
Mar. 1994	1.3	1.1
Jun. 1994	1.1	1.1
Sep. 1994	1.8	1.9
Dec. 1994	2.8	1.5
Mar. 1995	4.0	1.9
Jun. 1995	4.6	2.2
Sep. 1995	3.5	2.0
Dec. 1995	2.9	2.0
Mar. 1996	2.2	2.1

Sources: Underlying Inflation — Reserve Bank of New Zealand,
CPI Change — Statistics New Zealand.

stability would entail too rapid a rate of disinflation and too great a
cost in terms of unemployment, in a new PTA, the target date was
pushed back to the end of 1993 (4, p. 12). (In the year to December
1990, the underlying rate of inflation in New Zealand was 3.4 percent [11].) In February 1991, the Reserve Bank independently announced its own interim goals on the way to achieving price stability
by year-end 1993: year-on-year inflation rates of 2.5 to 4.5 percent
by December 1991; 1.5 to 3.5 percent by December 1992; and zero
to 2.0 percent by December 1993 (Fischer, 1995, p. 77). Notwithstanding the rise in the rate of underlying inflation in 1990 and the

postponement of the target date for achieving price stability by a year at the end of 1990, by December 1991—ahead of the Bank's original target date—the twelve-month underlying inflation rate had fallen to 1.7 percent (11). The CPI increase over the period December 1990 to December 1991, which Governor Brash calls the "headline" rate of inflation since it is featured in newspaper headlines, was only 1.0 percent. Because the headline inflation rate was in the middle of the range that the Reserve Bank defined as "price stability," its inflation-fighting achievement enhanced the institution's credibility (Fischer, 1995, pp. 78–79).

ASSESSING THE RESERVE BANK'S CREDIBILITY FROM THE RECORD

Expectations and Credibility

The public's expectations with respect to inflation, and, consequently, its behavior in both labor and product markets can be quite slow to change ("inelastic" in economists' jargon)—even in the face of changes in the factors that generate inflation. Moreover, the central bank's credibility as an inflation fighter is closely tied to public expectations regarding inflation. The more quickly economic agents (workers, businesspeople, investors, savers, and consumers) in New Zealand came to believe that the Reserve Bank meant what it said about achieving price stability, the more quickly and easily the Bank could reach its goal. In other words, the Reserve Bank had to make its crusade against inflation credible to economic agents in the financial, labor, and product markets of New Zealand, that is, in general, in the country's body politic. Governor Brash recognizes that the credibility of the central bank's efforts to achieve price stability is crucial to its ongoing success in that pursuit. He told the Canterbury Employers Chamber of Commerce:

> What is important, I believe, is not that the [inflation target] range is never breached under any circumstances but rather that the Bank is constantly aiming to deliver inflation outcomes within that range, and that all New Zealanders know and understand that fact, and act in that confidence. (8, p. 2)

The fastest way for a central bank to ascertain its credibility is to open financial markets because such markets perceive changing conditions and react to them nearly instantaneously (Fischer, 1995, p. 69). If financial markets sense a weakening of the monetary authority's commitment to price stability, market interest rates can spike upward (4, p. 8). It takes more time for central banks to achieve credibility in labor markets by discouraging nominal wage increases in excess of productivity gains.

Those who favor inflation targeting argue that credible inflation targeting facilitates rapid adjustment of inflation expectations, thereby reducing the output and unemployment costs over the period of disinflation. While it is clear that agreed-upon inflation targets can give the central bank greater autonomy and accountability, thereby yielding greater institutional credibility, it is not clear that the costs of disinflation, in terms of unemployment and lost output, are in fact appreciably lower with a rule-based anti-inflation strategy than without one (Fischer, 1995, provides references). In addition, studies show that inflationary expectations may be backward-looking, in which case only good performance in the battle against inflation, or high unemployment, will change inflationary expectations in labor markets (Fischer, 1995, p. 70).

Whether New Zealand's reduced wage-increases in recent years reflected an immediate increase in the credibility of the Reserve Bank's monetary policy is difficult to assess since high unemployment and a large gap between actual and potential output, which may have been attributable to an initial lack of credibility of the disinflation program, contributed to the reduction in wage increases (Fischer, 1995, p. 85). Another factor that may have contributed to moderating wage increases in the island nation's economy is the passage of the Employment Contracts Act (ECA) in 1991. Under the terms of this legislation, individual employees are free to negotiate all the terms and conditions of their employment directly with their employers. While employees may authorize a bargaining representative for any length of time, unions have no status under the ECA except as agents based on an employee's specific authorization (Dannin, 1995). This curtailment of union power may well have led to the negotiation of smaller wage increases than would have occurred had the act not been passed into law—with beneficial effects on the number of New Zealanders employed.

Governor Brash grants that the freeing of labor markets and historically high rates of unemployment may have contributed to the reduction in wage increases initially, but he notes that other (unnamed) nations with free labor markets and high unemployment rates have higher wage settlements than does New Zealand. He, therefore, concludes reasonably enough that reduced inflation expectations in the labor markets by now have kept wage increases in the country lower than they would have been if the Reserve Bank had not achieved inflation-fighting credibility with the nation's workers (2, p. 16).

The upper end of the Reserve Bank's inflation target zone was raised to 3 percent at the end of 1996. While, at first glance, the raising of the upper end of the Reserve Bank's inflation target zone by one percentage point would appear to provide scope for easing monetary policy, Governor Brash said that to the extent that the widening of the target band induces a rise in inflationary expectations, "the new inflation target gives much less scope for an easing . . . than might perhaps be assumed" (*Financial Times*, December 20, 1996, p. 4).

The Reserve Bank's Own Surveys of Inflation Expectations

Each quarter since September 1987, the Reserve Bank of New Zealand has asked approximately two hundred members of the business, financial, agricultural, and labor communities for their views on current and future monetary conditions. The questions posed include:

(1) What is your perception of monetary conditions at present?
(2) What expectations do you have for monetary conditions at the end of the next quarter (i.e., quarter t+1)?
(3) What expectations do you have for monetary conditions three quarters in the future (i.e., quarter t+3)?

Respondents are asked to indicate their expectations on a scale running from one (very tight) to seven (very relaxed). Using the methodology of Carlson and Parkin to perform quantitative analysis of qualitative data, Fischer and Orr (1994, pp. 5–6) draw several inferences from the Bank's survey data. They conclude that the Bank's policy announcements in the recent past have a significant influence on respondents' views of current monetary conditions but not on their expectations of future conditions and that respondents' uncertainty over the stance of monetary policy declines only after inflation falls.

Those authors compare changes in respondents' perceptions and expectations of monetary-policy conditions to movements in the yield curve on New Zealand debt instruments and in the Monetary Conditions Index (MCI). As in Canada, the latter is derived from a weighted average of the trade-weighted exchange rate of the domestic currency and interest rates. Survey responses track these economic variables but are more volatile than the variables themselves. Fischer and Orr (1994, pp. 7–8, 10) conclude that this survey evidence suggests that factors other than interest-rate and exchange-rate movements are important determinants of perceptions and expectations. With respect to perceptions of current monetary conditions—but not expectations of future conditions—the Bank's Monetary Policy Announcements were statistically significant at the 5-percent error level. Respondents appear to obtain information about the Bank's current policy stance from the announcements, an indication of the institution's credibility.

Public Education Activities

In order to achieve and maintain public acceptance of price stability as the sole appropriate objective of monetary policy, the Reserve Bank of New Zealand and Governor Brash have conducted a public-education program. To buttress the case for the single monetary-policy objective of price stability, the Bank's "public communication programme" confronts two major issues:

• Unemployment, which some would have monetary policy fight, was a "deep-seated problem" in New Zealand long before the Bank adopted its anti-inflationary monetary policy. Hence, the weakness in the labor market reflects the influence of structural factors rather than monetary policy. There is no way of buying lower unemployment with higher expected inflation. Instead, economic growth suffers under a regime with continuing high inflation.

• The Reserve Bank's anti-inflation policy, in its initial stages, may have produced some temporary real appreciation of the exchange rate (4, p. 10; 10). But while the anger and loss felt by the export sectors of the New Zealand economy as a result of these real transition costs is understandable, abandoning the fight against inflation would require that the costs of disinflation be paid again in the future. This at least applies unless New Zealand is prepared to tolerate high inflation and its economic costs indefinitely (4, p.11).

The PTAs, the *Monetary Policy Statements*, and the governor's testimony on the conduct of monetary policy before the Finance and Expenditures Committee of the Parliament are published; hence, these documents are part of the Bank's public-education efforts. In addition, the governor maintains an intensive public-speaking schedule during the course of which he appears before business and professional groups both in New Zealand and abroad explaining the "whys" and "wherefores" of the Bank's policies. Frequently, his addresses are really lectures on economic principles, in the course of which he points out what the Reserve Bank can and can not do to help achieve the economic goals of his audience and the country—and what the members of the audience must do for themselves. For example, he has discussed the exchange rate of the Kiwi and interest rates and their implications for the New Zealand economy before groups of manufacturers, business proprietors, and farmers (1, pp. 324-33; 6, pp. 2-9; 5, pp. 2-7).

Governor Brash told the Auckland Manufacturers' Association that, ultimately, employers and employees determine the real exchange rate of the New Zealand dollar since they determine the cost structure in the nation's economy, something he said was not generally understood in the private sector. He also told the group that, while a fall in the real exchange rate of the nation's currency increases the international competitiveness of New Zealand's manufacturers, it reduces the real wages of New Zealanders (1, p. 333):

> If you want a depreciation in the exchange rate, you are by implication saying you want to *reduce* real wages. You can't say you want both a reduced exchange rate and higher wages—or, at least, not with a straight face (1, p. 333).

Commenting on the inability of monetary policy to reduce the real exchange rate of the nation's currency, he said, "In other words, our capacity to beneficially influence the real exchange rate is limited to our capacity to fool people, or for as long as it takes for sticky prices to change" (4, pp. 12-13).

Turning to interest rates, Governor Brash told an audience of business people that, since nominal interest rates depend on the public's inflationary expectations:

> The best contribution which the Reserve Bank can make to lower interest rates in the long-term is to remain totally committed to delivering stable prices—even if, paradoxically, this requires *higher*

interest rates in the short-term to snuff out emerging inflationary pressures (6, p. 5).

He has reminded people who assert that reduced inflation in the recent past should lead to lower nominal interest rates that it is inflationary expectations that affect market interest rates: "last year's inflation has *no* direct effect on interest rates, and banks can be expected to ignore such information" (3, p. 5). In fact, if interest rates were "too high," saving would be rising strongly and bank lending falling, but, in fact, New Zealand's absorption has remained greater than its output; that is, on a net basis, the economy has remained a user of foreign saving (3, p. 5).

Governor Brash's Record

As shown in Table 2, Donald Brash's success in reducing the rate of underlying inflation in New Zealand was little short of phenomenal—at least through the first quarter of 1995. Underlying inflation, which had been 4.9 percent in the twelve months through December 1988, the year before he became governor of the Reserve Bank of New Zealand, was within his zero-to-2-percent target range by the end of 1991 and stayed there for more than three years. The target was missed, however, in June 1995 and again in March 1996, albeit by the smallest of margins (11). Governor Brash notes that "policy-driven government charges" had a role in the Bank's missing its inflation target over the year ending in March 1996. As we have noted above, when such government charges are deemed "significant," they are removed from measured CPI inflation in determining "underlying" inflation, and the Reserve Bank has settled on an impact on the CPI of at least 0.25 percent over twelve months as its working definition of "significant." Over the year ending in March 1996, such government charges added 0.23 percent to the CPI, so the Bank could not exclude them from its calculation of "underlying" inflation. The "underlying" inflation figure for the period was 2.1 percent (10).

In April of 1995, the governor called New Zealand's CPI, which recorded increases of 4.0 percent or more during the twelve months ending in March and June of that year, "a rather bad reflection of the rate at which private sector goods and services are increasing in price" because the index was "substantially inflated" by increases in inter-

New Zealand Inflation 1971–1997

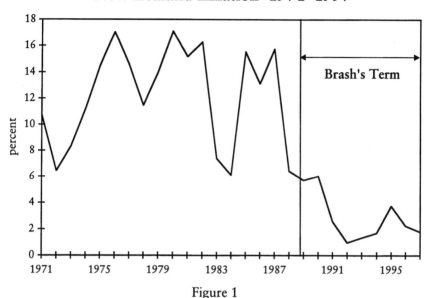

Figure 1

Note: Dr. Donald Brash's third, and not necessarily last,
five-year term expires in August, 2003.

Source: International Monetary Fund, *International Financial
Statistics Database*, March 25, 1998.

est rates and government charges. He estimated that, in the year to
March 1995, about half of the increase in the CPI had come from
those two sources (6, p. 10). At mid-year 1995, Brash noted that the
inflation rate would probably not fall within the Bank's target range
for the year and attributed this prospective failure to the fact that the
Bank did not tighten monetary policy sufficiently or sufficiently early
in 1994 (*Far Eastern Economic Review*, July 13, 1995, p. 72). The
governor thus showed a willingness to recognize quickly, to acknowl-
edge publicly, and to reverse policy mistakes.

During 1994, the Bank increased short-term interest rates substantially: The yield on 90-day bank bills (the most widely used measure of short-term interest rates) rose steadily from less than 4.5 percent in January 1994 to 9.5 percent, which was more than one percentage point above the rate on ten-year bonds by December of that
year. Seeing what appeared to be "decisive" signs that future inflation
was falling, the Reserve Bank eased in October 1995, and 90-day
rates fell below 8.5 percent. By December, the Bank realized it had

Table 3

Interest Rates on Ten-Year Government Bonds, 1987–1997
(annual averages)

Date	United States	New Zealand	Difference (NZ - US)
1987	8.4	15.7	7.3
1988	8.8	13.1	4.3
1989	8.5	12.8	4.3
1990	8.6	12.5	3.9
1991	7.9	9.9	2.0
1992	7.0	8.4	1.4
1993	5.9	6.9	1.0
1994	7.1	7.7	0.6
1995	6.6	7.7	1.1
1996	6.4	7.9	1.5
1997	6.4	7.2	0.8

Sources: Organisation for Economic Cooperation and Development, OECD Economic Outlook, 61, June 1997, and International Monetary Fund (1998a).

been too optimistic with its easing in October; in June 1996, the 90-day bill rate was 10.0 percent (10). Longer-term interest rates rose—albeit more modestly—between 1994:Q2 and 1994:Q4 and declined over the course of the following year. Subsequently, there was a two-quarter uptick in long rates, followed by a gradual decline through the remainder of 1996 and 1997 (International Monetary Fund, 1998a, pp. 510–11). Although the Bank missed its inflation targets in June 1995 and March 1966, Governor Brash remains on the job with his prestige intact. Figure 1 shows the inflation performance during his first two terms, compared with the earlier record.

In addition to wringing inflation out of the economy, Governor Brash appears to have reduced inflationary expectations and risks in New Zealand. That phenomenon is demonstrated in Table 3, which compares the interest rates on ten-year government bonds in New Zealand and the United States (OECD, 1997, p. A39). Clearly, the narrowing of the gap between the interest rates on these securities at a time when rates were trending down in both nations indicates a marked reduction in inflationary expectations and the allowance for inflation risk in New Zealand.

As one might expect, Donald Brash's pursuit of price stability has been controversial in New Zealand. Some New Zealanders think that he has done a superb job of bringing and keeping inflation under control. Others think that the objective is laudable but that the governor has not been sufficiently aggressive in its pursuit. Still a third group of people are convinced that the objective of monetary policy should not be only price stability and that price stability may have to be subordinated to other objectives.

David Richwhite of the firm of Fay, Richwhite rated Governor Brash's tenure at the Reserve Bank as "overall, an outstanding performance." He explained, "The Reserve Bank has established a high level of credibility for monetary management and enhanced financial market stability" (*Management*, February 1996, p. 46). While not criticizing the objective of stable prices or the zero-to-2-percent band defined as price stability by Governor Brash, Gareth Morgan of Infometrics asserted, "There is mounting market scepticism over whether the bank is, in fact, aiming for one per cent inflation, but rather is happy with results around two percent." He went on to warn:

> The apparent allergy to getting inflation results below the one per cent midpoint [of the target range] has given the market reason to build in higher inflation expectations than the declared objective would suggest. The danger with that is that the Reserve Bank is going to, over time, find it more and more difficult to meet its one per cent objective (*Management*, February 1996, p. 48).

Immediately after the Reserve Bank announced it had missed its inflation target by 0.1 percentage point in the year ending March 1966, the Governor's stewardship of monetary policy was called into question by Minister of Finance Bill Birch, who—notwithstanding the increase in government charges that added 0.23 percent to the CPI over the period—asked for a report from the Bank's nonexecutive governors on Governor Brash's performance. Birch said he would summon Governor Brash and ask for an explanation of the factors leading to the missing of the inflation target, the strategy for getting inflation back on track, and the steps the Bank would take to ensure that inflation remains within the target range in the future (*Australian Financial Review*, 18 April 1996).

On the other hand, there are those—both in the business world and outside it—who think that making price stability the sole focus of monetary policy is not a good idea. Sir Robert Jones, one of New Zealand's best-known property investors, called Brash a "misguided zealot" and finds the Reserve Bank Act of 1989 "one of the more foolish acts of the last 50 years" (*Management*, February 1996, p. 47). The Reserve Bank Act of 1989 itself became an issue in the 1996 election campaign, with many of its opponents favoring a broader scope of objectives for monetary policy, including such things as export growth, sustainable economic development, and maintenance of employment. In February 1996, Governor Brash told a parliamentary select committee that he would resign if he were asked to use monetary policy to achieve any goals other than price stability (*Otago Daily Times*, 15 February 1996).

THE LEGACY

All in all, Donald Brash has done a magnificent job of damping the inflationary fires in the New Zealand economy. In view of the tightening of monetary policy he administered during 1994 and 1995 and his single-minded devotion to price stability, it seems unlikely that underlying inflation will be allowed to regain momentum under the current regime. Far more important to the long-term future of New Zealand's economy than the reductions in inflation and inflationary expectations that Governor Brash effected, however, may be the education campaign that he and his colleagues at the Reserve Bank have conducted. The intensity of that education campaign appears unique among the central bankers surveyed in this volume, far ahead even of the considerable efforts made by Governor Crow. It stresses that the central bank cannot move the real interest rate, the real exchange rate, and the unemployment rate in the desired, downward, direction, except perhaps in the very short run and then only at considerable costs in the longer run. Educating the public about the dangers of inflation and inculcating the conviction that inflation is a deterrent to economic growth and economic efficiency and, thereby, to higher living standards, may well prove to be Dr. Brash's most important legacy to New Zealand.

As the governor makes clear in his public addresses, under the law, the government supplies the inflation target to the central bank. The central bank's job is to carry out the government's instructions with respect to monetary policy. The government, however, is responsible to the electorate. Hence, through educating the electorate about the dangers of inflation and investing in the institutional architecture undergirding inflation avoidance and public accountability, the governor helps to ensure that price stability will remain the objective of the Reserve Bank's monetary policy. As a result stable prices may well become an enduring feature of the New Zealand economy.

REFERENCES

Brash, Donald T.
(1) "The Exchange Rate and Monetary Policy." Speech delivered to the Auckland Manufacturers' Association, November 30, 1992. Published in *Reserve Bank Bulletin*, 55: 324–33.
(2) "Reconciling Central Bank Independence with Political Accountability—The New Zealand Experience." Address to the European Policy Forum, London, June 17, 1993.
(3) "New Zealand Interest Rates: 'Too High' Or 'Too Low'?" Address to the Christchurch Club Dinner, July 22, 1993 (with minor editing and updating).
(4) "The Role of Monetary Policy: Where Does Unemployment Fit In?" Address to the Jackson Hole Economic Symposium, Jackson Hole, Wyoming, August 26, 1994.
(5) "An Address to Federated Farmers Southland on Monetary Policy and the Export Sector." April 10, 1995.
(6) "A Presentation to Small and Medium-Sized Businesses in Whangarei." April 26, 1995.
(7) "The Role of the Reserve Bank in the New Zealand Economy." Address to the ADB Seminar "New Zealand: the Turnaround Economy," May 2, 1995.
(8) "An Address to the Canterbury Employers Chamber of Commerce." Christchurch, January 26, 1996.
(9) "New Zealand's Remarkable Reforms." Fifth Annual Hayek Memorial Lecture, Institute of Economic Affairs, London, June 4, 1996.
(10) Letter to G. M. von Furstenberg, Wellington, June 12, 1996.
(11) Table of New Zealand Consumer Price Index and underlying inflation rate data made available by Governor Brash, 1996, with "underlying inflation" from the Reserve Bank, and the CPI change data from Statistics New Zealand.
(12) Letter to G. M. von Furstenberg, Wellington, September 18, 1996.
(13) "The Implications of the Global Financial Market Place for New Zealand." Address to the Single Financial Services Market Conference, Wellington, November 19, 1997.
Dannin, Ellen J. 1995. "We Can't Overcome? A Case Study of Freedom of Contract and Labor Law Reform." *Berkeley Journal of Employment and Labor Law* 16 (1): 1–168.
Fischer, Andreas. 1995. "Inflation Targeting in Canada and New Zealand:

A Survey of the Issues and the Evidence." Pp. 67–91 in H.-H. Franke and E. Ketzel, eds., *Konzepte und Erfahrungen der Geldpolitik*, Beiheft Nr. 13 zu *Kredit und Kapital*. Berlin: Drucker & Humblot.

Fischer, Andreas and Orr, Adrian. 1994. "The Determinants and Properties of Monetary Conditions: Direct Survey Evidence from New Zealand," *OECD Working Paper Number 150*. Paris: Organisation for Economic Cooperation and Development.

International Monetary Fund. 1997. *International Financial Statistics Yearbook*. Washington, D.C.: International Monetary Fund.

_____. 1998a. *International Financial Statistics*. Washington, D.C.: International Monetary Fund (February).

_____. 1998b. *International Financial Statistics Database*. March 25.

OECD Economic Outlook 1997. Paris: Organisation for Economic Cooperation and Development, 61 (June).

Phillips, A. W. 1958. "The Relationship between Unemployment and the Rate of Change in Money Wages in the United Kingdom 1861–1957," *Economica* 25 (November): 283–99.

Walsh, Carl E. 1995. "Is New Zealand's Reserve Bank Act of 1989 an Optimal Central Bank Contract?" *Journal of Money Credit and Banking* 27, Part 1 (November): 155–62.